IBM Data

Handbook

Second Edition

Volume III: DataPower Development

John Rasmussen

Bill Hines

Jim Brennan

Ozair Sheik

Wild Lake Press

Also available! Volumes on DataPower Intro/Setup, Networking, and B2B/File Transfer.

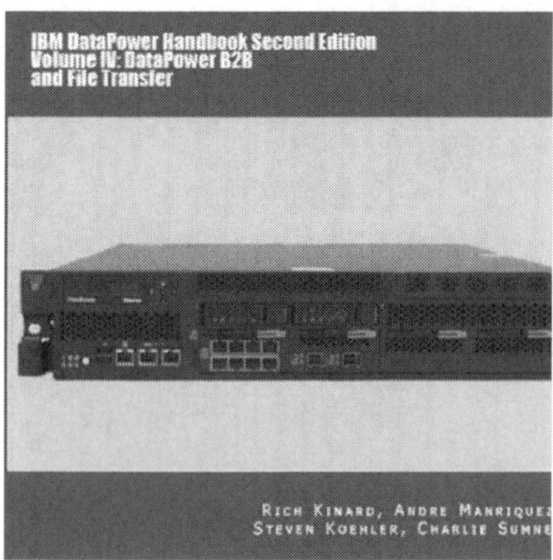

IBM DataPower Appliance Handbook, Second Edition, Volume III: DataPower Development

Version 1.0

ISBN: 0997219602

ISBN-13: 978-0997219609

Wild Lake Press

Lake Hopatcong, NJ, USA

www.wildlakepress.com

Please send questions to info@wildlakepress.com and errors/corrections to errata@wildlakepress.com and include the book title and page. Code listings and other resources in this book can be downloaded from http://wildlakepress.com/books/15-information-technology/18-datapower-handbook-resources

To my mother Marilyn, who has shown me the strength and joy of family and the skills of perseverance; and in memory of my father James, an Officer and a Gentleman, "born on the crest of a wave and rocked in the cradle of the deep." And most of all, to my sons Alex and Nick, who provide me with continuous pride and joy. —John Rasmussen

To my mother Carol, who encouraged me to learn, read, and write; to my wonderful, beautiful wife Lori who inspires me and makes me laugh when I need it most; to my children Jennifer, Brittany, and Derek and step-daughters Loriana and Marie; to my sisters Donna and Patty, and the rest of my extended family, who are always there for me; and last but not least, in memory of my beloved father. —Bill Hines

To my beautiful wife Jennifer and wonderful children Emily, Patrick, and Madison who have all been very patient and supportive of my goals and aspirations even when it meant weekends and late nights away from them. Also to my parents, who always encouraged me to learn and persevere. —Jim Brennan

To my dear wife Khadijah, for her unconditional love and support; and my son Yunus for bringing out the best in me; to my parents who instilled good values and a strong work ethic; and my siblings for their encouragement. —Ozair Sheikh

Contents

Preface

It is with great pleasure that I introduce the long-awaited development volume in our series of handbooks on IBM DataPower Gateway Appliances. We published Volume I of this series "DataPower Intro & Setup" in October of 2014, updated it in June 2015 for firmware version 7.2 and added a valuable new chapter on common use cases and deployment scenarios. We published Volume II, "DataPower Networking" in June 2015, and Volume IV, "DataPower B2B and File Transfer" in December 2015. Our concept of splitting the monolithic tome of the first edition DataPower Handbook into separate, more easily consumable volumes has finally come to fruition.

John has done a magnificent job in describing DataPower's development features, building on the work that we put into our original first edition hardcover book from 2008. Much has happened in DataPower development since then, and John and the rest of our team explore all of the nuances of XSLT, EXSLT, JavaScript/GatewayScript, JSON, XQuery, JSONiq, and much, much more.

—Bill Hines, January 12, 2016

I was first introduced to DataPower when all DataPower appliances were green. Yes, you may have read Bill Hines's history of the Easter-egg colored appliances in Volume I of this series, and how they have transitioned to today's arsenal of mean looking black powerhouses, with their sibling lineup of virtual appliances. But at that time the only DataPower appliance was the "John Deere Green" XA35. The XA35 was an amazing device.

Prior to my discovery of DataPower, I had been at another company, struggling to implement a Java Model View Controller pattern using this dense new tool, XSLT, to transform XML into HTML. And it was not cutting the cake. Our plans were at risk on a purely performance basis. I remember I was searching for alternatives when I found a company across the river in Cambridge, Massachusetts that had a way to do the same transformation in a fraction of the time, using the XSLT I'd developed. And I'm not talking about stripping 10% off the transaction, I mean doing it in 10% of the time or even less!

I soon came to meet Eugene Kuznetsov and the members of the DataPower team, a group of MIT engineers with creativity, passion, and a drive to outperform and out-engineer technical barriers and competitors. As an IT engineer, I had always hoped to have the experience of participating in the creation of a ground-breaking product. DataPower and its team of incredibly talented individuals enabled that.

And of course so much has changed since then. If you're an engineer or just someone with an interest in "the way things work," you'll find this volume of the DataPower Handbook interesting, I am sure.

Within the next three chapters we ...

- Review of relevant XML technologies such as XPath, XSLT and Regular Expressions
- Introduce XQuery and its FLOWR statement for XML query

- Cover the DataPower "Data Model" and the use of DataPower Extension Functions
- Cover the use of third party extensions such as EXSLT
- Introduce JSON technologies such as JavaScript, GatewayScript, and JSONiq
- Canvas programming within the DataPower environment
- Review the Multistep Processing Policy and its Actions and Contents
- Cover the use of system, service and context variables and access through XSLT and GatewayScript Functions
- Discuss debugging
- Cover basic actions such as Filtering and Routing

Having covered and demonstrated these fundamentals, we will continue in Chapter 3 with a set of complete example configurations demonstrating core techniques and best practices. These examples will be available for you to download, evaluation and to act as the basis for future projects should you wish, at http://wildlakepress.com/books/15-information-technology/18-datapower-handbook-resources.

I hope you learn from our work and I very much hope that you learn to appreciate the power, convenience and flexibility that the DataPower platform provides.

—John Rasmussen, On the beach at Windjammer Landing, Saint Lucia with Patty, Alex, Laura, Nick, Chandler, Joe, and Morgan. January 9, 2016

Chapter 1 Introduction to DataPower Development

Welcome to the world of IBM DataPower Gateway development. It's an exciting and dynamic landscape. If you've found yourself here, you're no doubt aware of the many DataPower security and integration services you can create for Mobile, Web and API workloads. Many of these services can be defined using DataPower's Web GUI with its simple property selection screens and drag and drop tooling. If you aren't familiar with these, please see the first book in this series "IBM DataPower Handbook, 2nd Edition Volume 1: Intro & Setup." You should also be familiar with the Command Line Interface (CLI) and XML Management Interface (XMI) which provide similar configuration capabilities in a more scripted fashion. Firmware version 7.2 has advanced your options by providing a REST Management Interface further extending configuration options. For many architectures, these tools will be sufficient to create secure and robust DataPower services.

But there's so much more! DataPower's firmware is built around libraries of functions, which comprise the core of its "purpose built" architecture. There are functions for parsing XML and JSON documents, cryptographic capabilities and transactional tools for filtering, load balancing and routing. You will often want to access runtime metadata such as URL and transaction headers. In most cases, you can access this metadata using the configuration tools. For example, you can inject an HTTP Header via the Multi-Protocol Gateway service, but you can also manipulate headers through programmatic processes and doing so often provides dynamic capabilities that are not readily accessible in the graphical tools.

For many years DataPower has been a powerhouse of XML parsing, inspection and transformation and has provided highly efficient transactional capabilities. Volume I of this series described how DataPower provides optimizations and hardware accelerators. DataPower's firmware features have always been available through the XML/XSLT programming model. As the world of Service Orientated Architecture (SOA) and Web services has matured, new standards have evolved. Mobile and dynamic web programming including API integration is much more dependent on JavaScript than XSLT and JavaScript Object Notation (JSON) over XML for transporting payloads while RESTful service invocations and WebDAV have become increasingly popular.

DataPower has evolved as well. No longer are you required to use XSLT and XPath 1.0 for customization, development, document transformation, and query. Some would prefer to use JavaScript rather than XSLT. And now you can! The GatewayScript, JavaScript based runtime in firmware 7.0 is a game changer, providing a fully integrated JavaScript capability at the Gateway tier. GatewayScript is the JavaScript language (ECMAScript 5.1) plus access to the DataPower runtime and platform. The XML world has evolved as well, including an SQL-like query facility called XQuery. DataPower now supports XQuery, XPath 2.0 and XQuery's sibling extension for the JSON world known as JSONiq.

These are exciting times in the world of DataPower development. Never before have you had such a range of protocol and specification support and the customization options to go with them. In this chapter we will lay the landscape of development options. We'll describe some of the new XML, REST, JSON, JavaScript and GatewayScript technologies and review some of the more mature XML ones as well.

This is not a document for learning these specifications. There are many resources for that, and we'll identify some. We will be showing you introductions and just enough to demonstrate some of their capabilities. In subsequent chapters, we'll show you how you can leverage them in your DataPower architectures.

Why the Need for DataPower Development?

Why do we need to "develop" within this easily administrated environment? Well, some of the typical reasons would include:

- Integration with other applications that are not compliant with current specifications and require transformation
- "Enriching" messages by doing database look-ups and providing more detailed transaction information
- Custom logging through dynamic message construction
- Custom security extension of the existing AAA (Authentication, Authorization and Auditing) framework

- Routing is a very typical use case and might involve determining the user's credentials from tokens or SSL certificates

The reasons are as varied as the implementations of DataPower, and each organization's architecture will have nuances which may very well be addressed by an extension of the standard DataPower actions.

Evolution of DataPower support for XML, JSON and Mobile technologies

As DataPower has evolved to meet the needs of dynamic client side web, mobile and new XML and JSON specifications, incremental feature improvements have been added to the firmware. For readers using firmware releases other than the current 7.2, and perhaps for historical purposes, it will be interesting to review the adaptation of these capabilities over the latest major release cycles.

Firmware Version 5.0

In order to provide a simple mapping of JSON documents into XML format DataPower supports the JSONx specification. JSONx provides a mapping of JSON into an XML format. This early adoption feature added the ability to quickly interrogate JSON requests through XSLT, while leaving the option of sending the original JSON payload or the new XML version to downstream applications.

A new “Request” and “Response” type was added to the XML Firewall and Multi-Protocol Gateway services to support JSON processing. The new JSON type provides:

- Validation as "well formed"JSON as described in RFC 4627
- Validation of JSONx using the jsonx.xsd built-in schema
- Conversion of input messages to JSONx via JSON Request/Response Type which is made available in the __JSONASJSONX context
- Optional conversion from JSON to JSONx via convert-http processing action within a processing policy
- Conversion of JSONx back to JSON through jsonx2json.xsl
- Support for RESTful processing model for document cache control

Firmware Version 6.0

Firmware 6.0 provided a signification expansion of JSON and advanced XML processing, including:

- Support for XQuery 1.0 and XPath 2.0 Data Model (XDM)
- XQuery queries, actions, filters, and transforms of data through the Transform Action
- Support for JSON Filtering, Query, and Extraction with the JSONiq extension version 0.4.42 to XQuery for JSON and XML data through the Transform Action
- Support for XPath 2.0 within XQuery and JSONiq scripts

- JSON Schema Validation for validation of JSON data draft version 0.3 through the Schema Validate Action

Firmware Version 6.0.1

This incremental release continued to expand XQuery and JSONiq support, including:

- Added support for JSONiq and XQuery scripts to read and write Multistep context and service variables and perform basic manipulation of protocol headers. This support significantly expanded the ability of XQuery and JSONiq to integrate with the DataPower "Data Model" and extension functions providing transactional metadata manipulation and routing.
- Increased tracing functionality fn:trace() for JSONiq and XQuery scripts.
- JSONiq and XQuery scripts can be configured using external parameters through the Transform Action advanced tab.

Firmware 7.0

This release provided a major advance in Mobile, Web and API workloads through the release of a JavaScript-based programming model. Features include:

- Support for GatewayScript – Highly secure and optimized JavaScript-based programming model
- Addition of GatewayScript action to Multistep Policy
- JavaScript debugging within the CLI

- ECMAScript 5.1 support
- CommonJS 1.0 module support
- Enhanced JSON Schema support
- Support for XPath 2.0 use in XQuery
- Support XQuery-transform() extension function from XSLT for execution of XQuery or JSONiq script transformation. This function can be used to off-load JSON processing from XSLT.

Firmware 7.2

This point release continued the advances in GatewayScript and XML technologies, including a significant focus in the areas of JSON cryptographic processing. Features include:

- Support for JSON Web Encryption (JWE) encryption and decryption APIs
- JSON Web Key (JWK) APIs
- JOSE and JSON Web Token (JWT) APIs for JWK, JSON decrypt, encrypt, sign, and verify processing actions
- Enhanced XQuery function support
- GatewayScript, fs module support
- dp:gatewayscript() extension function to execute GatewayScript from XSLT
- Execution of GatewayScript from dynamic content data
- Execution of GatewayScript from temporary:/// directory

While you're learning about development within DataPower, you'll want to have some resources on hand for reference. We list a complete set of DataPower resources in Appendix A for you. Those will include:

DataPower Knowledge Center, (http://www-01.ibm.com/support/knowledgecenter/SS9H2Y_7.2.0/com.ibm.dp.doc/welcome.html), especially the “Reference” and “Gateway programming model and GatewayScript” sections.

DataPower Gateway Forum, (https://www.ibm.com/developerworks/community/forums/html/forum?id=11111111-0000-0000-0000-000000001198) an active discussion on all areas of DataPower including development issues.

Hermann Stamm-Wilbrandt's Blog (https://www.ibm.com/developerworks/community/blogs/HermannSW/?lang=en) . Hermann provides a unique and always interesting perspective on DataPower development topics. He is very active on the DataPower Gateway Forum and his blog extends those discussions with in-depth product details.

Look into Hermann's “coproc2” tool for an example of development acceleration tooling. Using coproc2 you can test transformations using XSLT, XQuery, JSONiq and JavaScript using a Linux or Windows command line. This tool avoids having to upload new files to the DataPower file system in order to test them.

Review of XML Technologies

The following sections review some basic XML technologies, such as XPath, XSLT, Regular Expressions and XSLT extensions. We assume that you are familiar with basic XML document structure and tooling; however if not, please feel free to browse one of the many resources dedicated to these topics.

The XML document in Listing 1-1 is used in the introduction sections which follow and in the subsequent programming examples. It provides our inventory or "database" of books. We'll refer back to this document in those examples.

Listing 1-1 books.xml document.

```
<?xml version="1.0"?>

<books>

    <book name="The_Hunger_Games" author="Suzanne Collins" isbn-
13="9780439023481">

        <quantity>100</quantity>

        <price>1.23</price>

    </book>

    <book name="Harry_Potter_and_the_Order_of_the_Phoenix"
author="J.K. Rowling, Mary GrandPré" isbn-13="9780439358071">

        <quantity>100</quantity>

        <price>1.23</price>

    </book>

    <book name="IBM_DataPower_Handbook_Second_Edition" author="Bill
Hines, John Rasmussen, Jim Brennan, Ozair Sheikh, Harley Stenzel"
isbn-13="9780137148196">

        <quantity>1000</quantity>

        <price>3.21</price>

    </book>

</books>
```

Notice that Listing 1-1 contains an XML document declaration on the first line that defines information about the version and encoding. There are seven types of nodes in an XML document; each type may be uniquely identified and processed:

- Root nodes
- Element nodes
- Text nodes
- Attribute nodes
- Namespace nodes
- Processing instruction nodes
- Comment nodes

Looking back at our sample XML document in Listing 1-1, we can see that not only does the document contain the document declaration, but it also contains a “books” element containing a set of “book” elements. Attributes are defined within the book elements to define “name”, “author” and “isbn-13.” Additional elements “quantity” and “price” are children of book.

Namespaces

XML namespaces are used to provide uniqueness to a collection, or vocabulary of XML elements and attributes. When we are dealing with a simple document such as our sample, this is not much of an issue. However, in a real industrial-strength document, you will find elements from multiple sources. You may see WS-Security headers or payroll information from your Human Resources vendor. What if these applications decided to use the same name for an element, and then these elements became intermixed? In order to avoid this problem, namespaces are provided to make the various element sources unambiguous. A namespace is simply defined in the XML document, either at the document root or within a particular element.

You'll need to include a declaration of namespaces when programming in the DataPower environment. Listing 1-2 shows an example of an XSLT stylesheet with the DataPower extensions and configuration namespaces. This example includes the basic “dp” namespace declaration as well as the “dpconfig” namespace that provides access to parameters associated with a service configuration. As you include other libraries you’ll need to declare them as well as you’ll see in subsequent examples.

Listing 1-2 Standard XSLT Stylesheet declaration with DataPower namespaces.

```
<?xml version="1.0" encoding="utf-8"?>

<xsl:stylesheet version="1.0"
xmlns:xsl="http://www.w3.org/1999/XSL/Transform"
xmlns:dp="http://www.datapower.com/extensions"
xmlns:dpconfig="http://www.datapower.com/param/config">
```

XPath Expressions

XPath (specifically 1.0) was defined as a mechanism to address parts of an XML document. It also provides node set and basic string manipulation functions, as well as numeric and Boolean operations. It uses a very compact syntax and can quite literally identify any set or a combination of the node types listed previously. In a single word, XPath is cool! However, a word of caution: XPath can be used efficiently and with purpose, or it can be used naively and inefficiently.

Let's look at a simple task and see some XPath alternatives. Referring back to our sample XML document in Listing 1-1, what if we wanted to fetch the element named "book" within the books node that contained an attribute named "name" with the value of "The_Hunger_Games"? The following list shows some examples:

Listing 1-3 XPath expressions for book.

```
/books/book[@name='The_Hunger_Games']

//book[@name='The_Hunger_Games']

/books/child::book[attribute::name='The_Hunger_Games']

//descendant-or-self::*/book[attribute::name='The_Hunger_Games']
```

These expressions each return a nodeset containing the element publication that we are interested in. They do so by returning nodes named "book" and implementing a filtering construct known as a "predicate query" (the string within brackets) to examine the name attribute. However, there are some subtle differences in what these statements return and how they go about doing so. The most important differences are in the use of the "axes" such as "//", "child::book" and "descendant-or-self::*", and their efficiency.

You should use caution when performing XPath operations, just as you would with any programming tool. Choosing the more inefficient method can have significant performance impacts. For example in the choices in Listing 1-3, the use of the "descendent-or-self" or "//" axes performs a complete transverse of the entire document when the intent is far simpler.

CAUTION—Descendant-or-self Axes

You should never use the "descendant-or-self" or "//" axes without a specific reason, to avoid excessive and unnecessary document processing.

XSL Stylesheets

Now that we've completed our basic introduction to XML, namespaces and XPath, we can use them to construct an XSLT stylesheet. XSLT is used for the transformation of XML documents. The most common use case is producing a modified XML document. However, XSLT is not limited to producing XML, and it can be used to produce other data such as COBOL records or comma-delimited text.

Let's look at a simple XSLT stylesheet in Listing 1-4. We get our first look at a complete stylesheet—it's just XML! This is a simple stylesheet but it shows a couple things you'll need to do with each DataPower XSLT. First you need to declare the namespaces as we mentioned. The "extension-element-prefixes" and "exclude-result-prefixes" attributes are used to let the XSLT processor know about the DataPower functions. Specifically these declarations let the XSLT processor (DataPower) know which XSLT elements are to be processed as functions and are not to be written to the output or "result-set".

We use the XSLT document() function to read the books.xml document from the DataPower local:// directory, and then select the specific book using an XPath expression. The only real "DataPower" thing we're doing here is to emit a log entry and using a DataPower attribute "dp:priority" to set the log level.

Listing 1-4 XSLT Stylesheet with DataPower declarations.

```
<?xml version="1.0" encoding="UTF-8"?>
<xsl:stylesheet
    extension-element-prefixes="dp"
    exclude-result-prefixes="xsl dp"
    version="1.0"
    xmlns:dp="http://www.datapower.com/extensions"
    xmlns:xsl="http://www.w3.org/1999/XSL/Transform">
    <!-- -->
    <xsl:template match="/">
        <xsl:variable name="books"
select="document('local:///books.xml')"/>
        <xsl:variable name="book"
select="$books/books/book[@name='The_Hunger_Games']"/>
        <!-- -->
        <xsl:message dp:priority="info">
            <xsl:value-of select="concat('The_Hunger_Games has ',
$book/quantity, ' books')"/>
        </xsl:message>
    </xsl:template>
</xsl:stylesheet>
```

The execution of the stylesheet in Listing 1-4 results in the following message being emitted into the logging system with, as requested, a priority of "info". The log message is shown in Figure 1-1 with only "xsltmsg" category messages displayed.

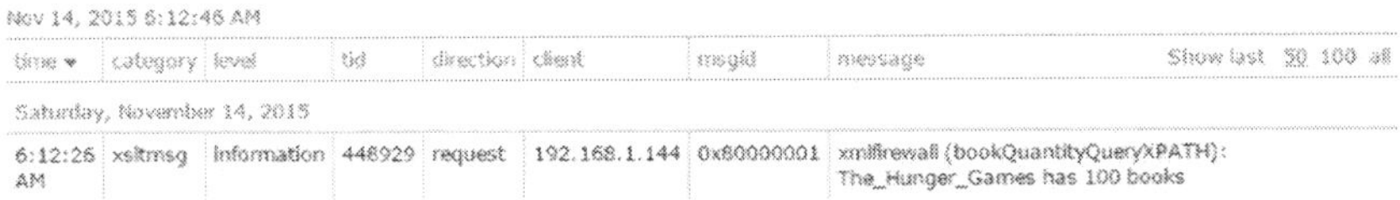

Nov 14, 2015 6:12:46 AM

time	category	level	tid	direction	client	msgid	message	Show last 50 100 all
Saturday, November 14, 2015								
6:12:26 AM	xsltmsg	information	448929	request	192.168.1.144	0x80000001	xmlfirewall (bookQuantityQueryXPATH): The_Hunger_Games has 100 books	

Figure 1-1 Priority “info” log message written to DataPower log.

Introduction to EXSLT Extension Function and Elements

EXSLT is a widely utilized collection of extensions for XSLT. It is supported by a community of people and organizations who have contributed implementations of functions and features that they feel are valuable. Its wide distribution means many XSLT processors implement its extensions either by importing packages or rewriting implementations while conforming to its extension signatures.

EXSLT provides quite a few extensions to support dates and times (as shown in Listing 1-5), math, regular expressions, string manipulation, and others. DataPower does not support all EXSLT extensions, but most of the date and time extensions are supported, as are several of the string and other types. You’ll find the supported EXSLT extensions in the DataPower Extension Elements and Functions Catalog documentation available from the DataPower Knowledge Center.

Listing 1-5 XSLT Template with EXSLT date-time() function.

```
<xsl:template name="timeStamp">
    <xsl:value-of select="date:date-time()"/>
</xsl:template>
```

Regular Expressions

We've seen how XPath provides searching and filtering of XML data models. Regular expressions have been used for many years for similar processing of strings. Regular expressions are suited for the searching of character classes, sets of character classes, and patterns such as word boundaries or preceding and following characters, among other string characteristics.

There are many objects within the DataPower system that utilize regular expressions. The Match Rule is an example. Figure 1-2 shows an example. Here, a regular expression is created to match URLs that end with "js" in upper or lower case. Use of regular expression patterns on the URL Match Rule allows for the implementation of complex matching rules for the selection of processing rules.

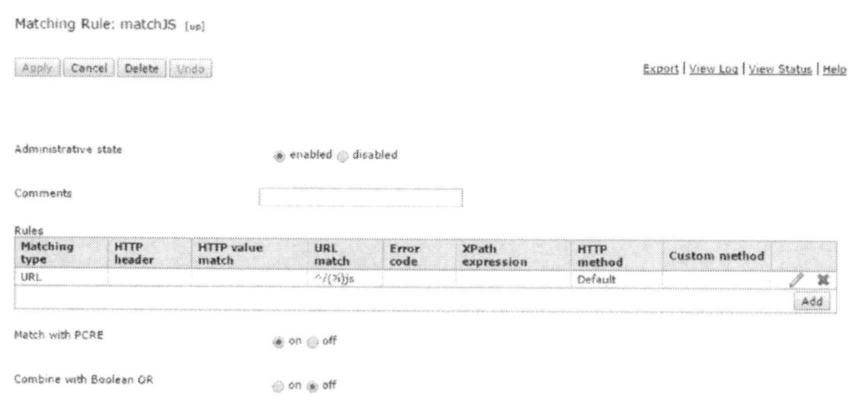

Figure 1- 2 Example of Match Rule using regular expression.

DataPower functions typically support the PCRE (Perl compatible regular expressions) style of regular expression rather than the JavaScript version. While they are closely related syntactically, you may need to know which version is supported in any given function, and you may need to tweak your patterns to comply with the supported version. The Knowledge Center provides the detailed descriptions you may need. Regular expression support is not limited to EXSLT, there's also support within XQuery and its XPath 2.0 sibling.

Listing 1-6 demonstrates a typical DataPower use case, the parsing of an incoming URL. We'll describe the “dp:variable()” syntax shortly. It also demonstrates a powerful feature of a PCRE: the ability to capture a back reference, or the contents of grouping parentheses.

Listing 1-6 Sample XSLT Using EXSLT Regular Expression Function.

```
<xsl:template match="/">

    <xsl:variable name="url" select="dp:variable('var://service/URL-
in')"/>

    <xsl:variable name="destinationHost">

        <xsl:value-of
select="regexp:replace($url,'(http://)([^:]*)(:)([0-
9]*)(.*)','','$2')"/>

    </xsl:variable>

    <xsl:message>

        <xsl:value-of select="concat('url=', $url, ',
destinationHost=', $destinationHost)"/>

    </xsl:message>

</xsl:template>
```

Each of the groupings can be individually identified by the regular expression processor, and are often referenced as “$1”, “$2”, and so on. Therefore, in our example, the “$2” used in the “regexp:replace()” function will contain the hostname of the incoming request. And given a request URL such as "http://MYHOST:2053/first/second" will result in the following log entry in Listing 1-7 as the destination host is extracted from the incoming URL. This is a frequently used technique for routing designation.

Listing 1-7 Log message showing results of parsing URL with regex.

```
xmlfirewall (regEx): url=http://MYHOST:2053/first/second,
destinationHost=MYHOST
```

XPath 2.0 and XQuery

While XSLT is typically used for processing entire XML documents, XQuery is used to query structured and unstructured text, though typically XML. There are extensions for other types of data such as JSON (as we will see shortly) for Mobile and API technologies. While XQuery does not currently provide the ability to update documents, it can be used to create new ones.

XQuery is a superset of XPath 2.0 expressions and is used to identify parts of XML documents. You can use the XPath 1.0 and 2.0 functions and navigation features. DataPower's support of XPath 2.0 and XQuery have improved to support the XPath 2.0 and XQuery 1.0 Data Model (XDM), which is based on sequences of heterogeneous items including nodes and primitive types. This replaces and improves on the XPath 1.0 node-set support and becomes the foundation of XSLT 2.0 and XQuery 1.0 data navigation.

XPath 2.0 adds new data types, closer integration with Schema and other powerful features. DataPower supports

XPath 2.0 within the XQuery context. There are ways to integrate XQuery from within XSLT via the "dp:xquery-transform()" function introduced in 7.0.

XPath 2.0 has about eighty functions, including an extensive collection of functions and operators to allow for an easier programming experience. Many of these replace XPath 1.0 proprietary extension mechanisms. These functions and operators help with date and time handling, enhance string manipulation, support regular expression matching and tokenization, extended number handling, and additional functions for sequence manipulation. For example the EXSLT function used for the time-stamp could be replaced with the XQuery, XPath 2.0 function "fn:current-dateTime()".

XQuery extends this model by providing query syntax similar to SQL which is known as "FLWOR". Think "flower expression". The acronym stands for the five clauses that make up the query: For, Let, Where, Order By and Return. The example in Listing 1-8 shows the simple format of the FLWOR statement, not all parameters are required but this example shows all and returns a sequence of "book/quantity" items whose price is greater than 1.23 and ordered by name.

Listing 1-8 XQuery FLOWR Statement.

```
for $book in doc("books.xml")/books
where $book/price>1.23
order by $book/name
return $x/quantity
```

DataPower's support of XSLT 2.0 is limited to extended support for numeric data types. We'll see how to establish that in the following chapters. However, an interesting option is available through the use of the "dp:xquery-transform()" extension function. You can use it to execute XQuery and XPath 2.0 functions from within an XSLT 1.0 stylesheet. The FLOWR statement in Listing 1-9 summarizes the prices of all books in inventory.

Listing 1-9 SumForXQuery.xq XQuery Statement.

```
sum(for $book in /books/book return $book/price * $book/quantity)
```

This FLOWR statement (shown in Listing 1-10 and stored within the SumForXQuery.xq file) can be called from within XSLT. Listing 1-10 shows the "dp:xquery-transform() function which stores the results of the query in the xsl variable "$value". This extension function provides the ability to query XML from within XSLT.

Listing 1-10 XSLT using dp:xquery-transform() and SumForXQuery.xq.

```
<?xml version="1.0" encoding="UTF-8"?>

<xsl:stylesheet extension-element-prefixes="dp"

    version="1.0" xmlns:dp="http://www.datapower.com/extensions"
xmlns:xsl="http://www.w3.org/1999/XSL/Transform">

    <xsl:template match="/">

        <xsl:variable name="books"
select="document('local:///books.xml')"/>

        <xsl:variable name="value"

select="dp:xquery-transform('SumForXQuery.xq', $books)"/>

        <xsl:value-of select=" concat('The value of all books in
inventory is : ', $value)"/>

    </xsl:template>

</xsl:stylesheet>
```

The execution of the stylesheet results in the processing of the XQuery script. It performs the query on the "$books" variable which contains an XML node of book entries. The result is the simple message shown in the response in Listing 1-11.

Listing 1-11 XSLT, XQuery-transform() result.

```
The value of all books in inventory is : 249.21
```

Introduction to JSON and Mobile/API Technologies

JSON, or JavaScript Object Notation, has emerged as an alternative to XML. It is considered more human readable than XML and is widely used for transmission of data between Web applications and servers. It is platform independent, like XML, and there are many supporting implementations.

We can easily convert the books.xml document in Listing 1-1 from our earlier XML examples to JSON, the results might look like the following in Listing 1-12.

Listing 1-12 Books.json document.


```
{
  "books": [
      {
        "name": "The_Hunger_Games",
        "author": "Suzanne Collins",
        "isbn-13": "9780439023481",
        "quantity": "100",
        "price": "1.23"
      },
      {
```

```
        "name": "Harry_Potter_and_the_Order_of_the_Phoenix",
        "author": "J.K. Rowling, Mary GrandPré",
        "isbn-13": "9780439358071",
        "quantity": "100",
        "price": "1.23"
      },
      {
        "name": "IBM_DataPower_Handbook_Second_Edition",
        "author": "Bill Hines, John Rasmussen, Jim Brennan, Ozair
Sheikh, Harley Stenzel",
        "isbn-13": "9780137148196",
        "quantity": "1000",
        "price": "3.21"
      }
    ]
}
```

There is no exact conversion from XML to JSON. There is the IBM JSONx specification mentioned earlier in this chapter which describes a mapping. But there is not a definitive specification for mapping XML attributes to a JSON object. This results in some differences in the implementation. JSON does not have a concept of XML attributes. So, while name, author and isbn-13 are defined as attributes in the XML document, we've implemented them as properties of the JSON book object. The book object consists of an array (within []) of “book” objects.

JSON-related standards are not as mature as equivalent XML/Web service standards, and some of the supporting technologies are still emerging. The JSON Schema is still in Internet Draft form, but DataPower does support the specification. JSON documents can be validated similar to

XML using the Validate action and specifying a JSON Schema document.

JSON processing can be performed in three ways within DataPower services:

- XML Firewall or Multi-Protocol Gateway's request and response type of "JSON" which makes the JSON input stream available as an XML (JSONx) representation.
- JSONiq Extensions to XQuery. This specification supports the reading and writing of both XML and JSON documents including the Hybrid model of dynamic type determination introduced in firmware 7.0.
- JavaScript introduced as part of the GatewayScript feature of firmware 7.0

Introduction to JSONiq Extensions to XQuery

We introduced XQuery as a query language for documents including XML, and described the use of the FLOWR statement as the integral query component for returning data. JSONiq follows a similar data model and provides similar functionally for JSON documents. JSONiq is an extension to XQuery which provides for the ability to consume and produce either XML or JSON. As of firmware 7.2, DataPower provides support for the draft specification 0.4.42.

Introduction to GatewayScript

As was mentioned in the firmware feature list earlier in this chapter, release 7.0 of DataPower introduced the most significant Mobile/API development enhancement to date. “GatewayScript” (GWS) frees the developer from previous requirements to use XSLT and makes JavaScript a first class citizen in the world of DataPower development. Of course JavaScript is natural for processing JSON documents, but you can also use it to access many of the DataPower extension functions to effect service configuration, security and transaction optimization.

DataPower's implementation of JavaScript is based on ECMAScript 5.1 with some ECMAScript 6.0 features such as Block mode variable definitions via the “let” operator. The implementation has been developed with a security-first approach. For example:

- Each transaction is isolated from others. No GWS action can access the execution space of another.
- Limited File Access through “urlopen” and “fs” modules to access local://, store:// and temporary:// directories.
- Eval() statement, which is a potential vector for unrestricted code execution, is not available in GWS.
- Access to GWS resources such as JavaScript code is, as are all DataPower resources, protected by Role Based Management settings.

As you'd expect, GWS is provided the same high performance capabilities as you've appreciated for XSLT through pre compilation and caching. And error handling is quite similar to the previous XSLT implementation. In fact as GWS is implemented as another action within the Processing Policy Rule, you can use the On-Error Action, Error Rules, evaluate Error objects returned from Asynchronous DataPower function calls and set headers and status codes in error conditions. All this and extensive logging support provide a robust, efficient and JavaScript friendly environment.

GWS programming within JavaScript follows the CommonJS 1.0 module format. When you want to utilize an API you must first "require" the module. You may also create your own modules. While you should always consult the Knowledge Center for the latest product features, especially the Gateway programming model and GatewayScript sections. As of this writing some of the available APIs are listed in Table 1-1.

Table 1-1 GatewayScript APIs.

Assert	Throw an exception when an expectation is not met
Buffer	Contiguous binary array of data
Buffers	Collection of Buffer objects that give the appearance and (partial) API of a single Buffer
Console	Write a message to the system log with a printf-like interface
Context	DataPower context. Access input, output, and named contexts of a transaction
Error	Thrown by exceptions and returned in asynchronous callbacks
Header-metadata	Access the original or current headers of a transaction
Punycode	Converting Unicode to ASCII and vice versa
Querystring	Utilities for manipulating and interrogating a URL query string
Service-metadata	Access the large collection of DataPower service variables
Session	The object providing access to context variables
URL	Utilities for manipulating a URL string as an object
Urlopen	Send an HTTP request to a server and process the response
Util	General purpose utilities for formatting strings and inspecting objects

One more important feature of GWS is the use of its debugger. As we'll see in the next chapter, the debugger, which is similar to GDB (GNU Debugger), allows you to breakpoint a script, check variables, step through code and more, to get finer control over your GWS execution. Very cool!

Introduction to DataPower "Data Model"

DataPower extension functions and elements provide access to the core of many of DataPower's features. Early firmware exposed these features through XSLT and separated their functionality along the lines of those written as XSL/XML "elements" and those implemented with XPath "functions". This separation still exists when used within the XML/XSLT programming model.

However, with the expanded use of Web 2.0 and RESTful programming, DataPower's functions are now also available in XQuery including XPath 2.0 and JSONiq scripts. And while the term "Data Model" is not an official description of this metaphor it may be a useful way to think about the core of DataPower's controlling "variable" data, and the functions that are used to reference and maintain it. Let's take a quick look at some of the categories of functions available to you on DataPower shown in table 1-2.

DataPower extension functions and elements provide access to the core of many of DataPower's features. Early firmware exposed these features through XSLT and separated their functionality along the lines of those written as XSL/XML "elements" and those implemented with XPath "functions". This separation still exists when used within the XML/XSLT programming model.

However, with the expanded use of Web 2.0 and RESTful programming, DataPower's functions are now also available in

XQuery including XPath 2.0 and JSONiq scripts. And while the term “Data Model” is not an official description of this metaphor it may be a useful way to think about the core of DataPower's controlling “variable” data, and the functions that are used to reference and maintain it. Let's take a quick look at some of the categories of functions available to you on DataPower shown in table 1-2.

Table 1-2 Typical Extension Function Categories.

Metadata extension functions	Metadata extension functions are used to manipulate protocol headers and messages
Cryptographic extension functions	Cryptographic extension functions run standard cryptographic operations. Examples include BASE64Access to parameters encoding, Canonicalization, Hashing, Encrypting and Decrypting data, Kerberos integration and Certificate processing
Governance extension functions	Sets the value of the SLM threshold level for the current transaction
XSLT and XPath extensions	Support for XSLT 2.0 and XPath 2.0 decimal data type
XQuery extension functions	Variable ("Data Model") access, Transactional Status and Header Access with XQuery and JSONiq queries
EXSLT extensions	Support for the EXSLT community effort to provide a standardized set of common extensions
WebGUI extensions	Access to parameters

We've described the basics of programming support for XML and Mobile/API through the description of the specifications that DataPower supports. Let's pause a moment and discuss the specific functions that these programming tools are applied to. You know that XSLT and XQuery can be used to access and create XML documents and that JSONiq and JavaScript can be used to access and create JSON and XML documents. But beyond just reading and writing documents they also need to access the DataPower service variables (it's "Data Model" if you will) for transaction control. In many cases the variables are maintained and managed by the extension function which extends the data model.

We're going to dive deeper into these variables and function in the next chapter "Development within the DataPower environment" but for now let's take a look at a simple example and show how it can be used within XSLT, XQuery, JSONiq and GatewayScript.

We'll use a variable that configures a Multi-Protocol Gateway service to not send the request message to the backside service, but rather to just echo it back to the client. By the way, if you're familiar with the XML Firewall, this is the same as setting the XML Firewall to "loopback" mode. These samples are just snippets, and do not show namespace or other declarations.

The DataPower variables are written in a "slash notation", we'll show a "dot" notation used for GatewayScript shortly. In this example in Listing 1-13, the variable is set using the "dp:set-variable()" function.

Listing 1-13 XSLT Set Variable example.

```
<dp:set-variable name="'var://service/mpgw/skip-backside'"
value="1"/>
```

In the XQuery example in Listing 1-14, or its JSONiq extension a similar "slash notation" is used. In this example an

XQuery variable is declared to define the variable name (a stylistic choice) and then used in the actual "dp:set-variable()" execution.

Listing 1-14 XQuery Set Variable example.

```
declare variable $var_name as xs:string := "var://service/mpgw/skip-backside";

let $set_var := dp:set-variable($var_name, "1");
```

JavaScript used in GatewayScript, uses a "dot notation" and must include the module that provides variable support. In this example (shown in Listing 1-5) the "mpgw.skipBackside" property of the "service-metadata" module is used to set the variable.

Listing 1-15 GatewayScript Set Variable example.

```
var serviceVars = require ('service-metadata');

serviceVars.mpgw.skipBackside = true;
```

In essence, all three examples are using the same "data model" and in each case the execution, namely the skipping of the backside is the same. You have choices! Want to use XSLT? Do so. Want to use JavaScript? Go for it!

Examples of XML/XSLT & Web 2.0 processing on DataPower

There are many variables and functions to utilize while you're programming in the DataPower environment, we'll show more in the next chapter. For now, let's extend our discussion on development by concentrating on some of the core functions and in areas that have seen recent growth within the XML and Mobile/API environments. We'll use sample XML and JSON documents to demonstrate simple document processing capabilities. And in each case, we'll use native DataPower functions to access transaction metadata, and we'll use a variety of other functions to provide programming structure and execute non-native functions. These examples will set the ground for further development in each of the technologies.

Now, let's take a simple example, and show how it can be implemented. We'll use our books "database", in XML form for the XML models; XSLT, XQuery, and JSON for JSONiq and GatewayScript. The example will take the name of a book from the URI, use that to look up the quantity of that book and create a response document which will also contain a time stamp.

XSLT Example

Listing 1-16 puts all this together for our first example. The stylesheet declares the "xsl" and "dp" namespaces, as well as the EXSLT "date" namespace which we will use for the creation of a time-stamp. We're going to be querying the book's XML "database" and search for a book whose name matches the URI of the incoming transaction. The flow of the stylesheet is:

1. The document() function reads the books.xml document.
2. Read the URI with "dp:variable()" within an XPath expression.
3. Strip out the leading '/' to obtain the bookName from the URI.

4. Use another XPath and predicate query to get the 'bookName' book from the document.
5. Write some log messages.
6. Create an output document with a time-stamp via a template call which uses EXSLT date:date-time().

Listing 1-16 Sample XSLT demonstrating access of books database and time-stamp creation.

```
<?xml version="1.0" encoding="UTF-8"?>

<!-- This XSLT Script will retrieve the quantity of a book based on
the URI -->

<xsl:stylesheet

    exclude-result-prefixes="xsl dp" extension-element-prefixes="dp"
version="1.0" xmlns:date="http://exslt.org/dates-and-times"
xmlns:dp="http://www.datapower.com/extensions"
xmlns:xsl="http://www.w3.org/1999/XSL/Transform">

    <!-- -->

    <xsl:template match="/">

        <xsl:variable name="books"
select="document('local:///books.xml')"/>

        <xsl:variable name="uri"
select="dp:variable('var://service/URI')"/>

        <xsl:variable name="bookName" select="substring-after($uri,
'/')"/>

        <xsl:variable name="book"
select="$books/books/book[@name=$bookName]"/>

        <xsl:message>

            <xsl:value-of select="concat('Getting Book Quantity for
bookName = ', $bookName)" />

        </xsl:message>

        <!-- -->

        <xsl:element name="bookQuantity">

            <xsl:element name="book">

                <xsl:attribute name="name">

                    <xsl:value-of select="$book/@name"/>

                </xsl:attribute>

                <xsl:element name="quantity">
```

```
                <xsl:value-of select="$book/quantity"/>
            </xsl:element>
        </xsl:element>
        <xsl:element name="dateTime">
            <xsl:call-template name="timeStamp"/>
        </xsl:element>
    </xsl:element>
    <!-- -->
</xsl:template>
<!-- -->
<!-- Template for Time Stamp -->
<!-- -->
<xsl:template name="timeStamp">
    <xsl:value-of select="date:date-time()"/>
</xsl:template>
</xsl:stylesheet>
```

Executing this stylesheet against the sample books.xml document produces the output XML document shown in Listing 1-17. Notice that the book quantity was accessed through the use of an XPath statement and a time-stamp was produced through the use of the EXSLT “date:date-time()” function.

Listing 1-17 Results of XSLT producing bookQuantity XML node.

```
<bookQuantity>
    <book name="The_Hunger_Games">
        <quantity>100</quantity>
    </book>
    <dateTime>2014-12-27T16:13:05-05:00</dateTime>
</bookQuantity>
```

XQuery Example

Here's an XQuery version of our previous XSLT example with a FLWOR statement in place of the XPath statement. Listing 1-18 shows the FLOWR statement used to query the sample books.xml document. In this example, we:

- Declared the "dp" namespace
- Declared a function to create the time-stamp
- Use the Xpath 2.0 fn:current-dateTime() to obtain the date-time
- Extracted and trimmed the bookname from URI via dp:variable and XPath 2.0 fn:substring-after() function
- Use a FLOWR statement to query the books.xml document
- Created the response document with time stamp

Listing 1-18 Sample XQuery to produce book quantity and time stamp.

```
(: XQuery script to find book quantity. Name taken from URI :)

declare namespace dp = "http://www.datapower.com/extensions";

declare function local:timeStamp() as xs:string?
{
let $dt := fn:current-dateTime()
return string($dt)
};

let $uri := dp:variable("var://service/URI")
let $bookName := fn:substring-after($uri, "/")
let $books := doc('books.xml')/books/book
```

```
for $book in $books
    where $book/@name = $bookName
    return
      <bookQuantity>
        <book>
            {$book/@name}
            {$book/quantity}
        </book>
        <dateTime>{local:timeStamp()}</dateTime>
      </bookQuantity>
```

Listing 1-19 shows the results of the transformation. An XML document with the structure that was defined within the XQuery code. As in the XSLT example, the book quantity is returned as an XML document along with a time stamp. However in this example the timestamp is produced through the XPath 2.0 “fn:current-dateTime()” function.

Listing 1-19 Sample XQuery Output.

```
<bookQuantity>
    <book name="The_Hunger_Games">
        <quantity>100</quantity>
    </book>
    <dateTime>2014-12-27T16:18:49-05:00</dateTime>
</bookQuantity>
```

JSONiq Example

We can convert our earlier XQuery example to a JSONiq implementation as we’ve done in listing 1-20. We've changed the books.xml inventory document to our new books.json JSON conversion. The flow of our process is very similar:

1. Declare the "DP" namespace
2. Declare the JSONiq option and version
3. Declare a function for time-stamp again using the XPath 2.0 fn:current-dataTime() function
4. Fetch and strip the bookname from the URI using DataPower and XPath 2.0 functions
5. We've converted the FLOWR statement to use the JSONiq jn:members function
6. Returned JSON Object with time-stamp

Listing 1-20 Sample JSONiq query to produce book quantity and time stamp.

```
declare namespace dp = "http://www.datapower.com/extensions";

declare option jsoniq-version "0.4.42";

declare function local:timeStamp() as xs:string?

{

let $dt := fn:current-dateTime()

return string($dt)

};


let $uri := dp:variable("var://service/URI")

let $bookName := fn:substring-after($uri, "/")

(: fn:trace("x", "y") :)

let $logMesg := fn:concat("Getting Book Quantity for bookName =",
$bookName)

let $null := fn:trace($logMesg, "BKQNTQRY")


let $books := jn:json-doc('local:///books.json')("books")


for $book in jn:members($books)

where $book("name") = $bookName
```

```
return
{
    "bookQuantity" : {
        "book" : $book("name"),
        "quantity" : $book("quantity"),
        "dateTime" : local:timeStamp()
    }
}
```

As in the case of the XSLT stylesheet and the XQuery example, the results of the JSONiq query are similar. But in this case instead of producing an XML document, we've produced a JSON object. The result is in listing 1-21,a JSON document with the structure that was defined within the JSONiq code. As in the previous examples, the book quantity is retuned and along with a time stamp through XPath 2.0 "fn:curren-dateTime()" function wrapped in a local function.

Listing 1-21 Sample JSONiq Output.

```
{
  "bookQuantity":{
    "book":"The_Hunger_Games",
    "quantity":"100",
    "dateTime":"2014-12-27T16:25:20-05:00"
  }
}
```

GatewayScript Example

Now we'll perform the same book query with GatewayScript. Here we've started by "requiring" the "service-metadata" module which gives you access to the transaction's metadata including the URL. We also require the “urlopen” library which will allow us to read files from the “local:///” directories which we'll need to read the books.json document. We’ll learn more about these and other GWS modules in the next chapter. Listing 1-22 shows the complete GatewayScript code.

We create a GWS function “getBook” to retrieve the specific book from the array of books. And another to produce a timestamp in ISO format.

Notice the execution of urlopen, it utilizes asynchronous call backs for processing returned data, and we've defined those functions in-line in our example. We've also coded an error handling function. Notice that we parse the JSON document via the “reponse.readAsJSON()” invocation, and we write our new “bookQuantity” document out via the “session.output.write()” method. We'll learn more about accessing, parsing and creating context in the next chapters.

A summary of the processing:

1. Declare variables including the 'service-metadata' and 'header-metadata' and 'urlopen' modules.
2. Get and trim (using JavaScript's string split function) the bookname
3. Implement a function 'getBook' to loop through the books for our book matching bookname
4. Implement a function to produce a time stamp and convert it to ISO format
5. Do some logging
6. Use “urlopen” to read the books.json document
7. Made provision for error events

8. Produced the response Object and write it to the response stream. More on this to come as well.

Listing 1-22 Sample GatewayScript to produce book quantity and time stamp.

```
/*
    This Gateway Script to find book quantity. Name taken from URI
 */
var sm = require('service-metadata'), hm = require('header-metadata'), urlopen = require('urlopen');
var uri = sm.getVar('var://service/URI');
var uriSplit = uri.split("/");
var bookName = uriSplit[1];

function getBook(books, bookName) {
  for (var i = 0; i < books.length; i++) {
    if (books[i]['name'] == bookName) {
      return books[i]
    }
  }
  return null;
}

function getTimeStamp() {
  var d = new Date();
  return d.toISOString();
}

console.debug("Getting Book Quantity for bookName = " + bookName);

urlopen.open("local:///books.json", function(error, response) {
  if (error) {
    console.debug("urlopen error: " + JSON.stringify(error));
  } else {
```

```
    console.debug("urlopen response.statusCode = " +
response.statusCode);

    response.readAsJSON(function(error, books) {

      if (error) {

        session.output.write("readAsJSSON error: "

            + JSON.stringify(error));

      } else {

        var book = getBook(books['books'], bookName);

        if (book) {

          var bookQuantity = {};

          bookQuantity.book = book['name'];

          bookQuantity.quantity = book['quantity'];

          bookQuantity.dateTime = getTimeStamp();

          session.output.write(JSON.stringify(bookQuantity, null,
'\t'));

        }

      }

    });

  }

});
```

Here's the JSON document returned by the GatewayScript. Just like those we've produced in other examples complete with book quantity and time-stamp. The time stamp in this case was produced by native JavaScript date processing. Listing 1-23 shows the complete JSON response.

Listing 1-23 Sample GatewayScript Output

```
{

        "book": "The_Hunger_Games",

        "quantity": "100",

        "dateTime": "2016-01-14T14:37:41.274Z"

}
```

Summary

We've shown you the latest generation of development technologies available on DataPower. We've described the additions of JavaScript and the GatewayScript programming models, and the new Query features of XQuery and JSONiq extensions. We have also introduced the DataPower "Data Model" and its use of variables and functions to dynamically modify service configuration, perform cryptographic operations, optimize transactions, and more. Finally we demonstrated each of the programming languages; XSLT, XQuery, JSONiq and GatewayScript with complete working examples.

But there's more to do. The next chapter will show how to integrate these technologies into the DataPower service configuration, and in particular the Transform action and GatewayScript action, and how to utilize the multiple "Contexts" that may be available to a Transform action. You will also learn how to handle errors, parse different types of data in the GatewayScript environment, and more!

Chapter 2 Programming in the DataPower Environment

As you probably know by now, DataPower appliances offer many features that are easily configured through the use of its graphical interfaces and other configuration options. Perhaps you've configured digital signature verification or encrypted a message by simply dropping an action onto a policy rule using the drag and drop editor. If you're using one of the recent firmware releases, you've likely used the advanced configuration options and Patterns exposed by the Blueprint Console.

With all these simple configuration options you may be wondering why it would be necessary to write custom procedures. The reasons are as varied as the environments in which the DataPower devices are deployed. An application may require a customized logging function to archive transaction details. You may want to perform complex message enrichment via a call to an external database. Or perhaps you need some special attention applied to that mission critical application by providing a unique routing pattern.

This chapter will provide you with a closer look at the Processing Policy (also known as the Multistep Policy) and its actions, in particular those actions associated with XSLT and GatewayScript (GWS) programming. You'll see code examples of how to perform customization including writing messages to the DataPower log and its file system. You'll see how to manipulate message contents (including XML and JSON) and to parse, serialize, and transform messages in a programmatic fashion. We'll show you how to access "off box" data as well, using HTTP, HTTPS and other protocols. And you'll learn to regulate message flow, accepting and rejecting transactions, and see how to access protocol headers and other metadata.

You have the background; you now have the tools, let's put them to work!

Context – Message, Metadata and Variables

DataPower custom programming may be implemented at several points within the configuration. You may need to implement a custom Lightweight Directory Access Protocol (LDAP) process as part of the Authentication phase of AAA (Authentication, Authorization, and Auditing). The majority of custom programming is invoked via the Transform and GatewayScript (GWS) actions of the multistep rule.

Figure 2-1 shows an example of a rule that contains three Transform actions. Transformations, whether using XSLT, JavaScript, XQuery or JSONiq, all operate on context as it is created and passed within the Multistep Policy rule.

The selected rule, which is expanded in the display, is a Client to Server (request) rule. A Server to Client (response) rule with a single Transform action is also defined and displayed in the Configured Rules table. The following sections will introduce the way in which context, which includes message data and user defined "variable" data, is created and accessed within the policy.

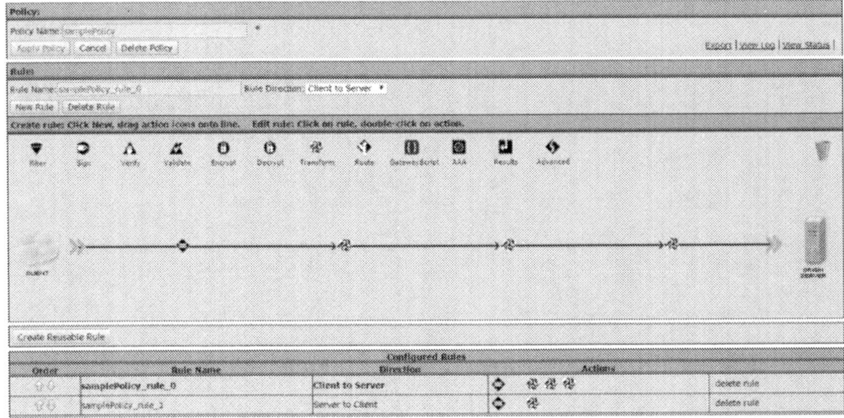

Figure 2-1 Processing Policy rule.

In order to fully utilize the context environment, we need to delve deeper into the way that context flows between the processing policy actions. This affects what data is available to the Transformation process.

The context that is created and passed within the policy rule contains not only the message data (if any), but also metadata about the transaction such as message properties, protocol headers, and any attachments that may have been submitted.

This data is provided to the actions within the rule, and they, in turn, may create new contexts. This allows for multiple active contexts within a rule. You could have an "INPUT" context, a "signedInput" context, and so on. In Figure 2-2, one of the Transform actions from the rule is shown; it uses INPUT as the input context and NULL as the output. (We talk about these contexts later.)

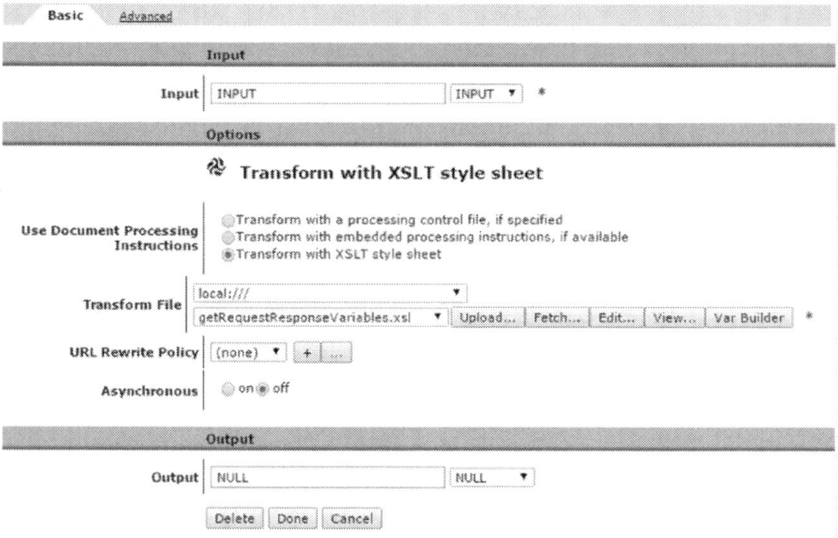

Figure 2-2 Sample input and output context assignments.

The context may be modified within each processing action. Context flow is not necessarily contiguous, and each action may access any of the previously created contexts. Figure 2-3 demonstrates this principle with two Transform actions, each accessing the original request context (INPUT) and producing unique contexts (OutPutA and OutPutB) that may be accessed by contiguous or noncontiguous actions within the policy rules. This provides the ability to enhance the context and the ability to access the modified content after applicable actions have been performed.

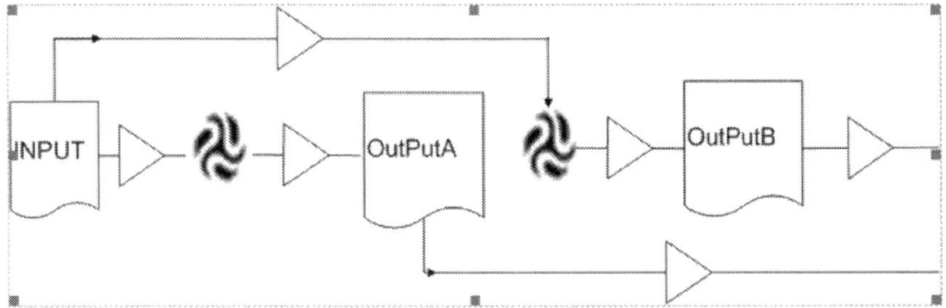

Figure 2-3 Document flow within a rule.

System, Service, and User-Defined Variables

In the previous chapter we introduced variables and the role they play in the DataPower data-model. Now let's take a closer look. Important information about the device, the service, and the transaction can be obtained and set using them. They are accessible from processing actions whether you use XSLT, GatewayScript, XQuery or JSONiq.

There are three primary classes of variables; system, service and context. The context class that we have been describing can contain variables that you can control. Each of these classes is unique in scope (lifespan) and accessibility. They may also be set graphically via a Set Variable action of a Multistep Policy.

Service variables define characteristics of the service associated with the current transaction. These variables are available to all actions within the policy to read and some to modify, but new service variables cannot be created. While using the XSLT programming model, variables take the form of "var://service/{VariableName}", referred to as "slash notation." For example, var://service/multistep/input-context-name is used to access the name of the input context of the current multistep action. While using the GatewayScript programming model, the variables take a "dot notation" form. Our input-context-name would be referenced as "serviceVars.multistep.inputContextName." We'll focus on slash notation for the remainder of our variable format discussion.

While service variables allow for the definition and access of service information, system variables provide a similar capability for system-wide metadata. However, while service variables exist only for the duration of the transaction, system variables are long lived. They take the form of var://system/{VariableName}. These variables exist until explicitly assigned a null value. It should be noted that if the DataPower system is restart or reloaded these variables will be reassigned. One characteristic of system variables is that they may be accessed not only by the current service, but by any service on the device, at any time. System variables require a minimum three-tiered name such as var://system/globalContext/performDefaultRouting.

Using system variable as a "global white board" provides a useful technique for multi service control. You could for example have a system variable define a flag which is used in conditional processing, extended logging perhaps. But as system variable modification is not synchronized, you need to avoid race conditions which risk modification collisions by centralizing their update. Having a scheduled rule which executes at start up or similar process is a good option.

A complete list of service and system variables is available in the Extension Functions and Elements Catalog available from the DataPower Knowledge Center. You should definitely become familiar with this resource; it's well-organized and presents valuable information on each variable, including "slash" and "dot" notation and whether the variable is read-only, write-only, or read-write.

User variables can be created as local to a particular context and accessible only when that context is assigned as the input of a processing action. For example, var://local/localVariable, If set it will be written to the output context specified on the action. This may be the same as the input context or it may be a new or existing context. Local variables were introduced prior to context variables and have several restrictions. For example then can only be accessed when the context they were created in is used as the input context. For example, consider a Transform action that reads the original INPUT context and creates a local variable in a new context named "newContext." The local variable created will be accessible only to subsequent actions that have access to the "newContext" context.

Named context variables are created in an independent context, and are accessible from any action within the multistep rule, including across request, response, and error phases. For example, var://context/myContext/contextVariable, defines a variable named context Variable within the myContext context. Using the hierarchical naming structure, "myContext/contextVariable", provides a means for organizing variables. You can define any number of variables within a context. The context can be newly defined, or one of the contexts previously created within the multistep rule.

While the local and context variable examples used a single level (after var://context/{contextName}) variable name, additional levels can be used. You can use this as a technique for variable organization. For example, var://context/myContext/Routing/CurrentEndPoint and var:// context/myContext/Routing/PreviousEndpoint are also acceptable context variable names.

TIP — Use Context Variables for Most Variable Use Cases

Use context variables unless you specifically want a local variable tied directly to a context and accessible only from that context. Context variables are more powerful and less restrictive than local variables. Local variables do not have the life span of a context variable and are lost on the request response cycle.

Variables are set within XSLT using the DataPower "dp:set-variable()" extension element and read via the "dp:variable()" extension function. Listing 2-1 shows an example of getting context variables "contextVariable" and "accessCount" from the myContext context. Special processing is performed on "accessCount." It will not be found on the first access attempt and we need to initialize it in this case. It is then incremented and set back into the context. The XSLT "number()" function will return a "NaN" string if the variable if not previous set with a valid number.

Listing 2-1 XSLT to access and modify variables.

```
<xsl:variable name="accessCount">
    <xsl:choose>
        <xsl:when
test="number(dp:variable('var://context/myContext/accessCount')>-1)">
            <xsl:value-of
select="number(dp:variable('var://context/myContext/accessCount'))"/>
        </xsl:when>
        <xsl:otherwise>
            <xsl:value-of select="number(0)"/>
        </xsl:otherwise>
    </xsl:choose>
</xsl:variable>
<dp:set-variable name="'var://context/myContext/accessCount'"
value="$accessCount+1"/>
```

GatewayScript provides a similar model. Within GatewayScript we rely on JavaScript objects that provide access to the methods and properties necessary for access and manipulation of the DataPower data-model. In the example in Listing 2-2, the session object is used to gain access to the context named "myContext", and its "getVar" method is used to get "contextVariable" and "accessCount" and subsequently to increment and set the "accessCount" just as was done in the XLST example.

Listing 2-2 GatewayScript to access and modify variables.

```
var myContext = session.name('myContext') ||
session.createContext('myContext');
var contextVariable = myContext.getVar('contextVariable');
```

```
/* If accessCount is unset, initialize it to 0 */
var accessCount = Number(myContext.getVar('accessCount'));
if (isNaN(accessCount)) {
    accessCount=0;
}
accessCount++;
myContext.setVar('accessCount', accessCount);
```

Variable access is not limited to processing through the Transform action. The Set Variable action (found within the advanced icon) may be used as well, and Figure 2-4 demonstrates this alternative method. One advantage to this approach is that you do not have to look into the processing code to see what variables are being set, and it provides some self-documentation to the policy. Variables set in this fashion are accessible by either the XSLT or GatewayScript programming models.

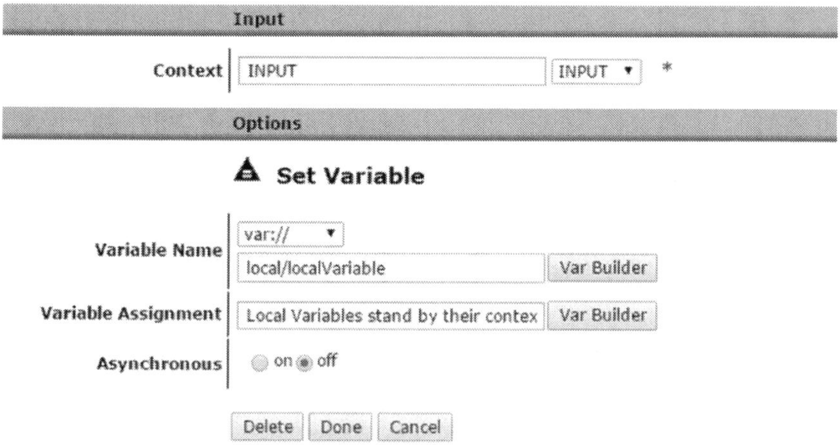

Input
Context INPUT INPUT *
Options
Set Variable
Variable Name var:// local/localVariable Var Builder
Variable Assignment Local Variables stand by their contex Var Builder
Asynchronous on off
Delete Done Cancel

Figure 2-4 Set Variable action.

The Set Variable action also provides a Variable Builder button ("Var Builder") that takes the guesswork out of variable assignment. It displays all the service, extension, and system variables that may be used as the target or source of set requests (some variables are read-only or write-only as will be noted) and provides input fields for the creation of context variables. Notice that the Var Builder does not provide for a way to create local variables and enforces the preferred context variable. The Set Variable action also does not provide some of the dynamic capabilities of variable setting with XSLT and GWS such as setting values via XPath or regular expressions. You can see the Var Builder in Figure 2-5.

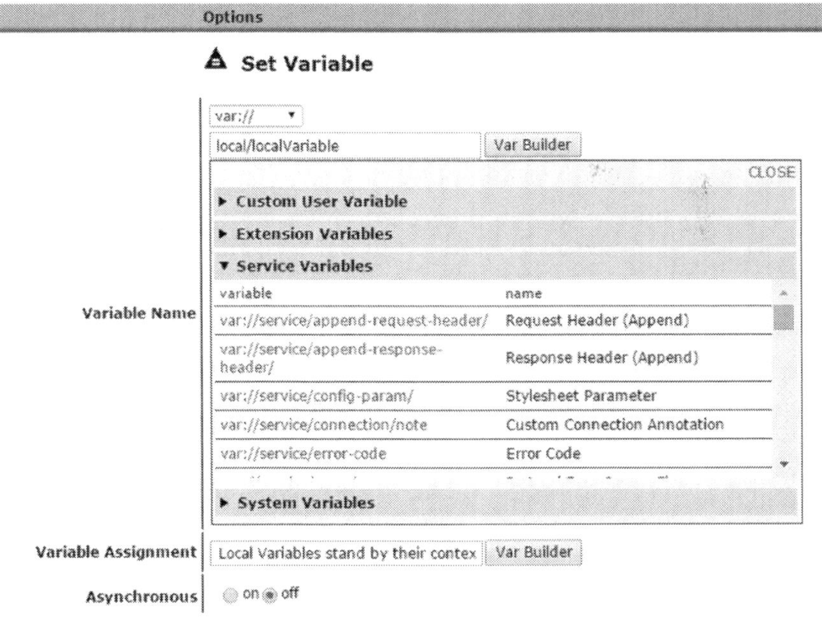

Figure 2-5 Set Variable, Variable Builder.

Set-Local-Variable

One final note on XSLT utilization of DataPower variables; it may be tempting to use DataPower variables as a convenient enhancement to the immutability characteristic of XSL variables. As you may know, XSL variables may not be changed after they are created. Many people struggle with this issue when learning XSLT. However there are patterns within XSLT such as recursive templates that are well-suited solutions for this problem. DataPower does provide a variant to the set-variable function, “set-local-variable().”

Don’t confuse this feature with local variables; they are “local” to the single XSLT in which they are created, not the context as local variables are. “Set-local-variable()” does not persist the variable beyond the current execution context, and it is not written to the output context. It may be used to set and reset a variable within a single XSLT stylesheet and is more efficient than the standard dp:variable and dp:set-variable functions. As of the current firmware “set-local-variable()” is only supported in XSLT.

TIP — dp:set-local-variable()

If you have a XSLT process which does a lot of dp-set-variable() commands for variables only used within the single processing action, you may find dp:set-local-variable() a more efficient option.

Predefined Contexts

By now you should have an understanding of the relationship between the processing (a.k.a. Multistep) policy context and the message data, metadata and variables it can contain. We've shown a few example of creating new named context like OutPutA and OutPutB. There are a few predefined contexts that you'll need to understand. You are probably already familiar with INPUT, it defines the context of the request. It also defines the input on response rules, which, of course, is not the same as the original input! So a Transform action on a request rule using INPUT sees the client's request. A transformation on the response side using the INPUT context sees the server's response.

OUTPUT defines the message sent to the backend server on a request rule and the response to the client on a response rule. Every rule that intends to produce a message should write to OUTPUT in some action.

NULL is a special use case that defines an empty context and can be used when an action does not produce meaningful output, or when it does not read from any previous context. It's an efficiency mechanism as well, as no context processing will be attempted. Think of it as the "bit bucket." Even in a Transform action that uses NULL, you'll be able to read system, context and service variables and execute DataPower extensions. If you don't need access to a message context, or the action won't change it, use NULL!

Finally, PIPE is another special case; it is another efficiency mechanism that describes two contiguous actions that produce and consume a context. The efficiency comes from the second action being prepared to receive its predecessor's output and not going through extra context processing. One side effect of PIPE is that you cannot define local variables, (those defined as var://local) within it. But as we've said previously there's limited reason to use local variables anyway.

TIP — Using NULL and PIPE

Use NULL as an output when you will not be producing an output context. Use PIPE when you are passing context between contiguous actions.

Use NULL as output when you will not produce an output context. It's more efficient and self-documents your actions. Use PIPE if two contiguous actions produce and consume a context.

Writing Messages to the DataPower Log

Writing messages to logging systems is a central part of any application architecture. You'll often need to log messages for accountability, providing a historical rendering to transaction records. And, in particular during application development, you may want to write messages for debugging purposes. All of the DataPower processing options (XSLT, GatewayScript, XQuery and JSONiq) provide logging capabilities. And logging within DataPower is so much more than just writing and reading messages. It's all about writing to message categories and publishing those to recording systems such as SYSLOG.

TIP — DataPower Logging Reliability

DataPower logging is "best effort", so the possibility exists that log messages may not be delivered. Options such as using SYSLOG over TCP, instead of SYSLOG over UDP, and controlling excessive logging will help. You should also be aware of the Log Action and its use for mission critical logging events. Please refer to the Knowledge Center for more information on DataPower Logging issues.

Within XLST, DataPower provides an implementation of the "<xsl:message>" element for this purpose. It accepts two attributes defined in the DataPower extensions namespace. The message's log level is assigned via dp:priority, and dp:type can be used to assign its log category. Listing 2-3 demonstrates the writing of a warning message to the default logging target. It uses the xsl:value-of element and concat() XPath function to print out the XSL variables previously established. One interesting XSL attribute of xsl:message (not demonstrated here) is "terminate", which, if it is set to "yes" will cause the transaction to fail and end processing of the current XSLT Transform action. It's a standard XSLT attribute, not a DataPower attribute and does not require the "dp" namespace. You can use this attribute yourself to force the failure of a transaction, though other techniques such as the use of the Filter action and "dp:reject()" are preferred.

TIP — terminate and dp:reject()

Many people are confused by the effects of terminate and dp:reject(). While they both will cause the current transaction to fail and end execution of subsequent actions in the rule, terminate will end execution of the processing process immediately, dp:reject() does not.

Listing 2-3 XSL Producing Logging Message.

```
<xsl:message dp:priority="'warn'">

    <xsl:value-of select="concat('on Request, Input Context Name= ',
$inputContextName,

        ', Output Context Name= ', $outputContextName, ',
var://local/localVariable=

        ', $localVariable, ',
var://context/myContext/contextVariable=

        ', $contextVariable)"/>

</xsl:message>
```

Of course GatewayScript also provides log messaging capabilities. The "console" module provides this functionality. Its use will be very familiar to anyone who has used the C language "printf()" function and the various format specifiers to construct message strings. You use "%s" for string, "%i" for a signed decimal integer and so on. The log level is assigned through various methods (alert, critical, error, ...) of the console object. Listing 2-4 shows an example of a debug message within GatewayScript that formats strings via the "%s" format specifiers.

Listing 2-4 GatewayScript Producing Logging Message.

```
console.debug("on Request, Input Context Name=%s, Output Context
Name=%s, var://context/myContext/contextVariable=%s",
inputContextName, outputContextName, contextVariable);
```

Demonstration of Context, Variable Access and Logging

Let's put these techniques to use in an example configuration. We're going to demonstrate the setting and accessing of context and service variables across the request and response cycle. You'll remember that local variables are associated with a specific context and only accessible when that context is the input to a Transform/GWS action. Context and service variables are accessible from any Transform/GWS action, regardless of the input context, including NULL.

We've described the use of XSLT and GatewayScript to access and set variables, and we'll show complete examples of each here. On the request, a "Set Variable" action is used to create the context variable var://context/myContext/contextVariable. It will then be accessed, and another context variable is created in a Transform/GWS action.

The same code (XSLT & GatewayScript) will be used in both the request and the response cycles and will demonstrate the accessibility and lifetime of context variable. Service variables, such as var://service/transaction-rule-type will be used to determine the direction and other information about the transaction processing.

Table 2-1 shows the flow of the Multistep Policy rules including the action type, input and output context and the action performed at each step.

Table 2-1 SetVariables Policy Actions.

Request Actions

Action	Input Context	Output Context	Content
SetVar	INPUT		var://context/myContext/contextVariable="Context Variables Rule the Policy!"
Transform/GWS	NULL	NULL	getRequestResponseVariables.{xsl/js}
Transform/GWS	INPUT	OUTPUT	getRequestResponseVariables.{xsl|js}

Response Actions

Action	Input Context	Output Context	Content
Transform/GWS	INPUT	OUTPUT	getRequestResponseVariables.{ xsl|js }

Using XSLT for Variable Access

Figure 2-6 shows how the rules would look in the WebGUI drag and drop policy editor. The request "Client to Server" rule with a Match, SetVar and two Transforms, there are the first and forth rule in the policy. There is also a response "Server to Client" with a Match and a single Transform action. There are similar rules for GatewayScript which we'll discuss later.

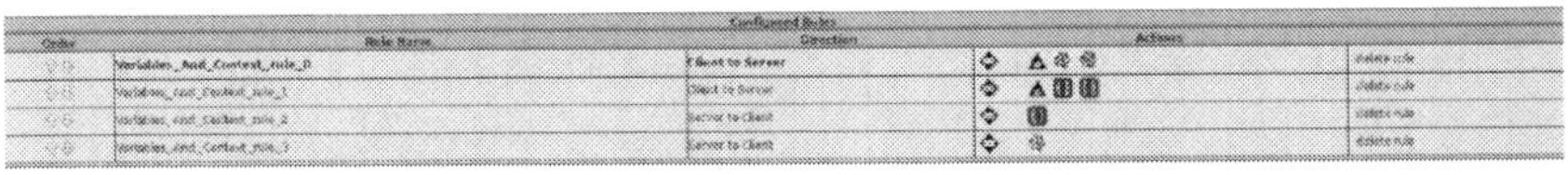

Figure 2-6 Get and Set Variables through XSLT.

The simple yet complete XSLT stylesheet shown in Listing 2-5 shows several functions that you will use again and again in your DataPower development. The stylesheet declaration contains the “dp” namespace and is identified in the “extension-element-prefixes” which tells the XSLT processor that elements in this namespace are functions. You may have to modify these when you use other libraries like EXSLT.

After matching the root of the input document (importantly, we’re not actually processing any of its nodes, they might not even be XML!), we determine the rule direction and Input and Output Context Names using three service variables “transaction-rule-type, input-context-name and output-context-name.” Notice some extra coding around the output context name. It’s empty in the case of “NULL”, for our printing purposes we initialize it in this case.

Next, we get the context variable that was previously set in the “SetVar” action, “myContext/contextVariable.” We're going to track it through the request/response cycle to make sure it is accessible from both directions and while using any input context. Remember that’s one of the features of the context variable.

Then we get and increment the context variables “/myContext/accessCount.” It is used as a counter for the execution of this stylesheet. On the first execution, the variable will not be found, so we wrap its access in an “xsl:choose” statement, and initialize the xsl:variable to 0 in that case. It is incremented and set back into the “myContext” context. A debug level log message is used to track our progress.

Now that we've gathered up the information on the rule direction, input and output context names and read (and set in the case of accessCount) the myContext variables, we'll print the request and response variables in the log. Notice that we use an debug level message and the “xsl:value-of” element and “concat()” function to format the message.

Listing 2-5 XSLT Demonstrating Variable Access.

```
<?xml version="1.0" encoding="UTF-8"?>

<xsl:stylesheet extension-element-prefixes="dp" version="1.0"
xmlns:dp="http://www.datapower.com/extensions"

    xmlns:xsl="http://www.w3.org/1999/XSL/Transform">

    <!-- -->

    <!-- This stylesheet gets and sets variables -->

    <!-- -->

    <xsl:template match="/">

        <!-- -->

        <!-- get the rule direction, Input and Output Context Names -
->

        <!-- -->

        <xsl:variable name="transaction-rule-type"
select="dp:variable('var://service/transaction-rule-type')"/>

        <xsl:variable name="inputContextName"
select="dp:variable('var://service/multistep/input-context-name')"/>

        <xsl:variable name="outputContextName">

            <xsl:choose>

                <xsl:when
test="dp:variable('var://service/multistep/output-context-name')">
```

```
                    <xsl:copy-of
select="dp:variable('var://service/multistep/output-context-name')"/>
                </xsl:when>
                <xsl:otherwise>
                    <xsl:text>NULL</xsl:text>
                </xsl:otherwise>
            </xsl:choose>
        </xsl:variable>
        <!-- -->
        <!-- get and increment the context variables -->
        <!-- -->
        <xsl:variable name="contextVariable"
select="dp:variable('var://context/myContext/contextVariable')"/>
        <xsl:variable name="accessCount">
            <xsl:choose>
                <xsl:when
test="number(dp:variable('var://context/myContext/accessCount')>-1)">
                    <xsl:value-of
select="number(dp:variable('var://context/myContext/accessCount'))"/>
                </xsl:when>
                <xsl:otherwise>
                    <xsl:value-of select="number(0)"/>
                </xsl:otherwise>
            </xsl:choose>
        </xsl:variable>
        <dp:set-variable name="'var://context/myContext/accessCount'"
value="$accessCount+1"/>
        <!-- -->
        <xsl:message dp:priority="'debug'">
            <xsl:value-of select="concat('accessCount= ',
$accessCount+1)"/>
        </xsl:message>
        <!-- -->
        <!-- print the request and response variables-->
        <!-- -->
        <xsl:message dp:priority="'debug'">
```

```
            <xsl:value-of select="concat('on ', $transaction-rule-type, ', Input Context Name=
                ', $inputContextName, ', Output Context Name= ', $outputContextName,
                ', var://context/myContext/contextVariable= ', $contextVariable)"/>
        </xsl:message>
        <!-- -->
    </xsl:template>
    <!-- -->
</xsl:stylesheet>
```

We can test out the XSLT using a variety of services. In this case, we'll just use two XML Firewalls. The first will use “Non-XML”, as the request and response types. This allows us to do HTTP Get or POST requests. You are probably familiar with the XMLFW's loopback capability, but to get the response rule to execute we can’t use loopback mode, we'll need to send the request to a backend service. We’ve used a second XMLFW in loopback mode as our backend. Setting its request and response type to “Pass Through” provides a simple implementation without the need for a policy rule while providing the backend service necessary for execution of the response rule in the first XMLFW

Executing a request against the service produces the following log messages; we've filtered out all but the “xsltmsg” category for readability. Reading from the bottom up, we can see the “myContext/accessCount” variable is read and incremented across the request/response cycle, even in those transformation steps that use NULL as input. Again, the context variable is accessible across the request response cycle. And the context variable that we set in the initial “SetVar” of the request rule ("myContext/contextVariable") is similarly available. Figure 2-7 shows the message as produced in the log.

time	category	level	tid	direction	client	msgid	message
Sunday, November 1, 2015							
6:43:57 AM	xsltmsg	information	268961	response	192.168.1.143	0x80000001	xmlfirewall (Variables_And_Context): on response, Input Context Name= INPUT, Output Context Name= OUTPUT, var://context/myContext/contextVariable= Context Variables rule the policy!
6:43:57 AM	xsltmsg	information	268961	response	192.168.1.143	0x80000001	xmlfirewall (Variables_And_Context): accessCount= 3
6:43:57 AM	xsltmsg	information	268961	request	192.168.1.143	0x80000001	xmlfirewall (Variables_And_Context): on request, Input Context Name= INPUT, Output Context Name= OUTPUT, var://context/myContext/contextVariable= Context Variables rule the policy!
6:43:57 AM	xsltmsg	information	268961	request	192.168.1.143	0x80000001	xmlfirewall (Variables_And_Context): accessCount= 2
6:43:57 AM	xsltmsg	information	268961	request	192.168.1.143	0x80000001	xmlfirewall (Variables_And_Context): on request, Input Context Name= NULL, Output Context Name= NULL, var://context/myContext/contextVariable= Context Variables rule the policy!
6:43:57 AM	xsltmsg	information	268961	request	192.168.1.143	0x80000001	xmlfirewall (Variables_And_Context): accessCount= 1

Figure 2-7 Log messages demonstrating context and variable access with XSLT.

Using GatewayScript

We need to 'require' modules that we'll be working with in GWS, in this case, all we need is the "service-metadata" module which give access to service variables. Context objects are created and accessed through the "session" object. This object provides access to context variables and service parameters. Service parameters can be added to the GWS action in the policy rule, just as they can be added to a Transform action using XSLT to provide parameters available within the processing code. Don't confuse service parameters with the service variables we've already discussed. The "session" object is not required; it is available to all GWS and is unique to each session of a GWS action. The service-metadata module is used to get the rule information; direction, input and output content names, just like in the XSLT example.

Listing 2-6 shows the complete GWS. We use the session object to get the "myContext" variables. Notice that we have to make provision (as we did in the XSLT example) for no previous "myContent/accessCount" context variable, and if it's not there (we use a "not a number" test) it is set to 0. The count is incremented and set back into the myContext context.

As in the XSLT example, we print information about the rule direction, input and output context and the variables in the log. In this case using the printf() like syntax and the console module's debug method.

Listing 2-6 GatewayScript Demonstrating Variable Access.

```
var sm = require('service-metadata');

/* */

/* get the rule direction, Input and Output Context Names */

/* */

var transactionRuleType = sm.getVar('var://service/transaction-rule-
type');

var inputContextName = sm.getVar('var://service/multistep/input-
context-name');

var outputContextName = "NULL";

if (sm.getVar('var://service/multistep/output-context-name')) {

    outputContextName = sm.getVar('var://service/multistep/output-
context-name');

}

/* */

/* get and increment the context variables */

/* */

var myContext = session.name('myContext') ||
session.createContext('myContext');

var contextVariable = myContext.getVar('contextVariable');
```

```
var accessCount = number(myContext.getVar('accessCount'));
if (isNaN(accessCount)) {
    accessCount = 0;
}
accessCount++;
myContext.setVar('accessCount', accessCount);
console.debug("accessCount = %i", accessCount);
/* */
/* log the request and response variables */
/* */
console.debug("on %s, Input Context Name=%s, Output Context Name=%s,
var://context/myContext/contextVariable=%s", transactionRuleType,
inputContextName, outputContextName, contextVariable);
```

Figure 2-8 shows the “gatewayscript-user” category messages produced by the GWS. You can filter the log output so that only “gatewayscript-user” messages are displayed in the log. Note the messages are filtered for display, showing only the “gatewayscript-user” category. As we saw in the XSLT example, the context variable's lifespan extends through the request/response cycle.

Sunday, November 1, 2015

6:56:43 AM	gatewayscript-user	debug	271537	response	192.168.1.143	0x8580005c	xmlfirewall (Variables_And_Context): on response, Input Context Name=NULL, Output Context Name=OUTPUT, var://context/myContext/contextVariable=Context Variables rule the policy!
6:56:43 AM	gatewayscript-user	debug	271537	response	192.168.1.143	0x8580005c	xmlfirewall (Variables_And_Context): accessCount = 3
6:56:43 AM	gatewayscript-user	debug	271537	request	192.168.1.143	0x8580005c	xmlfirewall (Variables_And_Context): on request, Input Context Name=INPUT, Output Context Name=OUTPUT, var://context/myContext/contextVariable=Context Variables rule the policy!
6:56:43 AM	gatewayscript-user	debug	271537	request	192.168.1.143	0x8580005c	xmlfirewall (Variables_And_Context): accessCount = 2
6:56:43 AM	gatewayscript-user	debug	271537	request	192.168.1.143	0x8580005c	xmlfirewall (Variables_And_Context): on request, Input Context Name=NULL, Output Context Name=NULL, var://context/myContext/contextVariable=Context Variables rule the policy!
6:56:43 AM	gatewayscript-user	debug	271537	request	192.168.1.143	0x8580005c	xmlfirewall (Variables_And_Context): accessCount = 1

Figure 2-8 Log messages demonstrating context and variable access with GWS.

We have demonstrated the ability to access and create several types of variables. We've put together a policy that accesses and updates them and we've used service variables to determine rule direction and to determine the input and output context name. And finally we used DataPower's XSLT <xsl:message> implementation and GWS's console.debug to write messages to the log.

So which do you prefer? In this example there was no accessing of the message content, we only accessed variables and wrote messages to the log. You could have used XSLT, GWS, XQuery or JSONiq. DataPower leaves that choice up to you!

Debugging Methods

Using the Probe for Variable Display

Now that we're on the path to development, let's pause for a moment to review some of the debugging methods you can use.

The “Probe” is a very effective tool to analyze traffic and for following request and response messages through the Multistep policy. You can see protocol headers and content modification between actions within the policy, view system, service, local and context variables. You can see the results of function calls within the policy rules. And the Probe is not just for XSLT either. You can still step through policy rules that invoke GWS, XQuery or JSONiq as well.

Using the GatewayScript Debugger

When you're using GWS you have another option. The very powerful GWS debugger, which is implemented in a fashion similar to GDB (GNU Debugger) allows you to step through your GWS code, view variables and execute GWS commands. It’s an extremely valuable tool. You can see more about the Probe and GWS debugger in the “Development Tools” chapter later in this volume.

Writing Documents to the File System

Writing data to the DataPower file system is often a helpful debugging method. It allows for the viewing of selective information long after the transaction has ended. While you can view context within the Probe as it flows through the policy rules, the data written to the file system may contain large document structures or other data not easily viewable from the Probe display.

TIP — Writing to the local: Directory

In some older firmware versions, you could have written to the "local:" directory which is contained within the DataPower flash drive. This is not a good practice. More recent firmware restricts write capabilities to the DataPower temporary: directory and potentially its RAID subdirectory if you have that enabled. And the temporary: directory is flushed with each reload of the device, so any unnecessary files or files that you have forgotten about will be removed automatically.

As of the current firmware release, writing to the file system is only available via XSLT extension functions. We could achieve this file system functionality though some "fancy foot work", perhaps invoking other services, but there's a lot of new feature support going on in the GWS area so stay tuned. For now we'll demonstrate the XSLT capabilities.

We'll use the XSLT "book query" sample of the previous chapter. In this example, we simply create an XML node and return that document to the client. If we wanted to store that document for later retrieval we can use the "dp:dump-nodes()" extension function. The function takes a node set as the source, so we'll first create an XSLT variable to hold the book quantity response. Then we can use the variable in the "dp:dump-nodes()" function and simply use the "xsl:copy-of" element to return the document to the client. Pretty simple, Listing 2-7 shows the changes to the stylesheet.

Listing 2-7 XSLT Enhanced to Write File.

```
<xsl:variable name="bookQuantity">
    <xsl:element name="bookQuantity">
        <xsl:element name="book">
            <xsl:attribute name="name">
                <xsl:value-of select="$book/@name"/>
            </xsl:attribute>
            <xsl:element name="quantity">
                <xsl:value-of select="$book/quantity"/>
            </xsl:element>
        </xsl:element>
        <xsl:element name="dateTime">
            <xsl:call-template name="timeStamp"/>
        </xsl:element>
    </xsl:element>
</xsl:variable>
<!-->
<!- Dump the bookQuantity node to the temporary:/// directory -->
<!-->
<dp:dump-nodes file="concat('temporary:///bookQuantity.xml_',
date:date-time())" nodes="$bookQuantity">
```

Figure 2-9 shows the files as they are written to the file system. As we've added the date and time to the file name, we can refer back to them if required.

temporary:	Actions...		
bookQuantity.xml_2015-11-01T07:22:10-05:00	Edit	136	Nov 1, 2015 7:22:10 AM
books.xml	Edit	606	Nov 1, 2015 7:22:10 AM

Figure 2-9 Files written to temporary: file system.

If you want to view the file, just like any other file on the DataPower file system, you can either just click the file name, or use the edit button which would allow you to modify the file. Listing 2-8 shows the document, just as we'd expect to find it.

Listing 2-8 Book Quantity response document.

```
<bookQuantity><book
name="The_Hunger_Games"><quantity>100</quantity></book><dateTime>2015
-02-06T10:28:17-05:00</dateTime></bookQuantity>
```

Accessing Protocol Headers

There are many occasions when accessing protocol headers will be a vital part of transaction processing. Information about the request, such as the user-agent that made the request, can be used to determine the appropriate response format. A browser declares itself using this header, and knowing that you could potentially return an HTML document that it can consume. Other HTTP protocol values such as the client IP and content-type are part of the standard manifest of headers. Other protocols, such as IBM WebSphere MQ (MQ), send headers, such as the Message descriptor (MQMD), that carry not only information about the request type, but details about the queues and queue managers used.

DataPower services allow for header manipulation at configuration time, and we'll see examples of protocol header manipulation in actions in the Real World Examples Chapter, but for now, let's review the DataPower extension elements and functions available.

Many of the functions are available using XSLT, GatewayScript, XQuery and JSONiq. And there are extensions available to get, set, append, and remove protocol headers.

XSLT Support for protocol header access

Some of the typical XSLT functions include:

- dp:request-header()—Get a named header of all types
- dp:set-request-header()—Set a named header of all types
- dp:append-request-header()—Append a named header of all types

Listing 2-9 demonstrates an XSL snippet that obtains the value of the protocol headers. It fetches a header named “foo” and sets one named “bar.” Notice that headers are categorized as both request and response. You need to set a header in the response category for it to be returned to the client for example.

TIP — Efficiently Writing Headers

When working with protocol headers, there is an efficiency method that should be used. When a client is making requests to a server, DataPower cannot write the request stream out until all headers have been written. This delay can be minimized by committing the header stream, which is telling the DataPower processor you are finished with header manipulation. This is done by use of the "dp:freeze-headers()" extension element.

Listing 2-9 Header Retrieval in XSLT.

```
<!-- -->

<!-- Get the foo request header, remove it and set the response bar
header to its value -->

<!-- -->

<xsl:template match="/">

    <xsl:variable name="fooHeader" select="dp:request-header('foo')"
/>

    <dp:remove-request-header name="foo"/>

    <dp:set-response-header name="'bar'" value="$fooHeader"/>

    <dp:freeze-headers/>

</xsl:template>
```

Listing 2-10 shows the response from the header manipulating stylesheet. We've used curl and the -v "verbose" option to see the headers (this in a condensed listing). You can see that the request contains a "foo" header with a value of "foobar." The XSLT receives this, obtains the value of "foo", and creates a new header named "bar" with its value.

Listing 2-10 Response from Header Setting XSLT.

```
curl http://192.168.1.125:2054 -v -H "Foo:foobar"

> GET / HTTP/1.1

> Foo:foobar

< HTTP/1.1 200 Good

< bar: foobar
```

GatewayScript Support for protocol header access

Of course GWS provides the same capacity for header access, creation and removal. Using GWS you'll need to "require" the "header-metadata" module. Listing 2-11 shows the same functionality implemented in GWS. Quite simply we declare a variable "fooHeader" and use the header-metadata's "current.get()" method to populate it, and the "current.remove()" and "current.set()" to, well, remove and set the new "bar" header.

Listing 2-11 GatewayScript performing Header Manipulation.

```
/* Get the foo header, remove it and set the response bar header to
its value */

var hm = require('header-metadata');


var fooHeader = hm.current.get('foo');

hm.current.remove('foo');

hm.response.set('bar', String(fooHeader));
```

Listing 2-12 shows the same curl example and similar results as the XSLT example. In this curl example, the header "foo" is supplied and the responding "bar" header received.

Listing 2-12 GatewayScript Header Manipulation Results.

```
curl http://172.16.247.128:2067/js -H "foo: foo" -v

> GET /xslt HTTP/1.1
> foo: foo
< HTTP/1.1 200 Good
< bar: foo
```

The Filter Action

The Filter action is used to reject the current transaction and is available in all multistep policies. Just use the drag and drop editor to pull the Filter action down to your processing rule. The Filter action is a place holder for an XSLT script to determine whether the transaction should be rejected. When a transaction is rejected, a message and invalid status code is returned to the client. As of the current release, 7.2.0.1, the Filter action does not accept GWS. But, you can perform similar functions as we'll demonstrate using a GatewayScript action and executing GWS.

When using XSLT, filtering has a special relationship with two extension elements; “dp:accept()” and “dp:reject().” When using GWS you can reject the transaction using the “reject” method of the session object. Remember, the session object is available to all GWS processes. To reject a transaction simply use a GWS action and use the “reject” method of the session object.

When using XSLT you can use the “dp:accept” and “dp:reject” extensions in any Transform action, not just the

Filter action. However, it is preferred to use the Filter action, as this acts as a self-documenting feature of the multistep rule, and we suggest that you do just that. Use the Filter action anytime you want to verify whether a request should be allowed through the system.

Filtering in XSLT

Listing 2-13 demonstrates a code snippet that performs the filter function. We are using the EXSLT "date-in-week()" function to get the day of the week, and if it is not "Tuesday" which equates to the number "3", the transaction is rejected. Supplying a literal error message to the reject function returns the message to the client. We've printed a message into the log at the error log level when an exception occurs, but the dp:reject() function will print its own log message as well. Remember when we first introduced dp:reject, the processing flow does not stop at the dp:reject() statement, it the transaction is rejected after the action is completed. In fact you can execute a dp:accept() even after you've done a reject(). And as we mentioned, it would also be possible to end program execution with the terminate attribute of the xsl:message element. Personally, we prefer programs that do not have arbitrary end points and instead have well-structured processes that avoid these techniques.

Listing 2-13 Sample Filter Execution in XSLT.

```
<xsl:stylesheet exclude-result-prefixes="xsl dp env dpconfig"
extension-element-prefixes="dp" version="1.0"
xmlns:date="http://exslt.org/dates-and-times"
xmlns:dp="http://www.datapower.com/extensions"
xmlns:env="http://schemas.xmlsoap.org/soap/envelope/"
xmlns:xsl="http://www.w3.org/1999/XSL/Transform">
```

```
   <!-- -->
   <xsl:template match="/">
       <xsl:variable name="dayOfWeek" select="number(date:day-in-
week())"/>
       <xsl:variable name="TUESDAY" select="number(5)"/>
       <xsl:variable name="dayOfWeek" select="date:day-
name(date:date())"/>
       <!-- -->
       <xsl:message dp:priority="debug">
           <xsl:value-of select="concat('dayOfWeek = ',
$dayOfWeek)"/>
       </xsl:message>
       <xsl:if test="$dayOfWeek != $TUESDAY">
           <dp:reject>
               <xsl:value-of select="'Books are only sold on
Tuesday'"/>
           </dp:reject>
           <xsl:message dp:priority="error">
               <xsl:value-of select="'Books are only sold on
Tuesday'"/>
           </xsl:message>
       </xsl:if>
   </xsl:template>
</xsl:stylesheet>
```

Figure 2-10 shows the messages that are emitted to the log. The middle message is that emitted by the “dp:reject()” function under the “xsltmsg” category, the top and bottom are the result of the “xsl:message()” messages which are under the xsltmsg category.

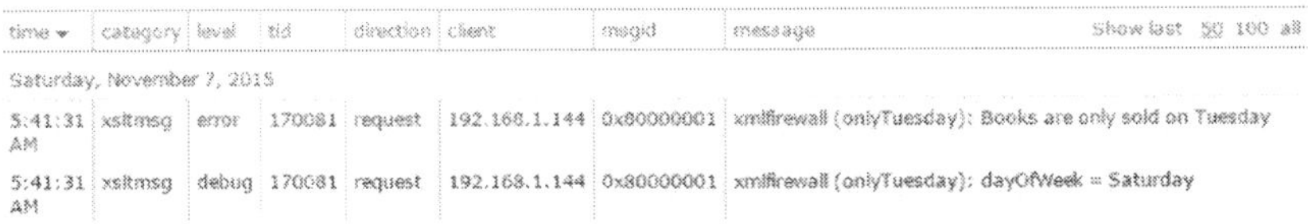

time ▾	category	level	tid	direction	client	msgid	message Show last 50 100 all
Saturday, November 7, 2015							
5:41:31 AM	xsltmsg	error	170081	request	192.168.1.144	0x80000001	xmlfirewall (onlyTuesday): Books are only sold on Tuesday
5:41:31 AM	xsltmsg	debug	170081	request	192.168.1.144	0x80000001	xmlfirewall (onlyTuesday): dayOfWeek = Saturday

Figure 2-10 Log showing results of dp:reject() and xsl:message at error priority.

Filtering in GWS

We mentioned that GWS is not supported in the Filter actions, and that we can perform filtering using the GWS action and simply using the "session.reject()" method. The example in Listing 2-14 shows processing similar to the previous XSLT example. We get the date of the week, this time just using the JavaScript "Date()" object and then using the "session.reject()" method when the day is not Tuesday.

Listing 2-14 GWS code determining the day of the week, and rejecting if not Tuesday.

```
var date = new Date();
var dayOfWeek = date.getDay();
const TUESDAY = 3;

console.debug("dayOfWeek = " + dayOfWeek);

if (dayOfWeek != TUESDAY) {
        console.error("Books are only sold on Tuesday");
        session.reject("Books are only sold on Tuesday");
}
```

Figure 2-11 shows the messages that are emitted to the log. All GWS console output messages are found in the “gatewayscript-user” log category, while the “session.reject” is under the “gatewayscript” category.

Saturday, November 7, 2015

5:34:26 AM	gatewayscript-user	error	168081	request	192.168.1.144	0x8580005c	xmlfirewall (onlyTuesday): Books are only sold on Tuesday
5:34:26 AM	gatewayscript-user	debug	168081	request	192.168.1.144	0x8580005c	xmlfirewall (onlyTuesday): dayOfWeek = 6

Figure 2-11 Log showing results of console.error and session.reject.

Routing

Dynamic Routing is a common operation on the DataPower device, and a widely used procedure. Routing can be performed for a variety of reasons. Perhaps you want to send your high value requests to a set of highly available, redundant, high-performance backend services, and some less critical requests to a less expensive platform. Of course DataPower allows you to do this with the Route action in a Multistep Policy and in several other highly configurable ways as well. For example you can use Load Balancer Groups with members statically defined and routed using methods such as “round-robin” or “least-connections.” You can use more advanced features such as the On Demand Router as well. But (maybe you’re seeing a pattern here), you can also perform routing directly within XSLT and GWS. As we know, the actions within a policy are supported by the extension functions, elements and GWS modules.

Let’s look at a couple examples of routing using XSLT and GWS. While we are doing so, we will also point out one more layer of detail within the DataPower configuration. We've spoken of extensions and variables, and we've exposed some interesting service variables that allowed us to do things like get the name of contexts, and so on. In many cases the extensions that we use are really methods for the settings of these service variables. The extensions provide a more structured mechanism and remove some of the peculiarities associated with setting the service variables directly. But there may be instances when setting the variables directly provides a little more flexibility.

Routing using XSLT

Let's see if the examples can make this clear. Our first example in Listing 2-15 shows the use of the "dp:xset-target()" extension element. It enables the setting of host, port, and SSL information via an SSL Proxy Profile object. Executing this XSLT changes the backend server address. There is another routing extension, "dp:set-target()." This is functionally the same as "dp:xset-target()", but does not enable the use of XPath statements in the attribute assignment, so you will probably just use "dp:xset-target()" in most cases.

Listing 2-15 Sample use of xset-target for Routing.

```
<xsl:variable name="ip" select="'10.10.10.15'"/>
<xsl:variable name="port" select="'88'"/>
<xsl:variable name="ssl" select="true()"/>
<xsl:variable name="sslid" select="'someSSLProxyProfile'"/>
<!- ->
<xsl:template match="/">
    <!- ->
```

```
    <dp:xset-target host="{$ip}" port="{$port}" ssl="{$ssl}"
sslid="{$sslid}"/>

    <xsl:message dp:priority="'info'">

        <xsl:value-of select="concat('Setting routing to ', $ip, ':',
$port)"/>

    </xsl:message>

</xsl:template>
```

The next example in Listing 2-16 shows how the same sort of routing can be performed via direct variable setting. In this case, the "var://service/routing-url" variable is directly modified. This is the core of the routing mechanism and is the variable that the "dp:xset-target()" extension modifies. However, modifying this variable directly allows us to not only change host and port, but also the protocol and Uniform Resource Identifier (URI). You can only change to supported protocols, of course.

Getting back to the ease of use that the extensions provide, an example is a secondary variable associated with routing, "var://service/routing-url-sslprofile." This is used to establish the SSL Proxy Profile used for SSL. It must be set prior to the setting of "var://service/routing-url." Using "dp:set-target()" or "dp:xset-target()" does this automatically for you by providing an attribute for the SSL Proxy Profile.

Listing 2-16 Sample Routing-URL Routing.

```
<xsl:variable name="newBackSideURL"
select="concat('dpmq://QueueManager/PUT?RequestQueue=',
$requestQueue)"/>

<xsl:message dp:priority="'info'">

    <xsl:value-of select="concat('Setting, var://service/routing-url
to ', $newBackSideURL)"/>

</xsl:message>
```

```
<!- ->

<dp:set-variable name="'var://service/routing-url'"
value="$newBackSideURL"/>
```

Routing using GatewayScript

Routing is performed in GWS in a very similar fashion as XSLT. You can use the similar variables to define the URL and optionally the URI, and SSL Crypto profile. In the example in Listing 2-17, you can see that all you need to do is "require" the "service-metadata" module and then modify its "routingUrlSslprofile" and "routingUrl" properties. Again, you can always refer to the Knowledge Center to find the variable names you are interested in.

Listing 2-17 Routing in GatewayScript.

```
var service = require('service-metadata');

service.routingUrlSslprofile = 'book2';

service.URI = '/book2';

service.routingUrl = 'https://127.0.0.1:2070';

console.debug('Routing set to https://127.0.0.1:2070');
```

URL Open

urlopen is an extremely powerful DataPower extension. If you have read the chapter on services you are aware of all the various protocols supported by the Multi-Protocol Gateway. Each of these protocols is implemented within the MPGW via Front Side Handlers and Backend URLs. Each of these objects in turn utilizes the URL Open Extension to implement protocol dependent IO. URL Open supports

- FTP/SFTP (File Transfer Protocol)
- HTTP/HTTPS (Hypertext Transfer Protocol)
- ICAP (Internet Content Adaptation Protocol)
- IBM WebSphere MQ (IBM WebSphere Message Queuing)
- NFS (Network File System)
- SMTP (Simple Mail Transfer Protocol)
- SNMP (Simple Network Management Protocol)
- SQL (Structured Query Language)
- TCP (Transmission Control Protocol)
- TIBCO-EMS (TIBCO Enterprise Message Service)
- WAS-JMS (WebSphere Application Server Java Messaging Services)
- IMS (IBM Information Management System)

You can also use the URL Opener within custom XSLT. We will see real-life examples in the next chapter, but for now let's take a closer look at the implementation. Each protocol used with url-open uses a slightly different URL, so you may need to look into the Extension Function Catalog to determine precisely what URL format to use. But all protocols share a common format and attributes as shown in Listing 2-18.

Listing 2-18 URL-Open Format.

```
<xsl:variable name="response">
    <dp:url-open target="url"
        response="xml | binaryNode | ignore |
            responsecode response code-ignore | savefile"
        resolve-mode="xml | ignore"
```

```
        base-uri-node="nodeSet"
        data-type="xml | ignore | filename"
        http-headers="xpathExpression"
        content-type="contentType"
        ssl-proxy="sslProxyName">
    </dp:url-open>
</xsl:variable>
```

The attributes shown in Table 2-2 describe all the potential parameters (attributes), you can use on the url-open element. Most of the parameters are optional; the only required parameter is the target.

Table 2-2 URL-Open Parameters

Parameter	Description
target	Target URL
response	Specifies how to handle response: • xml, parse • binaryNode, unparsed • ignore, discard response • responsecode, protocol response is returned with response data • responsecode-ignore, only protocol response is returned
resolve-mode	Only used if target is attachment, determines attachment type
base-uri-node	Only if target is relative, used to determine URL
data-type	XML—default Base64—input data is Base64 Filename—local file contains input
http-headers	Optional nodeset of protocol headers
content-type	Optional content-type
ssl-proxy	Optional SSL Proxy Profile to use for SSL

Listing 2-19 shows a simple MQ url-open element. It reads a message from the replyQueue and returns it into the variable "response." The MQ Queue Manager is named InventoryQM, and it describes where the actual Queue Manager resides. We could have added other parameters to the URL, including timeout values, credential information, and so on. You can read the formal definition of this URL in the Extension Functions Catalog.

Listing 2-19 Sample MQ URL-Open.

```
<xsl:variable name="response">
    <dp:url-open
target="dpmq://InventoryQM/mqGet?ReplyQueue=replyQueue"/>
</xsl:variable>
```

Any data submitted with the request is entered as a child of the url-open element. Listing 2-20 demonstrates the submission of a GET request over HTTP. It's the same book quantity service we demonstrated in listing 2-9. In this example, the service is hosted on port 2060 and the HTTP URL is defined as the target attribute of the dp:url-open element The response would be in the $response variable along with the response code due to the use of the response= "responsecode" attribute.

Listing 2-20 Sample HTTP URL-Open.

```
    <xsl:template match="/">
       <!-- -->
       <xsl:variable name="response">
           <dp:url-open
target="http://192.168.1.125:2060/The_Hunger_Games"
response="responsecode"/>
       </xsl:variable>
       <xsl:copy-of select="$response"/>
```

```
        <!-- -->
    </xsl:template>
```

Listing 2-21 shows the results of the url-open execution. The responsecode is available as a child of the url-open response as are the content-type and protocol headers. The bookQuantity is returned as a child of url-open as well. We could simply return that to the client or perform additional processing on the node as desired.

Listing 2-21 Sample HTTP URL-Open reponse.

```
<url-open>
   <responsecode>200</responsecode>
   <content-type>text/html</content-type>
   <headers>
       <header name="Cache-Control">no-transform</header>
       <header name="Host">127.0.0.1:2060</header>
       <header name="X-Global-Transaction-ID">178259</header>
       <header name="Via">1.1 bookQuantityXSLT</header>
       <header name="X-Client-IP">127.0.0.1</header>
       <header name="Content-Type">text/html</header>
       <header name="Date">Tue, 03 Nov 2015 08:52:03 GMT</header>
   </headers>
   <response>
       <bookQuantity>
           <book name="The_Hunger_Games">
               <quantity>100</quantity>
           </book>
           <dateTime>2015-11-03T03:52:03-05:00</dateTime>
       </bookQuantity>
   </response>
</url-open>
```

URL Open Using GatewayScript

GatewayScript supports the use of a similarly named function “urlopen” for accessing the DataPower file system and access of services over HTTP or HTTPS and with version 7.2.0.0 MQ. Other protocols will likely be added as the GWS model matures so keep an eye on new firmware releases for these and other GWS feature additions.

The use of urlopen requires the urlopen module. The basic implementation supports the use of a JSON object to contain options such as the target URL, the method to use, protocol headers and other parameters such as timeout values. A simpler implementation using just the target-url instead of the options object is also available. The urlopen module is implemented using a callback function to asynchronously obtain the results of the urlopen operation.

Listing 2-22 shows an example of urlopen use within GWS. It is executing a “GET” request against the service previously shown in Listing 2-11 which performed protocol header manipulation. If you refer back to that example you'll see that this service created a new header named “bar” using the contents of an incoming header, “foo.”

The GWS constructs a JSON object “options” to contain the “foo” header and other options controlling the service invocation. The callback function is implemented in-line, exposing the error and response data in like-named variables. You can see how the response headers from the service response are used to create a like-named “bar” header in the client response to this facade service.

Listing 2-22 GatewayScript use of urlopen.

```
var urlopen = require('urlopen');
var hm      = require('header-metadata');

var options = {
  target: 'http://192.168.1.129:2067/js',
  method: 'GET',
  headers: { 'foo' : 'foo' },
  timeout: 60,
};

urlopen.open(options, function(error, response) {
    if (error) {
        console.debug("urlopen error: " + JSON.stringify(error));
    } else {
        response.readAsBuffer(function(error, buffer) {
            if (error) {
                console.debug("readAsBuffer error: "
                        + JSON.stringify(error));
            } else {
                hm.response.set('bar', hm.response.headers.bar);
            }
        });
    }
});
```

Listing 2-23 shows the execution of the new service. The request is made using curl, no headers are supplied. The GWS is executed, performs the urlopen (supplying the “foo” header) and is returned the “bar” header with the contents of “foo.”

Listing 2-23 Facade Service Response showing new HTTP Header creation.

```
curl http://192.168.1.129:2071/js -v
> GET /js HTTP/1.1
< HTTP/1.1 200 Good
< bar: foo
```

Accessing and Processing Message Context

Our examples so far have dealt primarily with accessing metadata, for example the names of input and output contexts for a given action. There will be many occasions when this information and other metadata, such as protocol headers will be all that is needed to implement the functionality desired. Routing for example is often determined by the URI or transport headers such as the host name. There's no need to know the content of the message to make this routing determination.

However, these examples have not given much attention to the message data itself and in many cases we have simply copied the input context to the output. In many cases will need to do much more.

We'll demonstrate message processing in using both XML and JSON message formats by creating a Book Order service. This service will receive a request (in XML or JSON format) and produce a Purchase Order containing line items for each book and a total for the purchase. We'll make it a little more interesting by checking inventory (the books local XML database) to ensure we have enough to sell, and we'll use

XQuery to calculate the order total. XQuery is a great tool for the query functionality.

Book Purchase Order using XML and XSLT

So, let's take a look at the purchase order in XML format. It contains a "book_order" root and "book" children elements. There are attributes for name, author and isbn-13 and book has "quantity" as a child for the number of books to purchase. Listing 2-24 shows a complete sample.

Listing 2-24 Purchase Order in XML Format .

```
<book_order>
   <book name="The_Hunger_Games" author="Suzanne Collins" isbn-13="9780439023481">
         <quantity>5</quantity>
   </book>
   <book name="IBM_DataPower_Handbook_Second_Edition" author="Bill Hines, John Rasmussen, Jim Brennan, Ozair Sheikh, Harley Stenzel" isbn-13="9780137148196">
         <quantity>1001</quantity>
   </book>
</book_order>
```

You should be familiar with the opening declarations for XSLT processing on DataPower. Listing 2-25 shows the standard "xsl:stylesheet" construction. In this section we've accessed the books database (stored in $booksDB) and the root template creates a "books" element and "book" element in the output or "results" document for each book ordered. We'll see next how these book "line items" are processed.

Listing 2-25 Book Purchase Order root template.

```
<?xml version="1.0" encoding="UTF-8"?>
<xsl:stylesheet exclude-result-prefixes="xsl dp"
    extension-element-prefixes="dp"
    version="1.0"
    xmlns:dp="http://www.datapower.com/extensions"
    xmlns:xsl="http://www.w3.org/1999/XSL/Transform">
    <!-- -->
    <!-- Get the books database, it contains the quantity and price
of each book-->
    <!-- -->
    <xsl:variable name="booksDB"
select="document('local:///books.xml')"/>
    <!-- -->
    <!-- Build a "books" variable -->
    <!-- It contains a list of "book" elements with quantity and cost
-->
    <!-- -->
    <xsl:template match="/">
        <!-- -->
        <xsl:variable name="books">
            <xsl:element name="books">
                <xsl:apply-templates select="/book_order/book"/>
            </xsl:element>
        </xsl:variable>
        <!-- -->
        <!-- Use an XQuery to calculate the total cost of the ordered
books -->
        <!-- Create a Purchase Order with books/book list and total
cost -->
        <!-- -->
        <xsl:variable name="totalPrice" select="dp:xquery-
transform('SumForXQuery.xq', $books)"/>
        <xsl:element name="PurchaseOrder">
            <xsl:copy-of select="$books"/>
            <xsl:element name="Total">
```

```
              <xsl:value-of select="concat('Thanks for your order,
your total purchase price is
                  ', $totalPrice)"/>
          </xsl:element>
       </xsl:element>
    </xsl:template>
```

Continuing with Listing 2-26 we see that the total price of the order is calculated by using the "dp:xquery-transform()" function and passing it the "$books" list of purchased books and the name of an XQuery query. We'll describe that purchase list in detail next, but Listing 2-27 shows the simplicity of the XQuery that calculates the total purchase price. We use the simple FLWOR statement we described in Chapter 1, adding the price of each book with the quantity ordered.

Listing 2-26 XQuery to Calculate Total Purchase Price.

```
sum(for $book in /books/book return $book/@price * $book/@quantity)
```

Now circling back around to the creation of the book purchase list, we see the template, which matches "book" elements and is invoked by the "<xsl:apply-templates select="/book_order/book"/>" statement in Listing 2-27. It starts by simply creating a variable to hold the book's name (it's used in subsequent XPath statements) and by checking to ensure there are enough books in inventory to fulfill the order. If there are not, then we sell all we've got and make a comment in the final purchase order ('Your order was reduced').

Listing 2-27 Purchase order book template

```
<!-- -->

<!-- This template will produce each individual book PO line item-->

<!-- Make sure there are enough books in inventory to fulfill the
order! -->

<!-- -->

<xsl:template match="book">

    <xsl:variable name="name" select="@name"/>

    <xsl:variable name="purchaseQuantity">

        <xsl:choose>

            <xsl:when test="$booksDB/books/book[@name=$name]/quantity
&gt;= ./quantity">

                <xsl:value-of select="/quantity"/>

            </xsl:when>

            <xsl:otherwise>

                <xsl:value-of
select="$booksDB/books/book[@name=$name]/quantity"/>

            </xsl:otherwise>

        </xsl:choose>

    </xsl:variable>

    <!-- -->

    <xsl:element name="book">

        <xsl:attribute name="name">

            <xsl:value-of select="@name"/>

        </xsl:attribute>

        <xsl:attribute name="author">

            <xsl:value-of select="@author"/>

        </xsl:attribute>

        <xsl:attribute name="quantity">

            <xsl:value-of select="$purchaseQuantity"/>

        </xsl:attribute>

        <xsl:attribute name="price">

            <xsl:value-of
select="$booksDB/books/book[@name=$name]/price"/>

        </xsl:attribute>
```

```
        <xsl:if test="$purchaseQuantity != ./quantity">
            <xsl:attribute name="incompleteOrder">
                <xsl:value-of select="'Your order was reduced'"/>
            </xsl:attribute>
        </xsl:if>
    </xsl:element>
</xsl:template>
```

Let's test the service. We'll send it a request (using the Purchase Order in Listing 2-27). Listing 2-28 shows the response. You see the "book" entries matching the order. Note that the requested quantity of 1001 DataPower Handbooks was reduced to 1000 and a notice was added to the PO. We have such as hard time keeping those in inventory!

Listing 2-28 Purchase order response.

```
<PurchaseOrder>
    <books>
        <book name="The_Hunger_Games" author="Suzanne Collins"
quantity="5" price="1.23"/>
        <book name="IBM_DataPower_Handbook_Second_Edition"
author="Bill Hines, John Rasmussen, Jim Brennan, Ozair Sheikh, Harley
Stenzel" quantity="1000" price="3.21"
            incompleteOrder="Your order was reduced"/>
    </books>
    <Total>Thanks for your order, your total purchase price is
3216.15</Total>
</PurchaseOrder>
```

Message processing with JSON and GatewayScript

The purchase order in JSON format is similar to our XML example. It contains a "book_order" root and the "book" children are contained within a JSON array. The original XML attributes for name, author and isbn-13 as well as "quantity" are represented as name/value pairs, the quantity being a numeric value. Listing 2-29 shows a complete sample.

Listing 2-29 Purchase Order in JSON Format.

```
{

  "book_order": {
    "book": [
      {
        "name": "The_Hunger_Games",
        "author": "Suzanne Collins",
        "isbn-13": "9780439023481",
        "quantity": 5
      },
      {
        "name": " IBM_DataPower_Handbook_Second_Edition ",
        "author": "Bill Hines, John Rasmussen, Jim Brennan, Ozair
Sheikh, Harley Stenzel" ",
        "isbn-13": "9780137148196",
        "quantity": 1001
      }
    ]
  }
}
```

The GatewayScript processing is similar to the previous XSLT. There are a couple structural differences. The first task will be to read the books database; again we need it to check inventory quantity and the price of the books we're going to sell. While we used XPath's document() function in XSLT, we are using DataPower's urlopen.open() function in GWS.

urlopen.open() is implemented asynchronously. This requires that we establish a "call-back" function to process its response. Listing 2-30 demonstrates this implementation as an in-line function declaration. Another asynchronous function is used (and another in-line call-back function declared) to read the response from urlopen.open() and to parse it as JSON data.

Listing 2-30 GatewayScript builds book database from the books.json document and read purchase order from input context.

```
/*
    This Gateway Script will process a purchase order with line items
for each book purchased
 */


/* Get the books database (that requires urlopen) it contains the
quantity and price of each book */
/* If the books database is read successfully, begin processing the
book order */


var urlopen = require('urlopen');
urlopen.open("local:///books.json", function(error, response) {
  if (error) {
    console.debug("urlopen error: " + JSON.stringify(error));
  } else {
    response.readAsJSON(function(error, booksDB) {
      if (error) {
        console.debug("readAsJSSON error: " + JSON.stringify(error));
```

```
      } else {
        console.debug("The Books Database contains: %s", booksDB);
        readBookOrder(booksDB);
      }
    });
  }
});
```

If all goes well, the variable booksDB will now contain a JSON object representing the books.json data. Having completed these two asynchronous functions, we can now begin processing the book order. This requires us to parse the input message containing the order as shown in Listing 2-31. This is done by accessing the "session" object. It provides access to transaction information, including access to input, output and other context that have been created within a service, just as we've described earlier in this chapter. In the readBookOrder function, we use the session object's "input.readAsJSON()" method to parse (asynchronously again) the input book order message.

Listing 2-31 GatewayScript reading the input book order from the session object.

```
/*  read the book purchase request from the input context */
/*  it could have multiple book orders */
/*  Get the Purchase Order (PO) object and write it to the output
stream */

function readBookOrder(booksDB) {

  session.input.readAsJSON(function(error, bookOrder) {
    if (error) {
```

```
      console.debug("readAsJSSON error: " +
bookOrder.stringify(error));

    } else {

      var PO = producePurchaseOrder(bookOrder, booksDB);

      session.output.write(JSON.stringify(PO, null, '\t'));

    }

  });

}
```

The remainder of the GWS implements the guts of the book order processing. The producePurchaseOrder() function is the main routine and is passed a reference to the previously parsed bookOrder and booksDB. It builds the purchaseOrder object which contains an array of lineItem objects. Each lineItem contains the name, author, quantity and price of the individual books purchased. There could be more than one and based on inventory amounts the amount sold could be reduced from that requested. Finally, the total cost of all books is added to the purchase order. Listing 2-32 shows the implementation of the producePurchaseOrder function.

Listing 2-32 Function to build Purchase Order.

```
/*  Build a "PurchaseOrder" object */

/*  It contains a list of "books" elements, each with quantity and
cost */

/*  The lineItem object contains the details of each book purchase,
name, quantity, price */

/*  Calculate the TotalPrice */


function producePurchaseOrder(bookOrder, booksDB) {


  var purchaseOrder = {};
```

```
  purchaseOrder.books = new Array();
  var totalPrice = 0;

  for (var i = 0; i < bookOrder.book_order.book.length; i++) {
    var lineItem = produceLineItem(bookOrder.book_order.book[i],
booksDB);
    var totalPrice = totalPrice + (lineItem.price *
lineItem.quantity);
    purchaseOrder.books[i] = lineItem;
  }
  purchaseOrder.TotalLine = 'Total: Thanks for your order, your total
purchase price is '
      + totalPrice;
  return purchaseOrder;
}
```

Listing 2-33 shows the functions used to produce the PO line item and to check inventory. You'll notice that the “checkInventory” function returns an object containing the quantity and price. The quantity might be less than that originally requested. And if so, we add a name/value pair “incompleteOrder” indicating so

Listing 2-33 Produce Line Item processes checking inventory for book quantity and price.

```
/* This function will produce each individual book PO line item
object */
/* Make sure there are enough books in inventory to fulfill the
order! */
/* If the order was reduced or unfilled note it in lineItem object
*/

function produceLineItem(bookOrder, booksDB) {

  var inventoryItem = checkInventory(bookOrder.name,
bookOrder.quantity, booksDB)
```

```
  var lineItem = {name: bookOrder.name, author: bookOrder.author,
quantity: inventoryItem.quantity, price: inventoryItem.price};


  if (inventoryItem.quantity < Number(bookOrder.quantity)) {

    if (inventoryItem.quantity == 0) {

      lineItem.incompleteOrder = "Your order was unfilled";

    } else {

      lineItem.incompleteOrder = "Your order was reduced";

    }

  }

  return lineItem;

}


/* First build an empty inventoryItem in case there are no books in
inventory  */

/* Check the inventory to ensure there are enough books available */

/* if not, reduce the order to those available */


function checkInventory(name, quantity, booksDB) {


  var inventoryItem = {quantity: 0, price: 0};


  for (var i = 0; i < booksDB.books.length; i++) {

    console.debug("booksDB.books[i].name=" + booksDB.books[i].name);

    if (booksDB.books[i].name == name) {

      if (Number(quantity) <= Number(booksDB.books[i].quantity)) {

        inventoryItem.quantity = Number(quantity);

      } else {

        inventoryItem.quantity = Number(booksDB.books[i].quantity);

      }

      inventoryItem.price = Number(booksDB.books[i].price);

      break;

    }

  }
```

```
  return inventoryItem;
}
```

Listing 2-34 shows the results of the GWS purchase order processing. Very similar to the example using XML/XSLT, but of course in this case we're producing a JSON response. As we pretty printed the purchase order via JSON.stringify, it's in a nice human readable format.

Listing 2-34 Completed Purchase Order.


```
{
  "books": [
    {
      "name": "The_Hunger_Games",
      "author": "Suzanne Collins",
      "quantity": 5,
      "price": 1.23
    },
    {
      "name": "IBM_DataPower_Handbook_Second_Edition",
      "author": "Bill Hines, John Rasmussen, Jim Brennan, Ozair
Sheikh, Harley Stenzel",
      "quantity": 1000,
      "price": 3.21,
      "incompleteOrder": "Your order was reduced"
    }
  ],
  "TotalLine": "Total: Thanks for your order, your total purchase
price is 3216.15"
}
```


We've demonstrated the parsing and processing on incoming XML and JSON messages. We've shown how to traverse the messages using XPath, XQuery, XSLT templates and GWS. We've shown how to produce new messages in response to the client. In many cases your choice of processing will be dictated by the client message (XML or JSON), but in others, especially when you don't need to access the message content, the choice is yours!

Summary

This chapter introduced some key architectural components of the DataPower "data-model'. We've described the various types of variables and the Multistep Policy's use of context for message, metadata and variable containment and processing. We've discussed and demonstrated some core features of processing in both the traditional XSLT programming model and the newer and powerful GatewayScript API.

Of course we have not demonstrated all capabilities. But using these components of variable and context control, message parsing and manipulation, service invocation through url-open and the vast catalog of DataPower functions will open the door for an unlimited array of capabilities.

By now, you have the tools required to handle the corner cases and unique requirements that may be presented to you. Go forth and customize!

Chapter 3 Real World Programming Examples

Putting It Together: Sample DataPower Service Configurations

Now that you have read the preceding chapters, Chapter 1, "Introduction to DataPower Development" and Chapter 2, "Programming within the DataPower Environment"; you have been introduced to the fundamentals of DataPower development. You have seen the way DataPower extension functions provide access and control of the DataPower system while programming with both XSLT and GatewayScript (GWS). We've demonstrated the use and support of the EXSLT catalogs and JavaScript modules. Beyond these development models and APIs we have also introduced you to the latest Query capabilities for XML and JSON through DataPower's use of XQuery and its JSONiq extension. In firmware 7.2 DataPower has completed the loop allowing for XML parsing and query through GatewayScript and through XSLT. It also provides for JSON parsing and query using GatewayScript and XSLT. In some cases you'll choose the processing language based on your environment, for example you'd probably use GWS for JSON documents. But in other cases the choice may be more of a stylistic decision.

It's not that big green box (XA35) anymore focusing on super-fast XML/XSLT processing. DataPower has continued its significant advances in customization capabilities during the latest several firmware releases and now provides a powerhouse of development and customization capabilities matching the needs of the most demanding applications.

All you need now is a reason to customize; maybe the examples presented in this chapter will inspire you. Resist the urge to customize just for customization sake! Yea, we know its fun. But remember, DataPower has all sorts of built in capabilities out of the box. Signature verification, routing and conditional processing can be done just by using the Drag and Drop Policy Actions. Don't reinvent the wheel. But if you need to, you have the tools, you have the power, and you have the technology!

Sample Configuration Examples

This chapter presents examples that explore several aspects of DataPower customization. The examples are chosen to demonstrate core DataPower processing including; well used extension functions, document access and query, multistep parameter integration, message processing (both positive/accepted and negative/rejected) flows, dynamic processing and routing, and implementation of common security patterns. We will use these examples to demonstrate processing in both XML/XSLT and JSON/GWS. You will also be able to download the sample configurations to load onto your DataPower appliances and test on your own. Please see instructions at:

http://wildlakepress.com/books/15-information-technology/18-datapower-handbook-resources

Here are the examples that we'll use:

1) If This Is Tuesday, This Must Be Belgium - An example of protocol header inspection and message control using XSLT and GWS.

2) Dynamic Transaction Routing through SSL/TLS Certification interrogation with dynamic routing profile assignment using XSLT, XQuery and GWS.

If This Is Tuesday, This Must Be Belgium

We use the title of this 1969 film to demonstrate the ability to control transactions based on the content of protocol headers. In this implementation, the premise is that transactions are allowed to freely execute against a service, except on days that are designated for special control through values specified in control documents. For example on Tuesdays, we require that a protocol header named "THIS", if found on the request, must contain the value "Belgium". If it is not present, the value of Belgium will be used to create the header.

This fun sample enables us to explore XML and JSON document processing in XSLT and GatewayScript, and the use of core processing including XSLT and GWS date processing, the reading and setting of protocol headers and how to reject messages which do not meet our criteria. This example will also show how to externalize parameters in a multistep action providing for an enhanced dynamic configuration capability.

Figure 3-1 shows the multistep policy required to implement this example. There are two request rules, the first uses a PCRE expression to match URLs that contain "^/(?i)js" for GatewayScript processing and the second "^/(?i)xlst" for

XSLT processing. The PCRE uses an "ignore case" option, so either "XSLT" or "xslt" would work. The XSLT rule contains a "Filter" action to specify the XSLT. If you remember from previous discussions in Chapter XXX "Introduction to DataPower Services", the "Filter" action is a transformation (it executes an XSLT stylesheet) and has the capability to reject or accept incoming requests. The GatewayScript rule contains a single GWS action. As of the current firmware revision (7.2) the "Filter" action only works with XSLT. But the GWS action has all the capabilities of the "Filter" action as we will demonstrate.

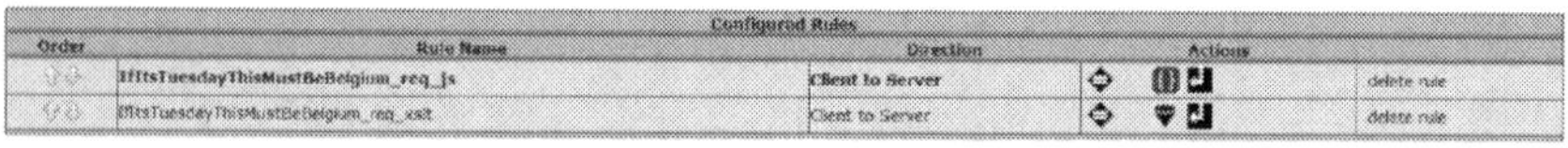

Configured Rules				
Order	Rule Name	Direction	Actions	
	IfItsTuesdayThisMustBeBelgium_req_js	Client to Server		delete rule
	IfItsTuesdayThisMustBeBelgium_req_xslt	Client to Server		delete rule

Figure 3-1 If This Is Tuesday Processing Policy.

We are focusing on the "accept/reject" processing component of our service and using an XML Firewall in "loopback" mode to do so. A complete implementation of this service would typically protect an application backend resource of the service. One of our goals in this example is to demonstrate the use of "Parameters" within multistep actions. Parameters allow for the assignment of values to be used within the processing XSLT/GWS, without having to modify the underlying code. This capability is shown with the "GatewayScript" Action in Figure 3-2. You can "Add Parameters" and enter values as we have done with the "whichHeaderName" field; you can do the same within an XSLT Transform action. We will show how to access this data shortly.

Figure 3-2 GatewayScript Action and Parameter definition.

Parsing and processing of XML and JSON control documents

Let's look at the control documents that will define our day of the week restrictions. We want to have the capabilities of defining the required value for any particular day of the week and to optionally add the header if it is not present. Let's look at the XML implementation first. Listing 3-1 shows the simple XML document. The day elements contain "dayOfWeek", attributes which will be matched to the EXLST date extension function week value and an "addIfNotSet" attribute which will determine if the header can be optionally created.

Listing 3-1 Day of Week Restrictions XML document.

```
<?xml version="1.0" encoding="UTF-8"?>
<dayOfWeekRestrictions>
    <!-- -->
    <!-- Sunday = 1, Monday = 2, ... -->
    <!-- -->
    <day dayOfWeek="1" mustBe="Boston" addIfNotSet="1"/>
    <day dayOfWeek="2" mustBe="Rockport" addIfNotSet="1"/>
```

```
    <day dayOfWeek="3" mustBe="Belgium"/>
    <day dayOfWeek="5" mustBe="Amsterdam" addIfNotSet="1"/>
    <day dayOfWeek="7" mustBe="Gloucester"/>
</dayOfWeekRestrictions>
```

We can do the same type of representation in JSON although the implementation is a little different. First of all, we can't put comments in the JSON document! Rather an odd restriction we think, regardless, this particular document (or external JSON object representation) is pretty straightforward. Listing 3-2 shows the object layout. It contains a "dayOfWeekRestrictions" property and a "day" property with an array of name values pairs. Notice that array indexes are different between the XML and JSON samples. As we will see the EXSLT and JavaScript day functions return different values to correspond to the '1' versus '0' base index values for their arrays.

Listing 3-2 Day of Week Restrictions JSON document.

```
{
  "dayOfWeekRestrictions": {
    "day": [
      {
        "dayOfWeek": "0",
        "mustBe": "Boston",
        "addIfNotSet": "1"
      },
      {
        "dayOfWeek": "1",
        "mustBe": "Rockport",
        "addIfNotSet": "0"
      },
```

```
      {
        "dayOfWeek": "2",
        "mustBe": "Amsterdam",
        "addIfNotSet": "1"
      },
      {
        "dayOfWeek": "4",
        "mustBe": "Belgium"
      },
      {
        "dayOfWeek": "6",
        "mustBe": "Gloucester"
      }
    ]
  }
}
```

ifItsTuesdayThisMustBeBelgium implementation in XSLT

Ok, so let's start looking at some code. Listing 3-3 shows the preface of our XSLT. It shows the standard namespace declarations required for DataPower processing, namely the "xsl" and "dp" namespaces. And as we are going to use EXSLT date functions we need to define the "date" namespace and its well defined URL for that. The "xsl:param" declaration is for the parameter we just configured in the multistep action. Here we can define a display literal and help for the "Transformation" Action advanced screen and a default value. GatewayScript at this time does not provide these display literals and help extensions to parameter definition. Though as we've said and will demonstrate, you can define parameters in the GWS action and access it though GWS processing.

Listing 3-3 XSLT declaring required name spaces.

```
<?xml version="1.0" encoding="UTF-8"?>

<!-- -->

<!-- This XSLT Script will check for the proper use of protocol
headers -->

<!-- The http Header to check is defined in this action, with a
default value defined below; dpconfig:whichHeaderName -->

<!-- An XML document (dayInWeekRestrictions.xml) will contain a list
of 'day' elements -->

<!-- <day dayInWeek="1" mustBe="Amsterdam" addIfNotSet="1"/> -->

<!-- These will control whether the Header is required, its value,
whether it should be created if not found -->

<!-- And whether it should be created ("addIfNotSet") if not found or
the transaction rejected in error  -->

<!-- -->

<xsl:stylesheet exclude-result-prefixes="xsl dp dpconfig" extension-
element-prefixes="dp" version="1.0"
xmlns:date="http://exslt.org/dates-and-times"
xmlns:dp="http://www.datapower.com/extensions"
xmlns:dpconfig="http://www.datapower.com/param/config"
xmlns:xsl="http://www.w3.org/1999/XSL/Transform">

    <!-- -->

    <xsl:param name="dpconfig:whichHeaderName" select="'THIS'"/>

    <dp:param name="dpconfig:whichHeaderName" type="dmString"
xmlns="">

        <display>Which Header to Check</display>

        <description>This is the HTTP Header to check</description>

    </dp:param>

    <!-- -->
```

Let's look at the remainder of the XSLT. We've broken down the main template into a couple sections. Listing 3-4 shows the requirements for accessing dates through EXSLT. And importantly we are reading and parsing the "dayOfWeekRestrictions.xml" document through the XSLT document() function. It will be available through the "todaysRestrictions" variable. The required header and its value and "addIfNotSet" option are fetched through XPath statements accessing the "dayOfWeekRestrictions" document. XPath is great for this. But, don't forget XQuery, we could have used that as well and we will in our next example.

Listing 3-4 XSLT accessing restrictions XML document.

```
    <xsl:template match="/">

        <!-- -->

        <!-- Get XML Restrictions document -->

        <!-- Get the day of the week, use it to find
todaysHeaderMustBe for this day (if any) -->

        <!-- Get the name of the day, 1 for Sunday, 2 for Monday, ...
-->

        <!-- Determine if the header MUST or MAY be set to particular
value -->

        <!-- See if its to be added if not found -->

        <!-- -->

        <xsl:variable name="dayInWeek" select="number(date:day-in-
week())"/>

        <xsl:variable name="dayOfWeek" select="date:day-
name(date:date())"/>

        <xsl:variable name="todaysRestrictions"
select="document('dayOfWeekRestrictions.xml')/dayOfWeekRestrictions/d
ay[@dayOfWeek = $dayInWeek]"/>

        <xsl:variable name="todaysHeaderMustBe"
select="$todaysRestrictions/@mustBe"/>

        <xsl:variable name="addIfNotSet"
select="boolean($todaysRestrictions/@addIfNotSet)"/>

        <xsl:variable name="dQ">"</xsl:variable>

        <!-- -->

        <!-- Get Action Paramaters "whichHeaderName", compare the
dayInWeek against any todaysHeaderMustBe restrictions -->

        <!-- -->
```

```
        <xsl:variable name="httpHeaderName"
select="$dpconfig:whichHeaderName"/>

        <xsl:variable name="httpHeaderValue" select="dp:request-
header($httpHeaderName)"/>

        <!-- -->

        <xsl:message dp:priority="debug">

            <xsl:value-of select="concat('Today is ', $dayOfWeek, ',
day # ', $dayInWeek)"/>

        </xsl:message>
```

The next step is to determine if the header is a requirement for today. Listing 3-5 shows the necessary XSLT. We know that there was a value specified for the day of the week, now we must determine if it MUST be provided or it MAY be created for the client if not provided based on the "addIfNotSet" optional attribute. All this information is rendered into the log through the "xsl:message" statement. Notice the use of the $dQ variable. We like to have nicely formatted log messages and wrapping the header name and value within double quotes is a good way to do this, especially if there are spaces in any of these values. Defining the double quote in an XSLT variable we find easier than using XML entities, for example """ which is another way of doing this.

Listing 3-5 XSLT Stylesheet date, document access, parameter and header access.

```
        <!-- -->

        <!-- Process the restrictions if necessary -->

        <!-- -->

        <xsl:if test="$todaysHeaderMustBe">

            <!-- -->

            <!-- Determine if the header MUST or MAY be set to
particular value -->
```

```
<!-- -->
<xsl:variable name="mustOrMay">
    <xsl:choose>
        <xsl:when test="$addIfNotSet">MAY</xsl:when>
        <xsl:otherwise>MUST</xsl:otherwise>
    </xsl:choose>
</xsl:variable>
<xsl:message dp:priority="info">
    <xsl:value-of select="concat('On ', $dayOfWeek, ', ',
$httpHeaderName, ' ', $mustOrMay, ' be set to ', $dQ,
$todaysHeaderMustBe, $dQ)"/>
</xsl:message>
<!-- -->
```

Listing 3-6 shows the final processing of the day restrictions. We use a xsl:choose statement to see when; 1) the header is equal to its requirement, 2) it's not found (its length is zero) and the optional "addIfNotSet" attribute has been provided or if 3) otherwise we dp:reject the transaction using the DataPower dp:reject() extension function.

Notice that when the header is created through the dp:set-request-header() extension element, it is followed by dp:freeze-headers(). The use of freeze-headers tell DataPower's firmware that we are done manipulating headers and it's OK to start sending data to the backend resource. It's an efficiency mechanism that you may choose to use.

Listing 3-6 XSLT Stylesheet performing restriction processing.

```
<xsl:choose>
    <xsl:when test="$todaysHeaderMustBe =
$httpHeaderValue">
        <xsl:message dp:priority="debug">
            <xsl:value-of select="concat('Header ', $dQ,
$httpHeaderName, $dQ, ' is set properly')"/>
        </xsl:message>
```

```
                </xsl:when>

                <xsl:when test="string-length($httpHeaderValue) = 0
and $addIfNotSet">

                    <dp:set-request-header name="$httpHeaderName"
value="$todaysHeaderMustBe"/>

                    <xsl:message dp:priority="info">

                        <xsl:value-of select="concat('Header ',
$httpHeaderName, ' not found. Adding and setting to ',
$todaysHeaderMustBe)"/>

                    </xsl:message>

                    <dp:freeze-headers/>

                </xsl:when>

                <xsl:otherwise>

                    <dp:reject>

                        <xsl:value-of select="concat('Header ', $dQ,
$httpHeaderName, $dQ, ' must equal ', $dQ, $todaysHeaderMustBe, $dQ,
' on ', $dayOfWeek, '. Message Rejected!')"/>

                    </dp:reject>

                </xsl:otherwise>

            </xsl:choose>

        </xsl:if>

    </xsl:template>
```

ifItsTuesdayThisMustBeBelgium implementation in XSLT, examples

We're done with the XSLT, let see some example. Listing 3-7 shows two slightly abbreviated requests via "curl". The first injects the "THIS" header with a value of "Gloucester" (America's oldest seaport). Which because it's Saturday and "Gloucester" is the proper setting, the transaction is accepted. The second example does not contain the right "THIS" header and is rejected with an error message.

Listing 3-7 ifItsTuesdayThisMustBeBelgium.xsl example processing via curl.

```
curl http://192.168.1.125:2048/XSLT -H "THIS: Gloucester" -v

> GET /XSLT HTTP/1.1
> Host: 192.168.1.125:2048
> Accept: */*
> THIS: Gloucester
>
< HTTP/1.1 200 Good
< Host: 192.168.1.125:2048
< THIS: Gloucester
< X-Global-Transaction-ID: 7441
< Via: 1.1 IfItsTuesdayThisMustBeBelgium
< X-Client-IP: 192.168.1.143

curl http://192.168.1.125:2048/XSLT -H "THIS: Boston" -v

> GET /XSLT HTTP/1.1
> Host: 192.168.1.125:2048
> Accept: */*
> THIS: Boston
>
< HTTP/1.1 200 Good
< Host: 192.168.1.125:2048
< X-Global-Transaction-ID: 7442
< Via: 1.1 IfItsTuesdayThisMustBeBelgium
< X-Client-IP: 192.168.1.143
<?xml version="1.0" encoding="UTF-8"?>
<env:Envelope
xmlns:env="http://schemas.xmlsoap.org/soap/envelope/"><env:Body><env:
Fault><faultcode>env:Client</faultcode><faultstring>Header "THIS"
must equal "Gloucester" on Saturday. Message Rejected! (from
client)</faultstring></env:Fault></env:Body></env:Envelope>
```

We've emphasized the importance of log messages, so let's see what our example has produced. Figure 3-3 shows some of the log messages produced by the failed transaction. We've trimmed them a bit for readability, read them from the bottom up. Don't forget that log messages are not just for sending to the default log. You can create Log Targets that capture message and send them to files, SYSLOG, or other destinations. See the discussion on Log Targets for additional information.

11:49:36 AM	multistep	error	236833		192.168.1.147	0x00d30003	xmlfirewall (IfItsTuesdayThisMustBeBelgium): Rejected by filter; SOAP fault sent
11:49:36 AM	multistep	error	236833	request	192.168.1.147	0x80c00009	xmlfirewall (IfItsTuesdayThisMustBeBelgium): request IfItsTuesdayThisMustBeBelgium_req_xslt #1 filter: 'INPUT local:///ifItsTuesdayThisMustBeBelgium.xsl' failed: Header "THIS" must equal "Gloucester" on Saturday. Message Rejected!
11:49:36 AM	multistep	error	236833	request	192.168.1.147	0x80c00078	xmlfirewall (IfItsTuesdayThisMustBeBelgium): Rejected by filter 'IfItsTuesdayThisMustBeBelgium_req_xslt_filter_0' of rule 'IfItsTuesdayThisMustBeBelgium_req_xslt'.
11:49:36 AM	xslt	error	236833	request	192.168.1.147	0x80c00010	xmlfirewall (IfItsTuesdayThisMustBeBelgium): Processing of 'local:///ifItsTuesdayThisMustBeBelgium.xsl' stopped: Header "THIS" must equal "Gloucester" on Saturday. Message Rejected!
11:49:36 AM	xmlfilter	information	236833	request	192.168.1.147	0x80c00037	xmlfirewall (IfItsTuesdayThisMustBeBelgium): Reject set: Header "THIS" must equal "Gloucester" on Saturday. Message Rejected!
11:49:36 AM	xsltmsg	information	236833	request	192.168.1.147	0x80000001	xmlfirewall (IfItsTuesdayThisMustBeBelgium): On Saturday, THIS MUST be set to "Gloucester"
11:49:36 AM	xmlfirewall	information	236833	request	192.168.1.147	0x80e000b4	xmlfirewall (IfItsTuesdayThisMustBeBelgium): rule (IfItsTuesdayThisMustBeBelgium_req_xslt): selected via match 'matchXSLT' from processing policy 'IfItsTuesdayThisMustBeBelgium'
11:49:36 AM	xmlfirewall	information	236833	request	192.168.1.147	0x80e00077	xmlfirewall (IfItsTuesdayThisMustBeBelgium): New transaction(conn use=1): GET http://192.168.1.125:2048/XSLT from 192.168.1.147

Figure 3-3 ifItsTuesdayThisMustBeBelgium.xsl Log messages.

ifItsTuesdayThisMustBeBelgium implementation in GatewayScript

Now let's look at the GatewayScript implementation. Listing 3-8 shows the required modules we will be using through the GWS's CommonJS 1.0 module support. The "header-metadata" module provides access to HTTP headers. The module "fs" provides file system access and finally the "sprintf" module is used to implement string manipulation that will be helpful in formatting logging messages.

GatewayScript date processing assigns the "dayInWeek" and "dayOfWeek" variables. The header to use is fetched from the session module and its parameters object. The header values themselves are available through the "header-metadata" implementation and our "hm" variable assignment. We noted previously that the GWS implementation and its underlying ECMA Script getDay() function returns a dayInWeek based on "0", while the EXSLT date functions are "1" based. We've adjusted this so that log messages produced by XSLT and GWS show a consistent value, i.e. "1" for Sunday in both cases.

Listing 3-8 ifItsTuesdayThisMustBeBelgium.js, require modules, date, HTTP Header and Session Parameter access.

```
var hm = require('header-metadata');
var fs = require('fs')
var sf = require('sprintf').sprintf;

var date = new Date();
var dayInWeek = date.getDay(); /* Sunday is 0, Monday is 1 ... */
var days = [ "Sunday", "Monday", "Tuesday", "Wednesday", "Thursday",
"Friday",
    "Saturday" ];
var dayOfWeek = days[dayInWeek];
var httpHeaderName = "";
/* Get the Header Name from the Actions parameter configuration */
if (session.parameters.whichHeaderName) {
  httpHeaderName = session.parameters.whichHeaderName;
}
var httpHeaderValue = "";
if (hm.current.get(httpHeaderName)) {
  httpHeaderValue = hm.current.get(httpHeaderName);
```

```
}

/* add 1 to the dayOfWeek so log message is the same as that produced
by XSLT */

console.debug('Today is %1$s, day # %2$s ', dayOfWeek, dayInWeek +
1);
```

This next section of ifItsTuesdayThisMustBeBelgium.js is the most critical to our processing and to your understanding of the process flow. As in the XSLT example, a document is used to control day of week restrictions. Within XSLT we used the XPath “document()” function. In firmware release 7.2 a new GWS module was added which makes reading JSON document an equally simple process. The “fs” or file system module provides the ability to read files in the local: and store: directories and to read, write or rename files in the temporary:// directory.

Listing 3-9 shows the use of the fs module to read the local://dayOfWeekRestrictions.json file. If the document is read successfully as a JSON object, it is passed to the findTodaysRestriction function for processing.

Listing 3-9 ifItsTuesdayThisMustBeBelgium.js, access JSON document through file system module.

```
/*

- Read the JSON dayOfWeekRestrictions document and look for today's
restrictions

*/

fs.readAsJSON("local:///dayOfWeekRestrictions.json", function(error,
dayOfWeekRestrictions) {

  if (error) {

    console.debug("urlopen error: " + JSON.stringify(error));
```

```
  } else {
    findTodaysRestriction(dayOfWeekRestrictions);
  }
});
```

Listing 3-10 shows the findTodaysRestriction function which is called when with the dayOfWeekRestrictions object contains the day array. We loop through it, looking for a day object that has a matching dayOfWeek property value. When we find a match we get the mustBe and addIfNotSet properties similar to our earlier XSLT processing.

Listing 3-10 ifItsTuesdayThisMustBeBelgium.js, finding today's restrictions and processing if available.

```
/*
- Find the JSON object for this day of the week
- Determine if the header MUST or MAY be set to particular value
- See if its to be added if not found
- Process the restrictions if necessary
*/
function findTodaysRestriction(dowr) {
  // debugger;
  for (var i = 0; i < dowr.dayOfWeekRestrictions.day.length; i++) {
    if (Number(dowr.dayOfWeekRestrictions.day[i].dayOfWeek) ==
dayInWeek) {
      var mustBe = (dowr.dayOfWeekRestrictions.day[i].mustBe != null
? dowr.dayOfWeekRestrictions.day[i].mustBe
          : '');
      var addIfNotSet =
(dowr.dayOfWeekRestrictions.day[i].addIfNotSet != null ?
dowr.dayOfWeekRestrictions.day[i].addIfNotSet
          : '');
      var mustOrMay = (addIfNotSet ? "MAY" : "MUST");
      console.debug('On %1$s, Header \"%2$s\" %3$s be set to
\"%4$s\"',
```

```
          dayOfWeek, httpHeaderName, mustOrMay, mustBe);
      if (mustBe) {
        processTodaysRestriction(mustBe, addIfNotSet);
      }
    }
  }
}
```

Listing 3-11 shows the final stage of our GWS implementation. The mustBe and addIfNotSet options are passed from the selected day object array, and verification is performed within the processTodaysRestriction function. We've taken care to ensure the messages are equivalent to the XSLT cases. This function demonstrates the ability to set protocol headers via the "hm.current.set" function, the ability to reject a transaction "session.reject", and use of the "sprintf" module to format the message returned to the client in rejection cases.

Listing 3-11 ifItsTuesdayThisMustBeBelgium.js, processing today's restrictions.

```
/*
 * - Perform checking of header and options as specified
 */
function processTodaysRestriction(mustBe, addIfNotSet) {
  debugger;
  console.info('Header Name \"%1$s\", Value \"%2$s\", mustBe
\"%3$s\", addIfNotSet \"%4$s\"',
          httpHeaderName, httpHeaderValue, mustBe, addIfNotSet);
  if (httpHeaderValue == mustBe) {
    console.info('Header \"%1$s\" is set properly', httpHeaderName,
        httpHeaderValue);
  } else {
```

```
    if (httpHeaderValue.length == 0 && addIfNotSet) {

      console.info('Header %1$s not found. Adding and setting to
\"%2$s\"',

          httpHeaderName, mustBe);

      hm.current.set(httpHeaderName, mustBe);

    } else {

      console.error('Header \"%1$s\" must equal \"%2$s\" on %3$s.
Message Rejected!',

              httpHeaderName, mustBe, dayOfWeek);

      session.reject(sf('Header \"%1$s\" must equal \"%2$s\" on %3$s.
Message Rejected!',

              httpHeaderName, mustBe, dayOfWeek));

    }

  }

}
```

Listing 3-12 shows two abbreviated examples of the GatewayScript configuration. The first does not supply a "THIS" header and is successful. It comes back with a "THIS: Boston" header, it was injected based on our "addIfNotSet" option for Sunday. The second example has a "THIS" supplied with a value of "Gloucester" which does not match the required value of "Boston". But the settings within our control document ignore that and cause the "THIS: Boston" header to be injected and returned to the client.

Listing 3-12 ifItsTuesdayThisMustBeBelgium implementation in GWS, examples.

```
curl http://192.168.1.125:2048/JS -v


> GET /JS HTTP/1.1

< HTTP/1.1 200 Good

< Host: 192.168.1.125:2048

< X-Global-Transaction-ID: 1569
```

```
< Via: 1.1 IfItsTuesdayThisMustBeBelgium
< X-Client-IP: 192.168.1.143
< THIS: Boston

curl http://192.168.1.125:2048/JS -H "THIS: Gloucester" -v
> GET /JS HTTP/1.1
> Host: 192.168.1.125:2048
> THIS: Gloucester
< HTTP/1.1 200 Good
< Host: 192.168.1.125:2048
< X-Global-Transaction-ID: 1585
< Via: 1.1 IfItsTuesdayThisMustBeBelgium
< X-Client-IP: 192.168.1.143
< THIS: Boston.
```

Example 1 Summary

This first "real world" example was chosen to demonstrate several common DataPower processing patterns, including:

- Reading XML and JSON control documents
- Fetching Parameters from Actions
- Module support in GWS
- Processing Dates in EXSLT and JavaScript
- The use of XPath and JavaScript array processing
- Header access and manipulation
- Transaction Rejection
- Emphasis of good log message format

Transaction throttling (rejection or acceptance) can be used in many ways. Our day of the week example might not be exactly what you need, but certainly this pattern will provide the basics for many such implementations. And now that we're done it occurs to us that we did not test this on "Tuesday". We've left that up to you!

Dynamic Routing using XSLT, XQuery and GateWayScript

Transaction routing is one of the core DataPower service patterns. Transactions may be routed for a variety of reasons. You may want to route to multiple servers for high availability and load balancing. You may want to route high value transactions to a higher performing or more feature rich service. A very frequently used pattern of transaction routing involves the authorization of requests within a "demilitarized zone" or DMZ. As was discussed in Volume I, this pattern ensures that only authorized traffic is allowed to enter the "trusted zone", and in doing so provides a higher level of security for that inner, trusted network space.

We will use dynamic routing as the final example of DataPower service development and configuration. Dynamic routing could be based on many message characteristics, and in many instances within a secured transport, the message encryption credentials can be used for this purpose.

In the example shown in Figure 3-4, clients make a request to an Award Service over HTTPS. The service will use the Distinguished Name from the client's SSL/TLS certificate to determine where the transaction will be routed. The request will be forwarded to a Bronze or a Gold Service depending on how that Distinguished Name is mapped within a Dynamic Routing document which contains host, port and SSL/TLS client profile information. In our example, the result of the transaction will be simple; you will be provided a response HTML document that will randomly contain either a circle or a star in bronze or gold depending on your SSL client credential.

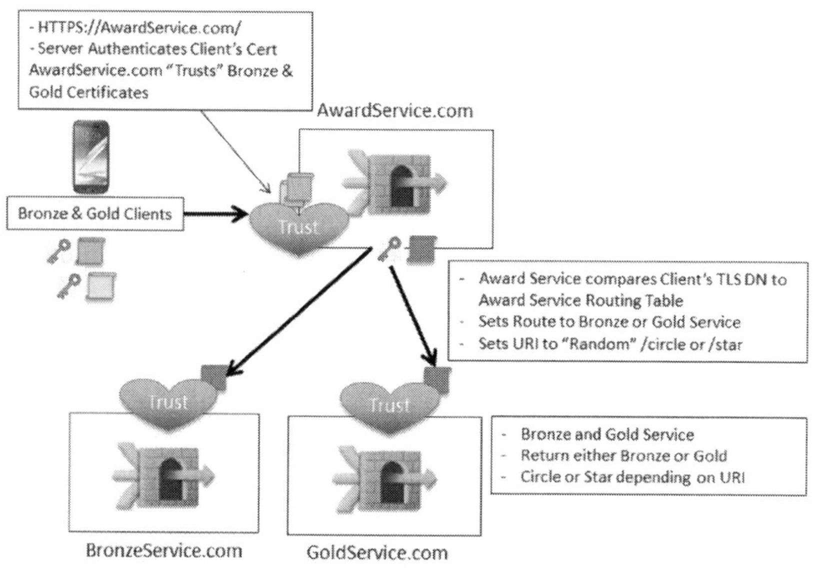

Figure 3-4 Dynamic Routing using Client Certificate.

This example will demonstrate several key fundamentals of security implementations, DataPower configuration best practices and DataPower development techniques, such as:

- SSL/TSL authentication best practices, client vs. server authentication
- Client / Browser Certificate and Key configuration issues
- DataPower crypto development and transaction control in XSLT, XQuery and GatewayScript
- Best Practices including the use of DNS Static Hosts and Host Alias for increased DataPower configuration portability

Let's start by reviewing the first phase of the transaction process; two classes of clients; bronze and gold will make requests to the Award Service. We will use DataPower's Crypto Tools, to generate the bronze and gold client keys and certificates and also for the Award Service. Figure 3-5 shows the details for the Bronze_Client certificate, including the Subject distinguished name of "CN=Bronze_Client". A similar key and certificate is created for the gold client, "CN=Gold_Client", and the Award Service "CN=Award_Service.com" that will receive the client requests.

Details of Crypto File *cert:///Bronze_Client-sscert.pem*

Basic Fields	
Fingerprint(SHA1)	18:5F:7F:F4:61:C0:39:A9:C3:16:9D:CD:5E:DD:28:15:B2:6E:C8:F6
Version	3
SerialNumber	6488684662274448010
SignatureAlgorithm	sha256WithRSAEncryption
Issuer	CN=Bronze_Client
NotBefore	2015-12-13T22:04:41Z
NotAfter	2025-12-10T22:04:41Z
Subject	CN=Bronze_Client
SubjectPublicKeyAlgorithm	rsaEncryption
SubjectPublicKeyBitLength	1024

Figure 3-5 Details of Bronze_Client Certificate.

DataPower creates “PEM” encoded, or a Privacy Enhanced Mail, Base64 encoded DER certificate. There are several key and certificate encoding and some clients and servers are selective about which encoding they will accept. Many browsers do not use PEM encoding, so we will convert the PEM certificates and keys into a PKCS12 file. PKCS #12 is one of the standards published by RSA Laboratories and packages one or more key and certificate together. There are many sources available to learn about these topics if you wish. For our exercise we’ll need to convert the PEM files into PKCS12 files using OPENSSL as Figure 3-6 demonstrates. Notice that you’ll be prompted for a password when creating the p12 file; we’ve chosen not to use one for simplicity’s sake.

```
asmussj@rasmussj-W520:~/book2$ openssl pkcs12 -export -in Award_Service.com-sscert.pem
-inkey Award_Service.com-privkey.pem -out Award_Service.com.p12
nter Export Password:
erifying - Enter Export Password:
asmussj@rasmussj-W520:~/book2$ ls *.p12
ward_Service.com.p12
asmussj@rasmussj-W520:~/book2$
```

Figure 3-6 Converting PEM to PKCS12 files.

Now that we have the PKCS12 files, let's start performing some DataPower configuration. We'll start by creating the Award Service's SSL Server Profile that's necessary to receive the client requests. DataPower 7.2 introduced new SSL/TLS configuration options, in particular to support Server Name Mapping Profile which allows a service to expose multiple certificates and hence domain names on the same IP/Port combination. We're not using that here, but we are using the new SSL Server Profile.

Figure 3-7 shows the Award Service SSL Server Profile. You may have to tweak the protocol and Ciphers used to be compatible with your client. We've removed "CBC" ciphers and restricted the protocol to only use TLS 1.2 for this example as the Chrome browser may complain about others being obsolete.

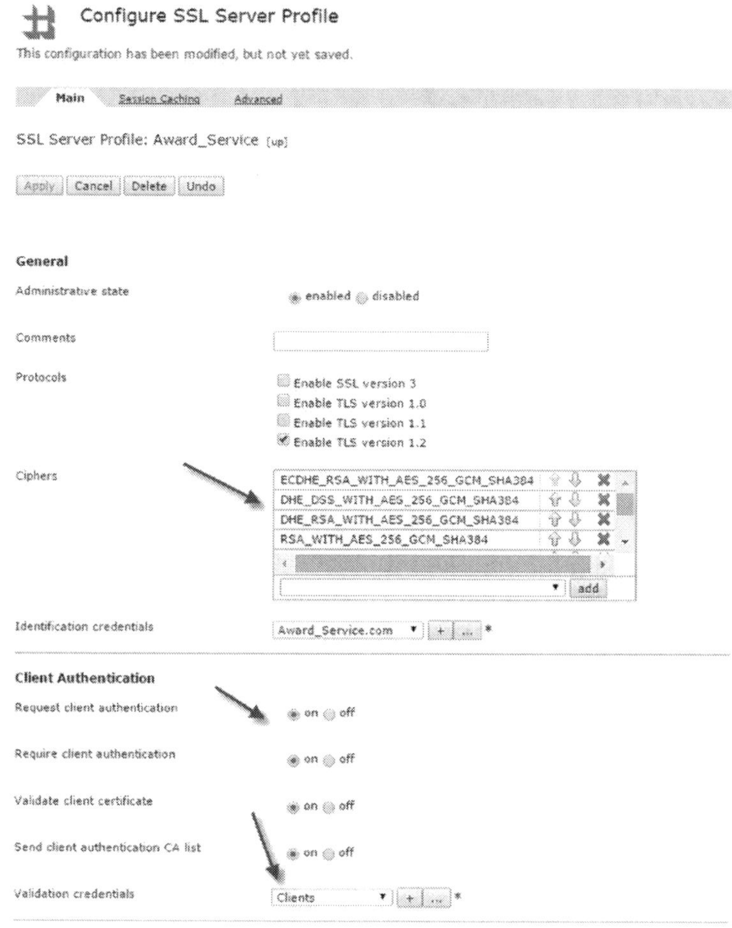

Figure 3-7 Award Service SSL Server Profile.

In addition to specifying the protocol and cipher suites, notice that the SSL Server Profile also has the "Request client authentication" toggle set and a "Validation credential" object specified. This is important for our 2-way authentication goals. We need to ensure that the client sends its TLS certificate so we can use it in our routing scheme and to verify that it is one of the accepted clients. Setting these parameters will ensure this. Figure 3-8 shows the crypto validation object which defines the valid client certificates.

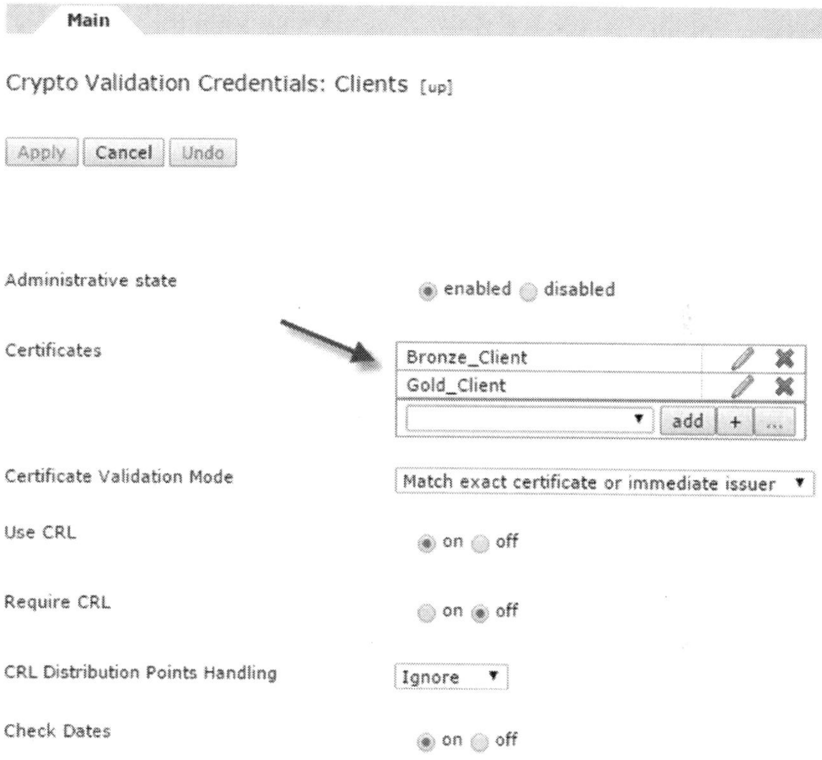

Main

Crypto Validation Credentials: Clients [up]

Apply Cancel Undo

Administrative state — enabled / disabled

Certificates — Bronze_Client, Gold_Client — add + ...

Certificate Validation Mode — Match exact certificate or immediate issuer

Use CRL — on / off

Require CRL — on / off

CRL Distribution Points Handling — Ignore

Check Dates — on / off

Figure 3-8 Crypto Validation Credentials used to verify Bronze and Gold Clients.

We will be using the Multi-Protocol-Gateway service for the Award Service and the Bronze and Gold Services that will respond with our awards. A real world application would typically route the requests to a WAS or other service. As you may know the MPGW uses a Front Side Protocol Handler for the configuration of all incoming transactions. Figure 3-9 shows the three Front Side Protocol Handlers that we'll need. Notice that each is defined on a separate port and that rather than specifying a numerical IP address, they each use a Host Alias for the definition of the Local IP Address and each has a SSL Server Profile definition.

Name	Status	Op-State	Logs	Administrative state	Comments	Local IP address	Port	SSL server type	SSL proxy profile (deprecated)	SSL server profile	SSL SNI server profile	Quiesce State
Award_Service	saved	up		enabled		public_interface	4433	Server Profile		Award_Service		
Bronze_Service	saved	up		enabled		trusted_interface	4434	Server Profile		Bronze_Service		
Gold_Service	saved	up		enabled		trusted_interface	4435	Server Profile		Gold_Service		

Figure 3-9 Front Side Protocol Handlers.

Figure 3-10 shows the Host Aliases created in the default domain. In a production ready implementation the 127.0.0.1 address would represent a physical interface rather than the loopback address we've used in this example.

public_interface	saved	up		enabled	192.168.1.125	
trusted_interface	saved	up		enabled	127.0.0.1	

Figure 3-10 Host Alias configuration.

Figure 3-11 shows the primary configuration of the MPGW. It's really pretty basic. The Service name, Policy and FSH are all named the same for manageability. Notice that the request type is "Non-XML" as we'll be sending HTTPS GET requests from a browser.

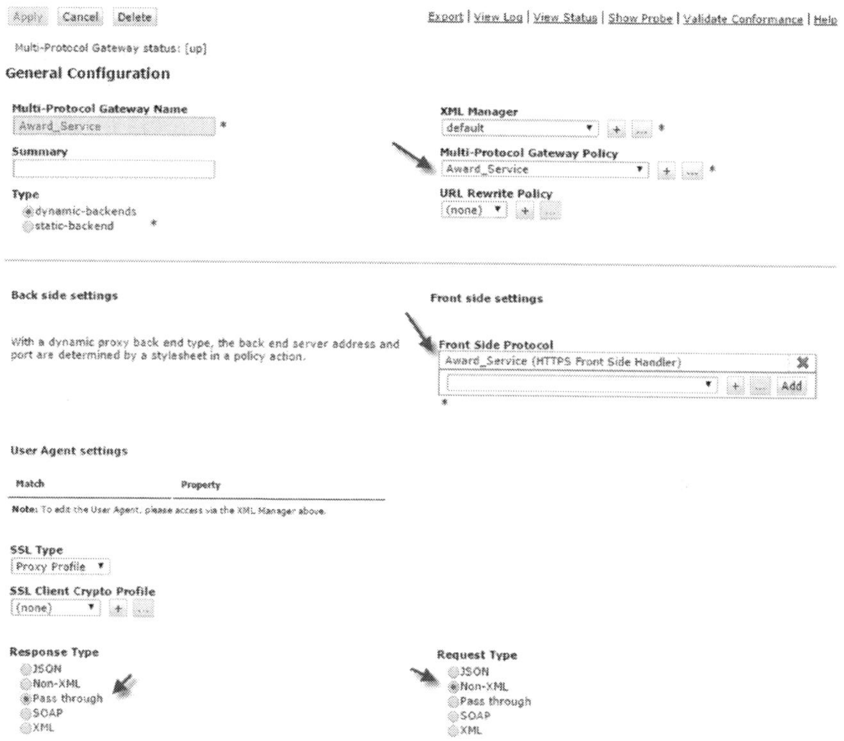

Figure 3-11 Service Award MPGW Configuration.

Now that we have the TLS and interface plumbing set up we can begin to look at the dynamic routing nature of the configuration. We've talked about the multiple ways to program DataPower services using XSLT, XQuery and GatewayScript, and the Processing Policy in Figure 3-12 contains rules for each. It also contains an image processing rule which we'll describe shortly to respond to browser image requests. Match rules are established to select images (^(?i).*\.ico|^(?i).*\.png) and URI values including "xslt", "xq" and "js" to match the appropriate rule.

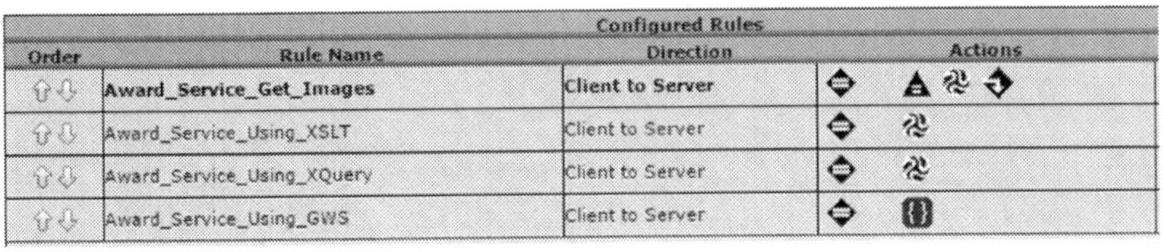

Configured Rules			
Order	Rule Name	Direction	Actions
	Award_Service_Get_Images	Client to Server	
	Award_Service_Using_XSLT	Client to Server	
	Award_Service_Using_XQuery	Client to Server	
	Award_Service_Using_GWS	Client to Server	

Figure 3-12 Processing Policy Rules for dynamic routing.

Our first example will use XSLT as the core programming language for dynamic routing. The first requirement is to fetch the client's TLS certificate and obtain the subject information. Listing -13 shows the use of the dp:auth-info() extension function for this. Notice that an XSL variable is created to hold not only the subject, but also the issuer and the cipher suite selected for TLS encryption. While not necessary for dynamic routing, we've captured this additional information for demonstration purposes. The subject is then individually extracted from that XSL variable and stored in anther variable $subjectCN.

Listing 3-13 dynamicRouting_with_XSLT.xsl Extracting Crypto Subject information.

```
    <xsl:template match="/">
        <!-- -->
        <!-- Get the clients Distinguished Name from SSL Certificate
-->
        <!-- This requires client authentication via Identification
Credentials -->
        <!-- Tokenize it and get the CN  -->
        <!-- -->
        <xsl:variable name="client-cert-info">
            <xsl:element name="client-cert-info">
                <xsl:element name="ssl-client-subject">
```

```
                    <xsl:value-of select="dp:auth-info('ssl-client-
subject')"/>
                </xsl:element>
                <xsl:element name="ssl-client-issuer">
                    <xsl:value-of select="dp:auth-info('ssl-client-
issuer')"/>
                </xsl:element>
                <xsl:element name="ssl-cipher-suite">
                    <xsl:value-of select="dp:auth-info('ssl-cipher-
suite')"/>
                </xsl:element>
            </xsl:element>
        </xsl:variable>
        <!-- -->
        <xsl:variable name="subjectCN" select="$client-cert-
info/client-cert-info/ssl-client-subject"/>
        <!-- -->
        <xsl:message dp:priority="debug">
            <xsl:value-of select="concat('client-cert-info=',
$client-cert-info)"/>
        </xsl:message>
        <!-- -->
```

Our routing information is contained within an XML document in this example. Listing 3-14 shows the document contains a node for each potential client. Each has a host name, port and SSL Client Profile to be used in the dynamic connection.

Listing 3-14 Dynamic Routing XML Document.

```
<!--  -->
<!-- Routing for Gold and Bronze Services -->
<!-- A match is made on the @subjectCN using the SSL/TLS Subject -->
<!-- Note this requires the client supplies certificate -->
<!--  -->
```

```
<routingDestinations>
    <destination subjectCN="/CN=Gold_Client">
        <host>Gold_Service</host>
        <port>4435</port>
        <sslid>client:Award_Service</sslid>
    </destination>
    <destination subjectCN="/CN=Bronze_Client">
        <host>Bronze_Service</host>
        <port>4434</port>
        <sslid>client:Award_Service</sslid>
    </destination>
</routingDestinations>
```

You'll notice that the hosts defined in the Dynamic Routing document are not numerical IP addresses. Just as we used Host Aliases for the Front Side Protocol Hander for configuration transportability, we are using DNS Static Host entries for routing. By doing so, when the configuration is migrated to another device, only the target device's DNS entries have to be changed, the XML and any associated XSLT, XQuery or GWS can be left alone. Figure 3-13 shows the configuration.

Host Name	IP Address	Type
Bronze_Service	127.0.0.1	Static Host
Gold_Service	127.0.0.1	Static Host

Figure 3-13 Host Alias configuration for Bronze and Gold Services.

Moving back to the XSLT in Listing 3-15 we can see how the destination for each transaction is made by using an XPath expression to select the Award Service Routing document node that contains a subjectCN that matches the incoming request. Again a log message is created and in this case, a serialized copy (with the human readable XML brackets) is written to the log by using the dp:serialize() extension function. The host, port and SSL/TLS profile are then extracted from the node.

Listing 3-15 dynamicRouting_with_XSLT.xsl Extracting Crypto Subject information.

```
        <xsl:variable name="destination"
select="document('AwardServiceRouting.xml')//routingDestinations/dest
ination[@subjectCN=$subjectCN]"/>

        <!-- -->

        <xsl:message dp:priority="debug">

            <xsl:value-of select="'destination='"/>

            <dp:serialize select="$destination" omit-xml-decl="yes"/>

        </xsl:message>

        <!-- -->

        <!-- Get the routing information from the routing doc based
on CN  -->

        <!-- -->

        <xsl:variable name="host"
select="$destination//host/text()"/>

        <xsl:variable name="port"
select="$destination//port/text()"/>

        <xsl:variable name="sslid"
select="$destination//sslid/text()"/>

        <!-- -->
```

Finally, having obtained the necessary routing information, the dp:xset-target() extension function is used to establish the dynamic route. Listing 3-16 shows the use of dp:xset-target() and includes two cases for instances with and without SSL.

Listing 3-16 dynamicRouting_with_XSLT.xsl Extracting Routing Details.

```
        <xsl:choose>
            <!-- -->
            <!-- If the routing requires SSL, use that format of the
dp:xset-target Ext Func  -->
            <!-- -->
            <xsl:when test="$sslid">
                <dp:xset-target host="$host" port="$port"
ssl="true()" sslid="{$sslid}"/>
                <xsl:message>
                    <xsl:value-of select="concat('Routed to ', $host,
':', $port, ', sslid=', $sslid)"/>
                </xsl:message>
            </xsl:when>
            <!-- -->
            <!-- Routing without SSL -->
            <!-- -->
            <xsl:otherwise>
                <xsl:message>
                    <xsl:value-of select="concat('Routed to ', $host,
':', $port)"/>
                </xsl:message>
                <dp:xset-target host="$host" port="$port"
ssl="false()"/>
            </xsl:otherwise>
        </xsl:choose>
```

Now, to add some variability to our sample, we've described the service as responding with a circle or a star. To do this we set the URI using a value determined by an XSLT function that will use the current time as a random seed. Listing 3-17 shows the setting of the URI and the invocation of the randomURI() function.

Listing 3-17 dynamicRouting_with_XSLT.xsl Extracting Routing Details.

```
        <!-- -->

        <!-- Assign the 'award' as randomly either a star or a circle
-->

        <!-- -->

        <xsl:variable name="randomURI" select="func:randomURI()"/>

        <dp:set-variable name="'var://service/URI'"
value="$randomURI"/>

        <!-- -->

        <xsl:message>

            <xsl:value-of select="concat('Set URL to ',
$randomURI)"/>

        </xsl:message>

        <!-- -->

    </xsl:template>
```

Listing 3-18 shows the implementation of the randomURI() function. Any cryptologist will tell you that this is poor man's version of randomness, but it's good enough for our circle vs. star decision. We use the EXSLT second-in-minute() function to get the current second value and use its odd or evenness for our choice.

Listing 3-18 dynamicRouting_with_XSLT.xsl Extracting Routing Details.

```
    <func:function name="func:randomURI">

        <!-- -->

        <!-- Generate a Pseudo Random Number 0/1 -->

        <!-- Get the current second using the exslt date:second-in-
minute() function -->

        <!-- Other options such as the dp:time-value() function could
have been used -->

        <!-- -->

        <xsl:variable name="seconds" select="date:second-in-
minute()"/>

        <xsl:message>
```

```
        <xsl:value-of select="concat('seconds = ', $seconds)"/>
    </xsl:message>
    <!-- -->
    <xsl:choose>
        <xsl:when test="$seconds mod 2 = 1">
            <func:result>
                <xsl:value-of select="'/star'"/>
            </func:result>
        </xsl:when>
        <xsl:otherwise>
            <func:result>
                <xsl:value-of select="'/circle'"/>
            </func:result>
        </xsl:otherwise>
    </xsl:choose>
</func:function>
```

The Bronze and Gold services are very similar to our Award Service. Each contains the Server Policy and Front side handler with client verification as the Award Service. Each service has a policy with two rules as shown in Figure 3-14, one matching /circle URI and one /star. Each of the rules contains a SETVAR action which sets the “var://service/mpgw/skip-backside” service variable to “1” to cause the rules to “loopback” rather than forward the request to a backside service, and each contains a FETCH action to get and return the Bronze or Gold Circle or Start HTML document.

Bronze_Service_Fetch_Circle	Client to Server	
Bronze_Service_Fetch_Star	Client to Server	

Figure 3-14 Bronze Service Policy for returning circle or star.

Before we complete and demonstrate our service, we have one more policy issue to deal with. Each of the HTML documents will contain an image tag to display the circle or star images, defined within the HTML as "<img src="bronzeStar.png" alt=""></img>". Referring back to Figure 3-12 there is a rule which matches *.png and *.ico images. The rule simply sets the loopback service variable via a SETVAR (as shown above), and executes the XSLT in Listing 3-19 to construct a URL into the local:/// directory, and then uses a FETCH action using that variable to obtain the image for the HTML page. Your browser will want to fetch a favicon, and this rule makes provision for that as well. A real production implementation would use an HTTP server for fetching data such as this, and would probably cache that data if it is highly fetched.

Listing 3-19 setImageURL.xsl Used to Set URL for Images from Local:// Directory.

```
    <xsl:template match="/">

        <!-- -->

        <!-- get the local and context variables -->

        <!-- -->

        <xsl:variable name="URI"
select="dp:variable('var://service/URI')"/>

        <dp:set-variable name="'var://context/myContext/imageURL'"
value="concat('local:///', substring-after($URI, '/'))"/>

    </xsl:template>
```

Ok, so all the work is done, let's test the service. In order for it all to work, there's a little housekeeping to be done on the client certificates. You'll need to configure the SSL component of your browser. We are using Chrome, you'll need to import the PKCS12 files that were created earlier into the Personal Certificates section of Chrome's HTTPS/SSL configuration for use as the Award Service bronze and gold clients. Figure 3-15 shows that done for the Gold_Client.

Figure 3-15 Personal Certificate Configuration in Chrome.

And to avoid warning messages suggesting improper HTTPS configuration in the browser's address bar, we will import the Award_Service.com certificate into Chrome's Trusted Root Certificate Authorities. Figure 3-16 shows that.

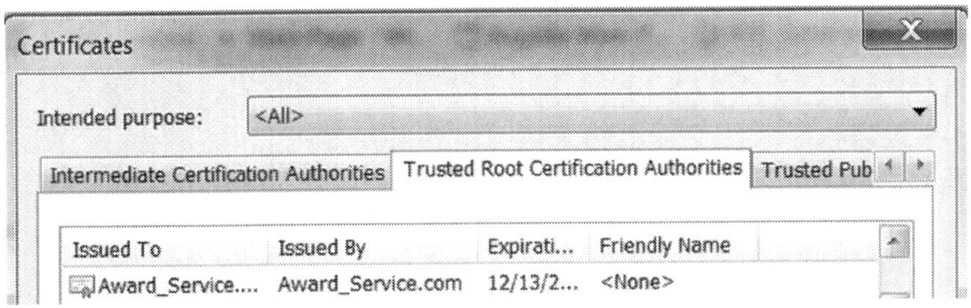

Figure 3-16 Award_Service.com Certificate Added to Trusted Root Certificates in Chrome.

Typically we'd register the domain name Award_Service.com with a DNS provider so we can have world wide access. But for our testing, that's not necessary. But before we enter Award_Service.com in the browser, we need to define a local DNS entry. You can simply add the following entry to your host file as we've shown in Listing 3-20.

Listing 3-20 Host DNS entry.

```
192.168.1.125
```

And away we go. Entering the https://award_service.com:4433/xslt in the browser and see what you get. Maybe you'll get a Gold Star! In Figure 3-17 you see in this case we've received a gold circle. Changing to the Bronze client certificate and you'll get a bronze star, or circle.

Figure 3-17 Award_Service Responses with a Gold Circle.

Figure 3-18 shows some of the log messages produced by the xsl:message statements in our XSLT code. Two separate requests are shown here. Notice the serialized destination XML node that was produced by the dp:serialize() function.

7:59:27 AM	xsltmsg	information	175233	request	192.168.1.147	0x80000001	mpgw (Award_Service): Set URL to /star
7:59:27 AM	xsltmsg	information	175233	request	192.168.1.147	0x80000001	mpgw (Award_Service): seconds = 27
7:59:27 AM	xsltmsg	information	175233	request	192.168.1.147	0x80000001	mpgw (Award_Service): Routed to Gold_Service:4435, sslid=client:Award_Service
7:59:27 AM	xsltmsg	debug	175233	request	192.168.1.147	0x80000001	mpgw (Award_Service): destination=<destination subjectCN="/CN=Gold_Client"> <host>Gold_Service</host> <port>4435</port> <sslid>client:Award_Service</sslid> </destination>
7:59:27 AM	xsltmsg	debug	175233	request	192.168.1.147	0x80000001	mpgw (Award_Service): client-cert-info=/CN=Gold_Client/CN=Gold_ClientECDHE-RSA-AES128-GCM-SHA256
7:59:16 AM	xsltmsg	information	460467	request	192.168.1.147	0x80000001	mpgw (Award_Service): Set URL to /circle
7:59:16 AM	xsltmsg	information	460467	request	192.168.1.147	0x80000001	mpgw (Award_Service): seconds = 16
7:59:16 AM	xsltmsg	information	460467	request	192.168.1.147	0x80000001	mpgw (Award_Service): Routed to Gold_Service:4435, sslid=client:Award_Service
7:59:16 AM	xsltmsg	debug	460467	request	192.168.1.147	0x80000001	mpgw (Award_Service): destination=<destination subjectCN="/CN=Gold_Client"> <host>Gold_Service</host> <port>4435</port> <sslid>client:Award_Service</sslid> </destination>
7:59:16 AM	xsltmsg	debug	460467	request	192.168.1.147	0x80000001	mpgw (Award_Service): client-cert-info=/CN=Gold_Client/CN=Gold_ClientECDHE-RSA-AES128-GCM-SHA256

Figure 3-18 Log messages produced by the XSLT Dynamic Routing.

Extending Dynamic Routing sample with XQuery

We can use XQuery in place of XPath while fetching the routing destination. Rather than using the XPath document function and statement to obtain the destination we can use the dp:xquery-transform() extension function as shown in Listing 3-21.

Listing 3-21 dynamicRouting_with_XSLT_For_GWS.xsl with dp:query-transform() in Place of XPath.

```
<xsl:variable name="destination" select="dp:xquery-
transform('routingDestinations_xml.xq', $client-cert-info)"/>
```

This dp:xquery-transform() use the XQuery defined in Listing 3-32. The FLOWR statement performs the equivalent function by getting the client subject from the TLS certificate, obtaining the routing document and returning the Host, Port and SSLID.

Listing 3-22 routingDestinations_xml.xq XQuery with FLOWR statement.

```
declare namespace dp = "http://www.datapower.com/extensions";


(:The following syntax must be used to specifically set the output
method to XML:)


declare namespace output = "http://www.w3.org/2010/xslt-xquery-
serialization";

declare option output:method "xml";


let $destinations :=
doc('AwardServiceRouting.xml')/routingDestinations/destination


(:Get the SSL/TLS Client Subject from the Inputput <client-cert-info>
node:)

(:The ssl-client-subject will be used to match to the
routingDestinations/destination node:)


let $subjectCN := /client-cert-info/ssl-client-subject


for $destination in $destinations

  where $destination/@subjectCN = $subjectCN

  return $destination
```

The randomURI function can also be rewritten using an XQuery transform. In this example in Listing 3-23 the time variable is obtained by execution of the 'currentTime.xq' XQuery.

Listing 3-23 routingDestinations_xml.xq XQuery with FLOWR statement.

```
    <func:function name="func:randomURI">
        <!-- -->
        <!-- Generate a Pseudo Random Number 0/1 -->
        <!-- XPATH 2.0 fn:current-time() returns (for example)
08:04:22-05:00 -->
        <!-- Get the milliseconds and see if they are odd/even -->
        <!-- Other options such as the dp:time-value() function could
have been used -->
        <!-- -->
        <xsl:variable name="time" select="dp:xquery-
transform('currentTime.xq', .)"/>
        <xsl:variable name="milliseconds" select="substring-
after(substring-after(substring-before($time, '-') , ':'), ':')"/>
        <xsl:message>
            <xsl:value-of select="concat('time = ', $time, ',
milliseconds = ', $milliseconds)"/>
        </xsl:message>
        <!-- -->
        <xsl:choose>
            <xsl:when test="$milliseconds mod 2 = 1">
                <func:result>
                    <xsl:value-of select="'/star'"/>
                </func:result>
            </xsl:when>
            <xsl:otherwise>
                <func:result>
                    <xsl:value-of select="'/circle'"/>
                </func:result>
            </xsl:otherwise>
        </xsl:choose>
    </func:function>
```

Listing 3-24 shows the XQuery XPath 2.0 function invocation. There's not much there, it's just a single like of XPath 2.0 which obtains the current-time. And as we did it in the XSLT example previously, it's used in the randomURI function to randomly generate the /circle or /star URI. There are many XPath 2.0 function supported and you can use them in this fashion.

Listing 3-24 XQuery XPath 2.0 function call.

```
fn:current-time()
```

The XQuery sample works just as the XSLT did. We simply use an https://Awards_Service:4433/xq request which contains the 'xq' matching string to execute the Award_Service_Using_XQuery rule.

Extending Dynamic Routing sample with GatewayScript

Our final demonstration of dynamic routing is performed with GWS. We've introduced GWS and demonstrated some of its functionality. GWS features are expanding rapidly in the DataPower Gateway product with some of the latest features including signing and verifying messages use JSON Web Signature (JWS) specifications. The current firmware 7.2.0.2 does not however provide access to the dp:auth-info('ssl-client-subject') extension function that we've been using to match the dynamic routing entries in the DynamicRouting.xml document.

But fear not! This gives us the opportunity to explore one more XSLT/XQuery/GWS interoperability option. GatewayScript does provide the ability to execute XSLT from within GWS. This gives us the ability to obtain the routing information. Listing 3-25 shows the necessary plumbing. The ‘transform’ module is required, and its XSLT function is invoked with the options object being used to describe the XML DOM to transform (none in this case) and the XSLT to execute.

Listing 3-25 GatewayScript executing XSLT to Crypto information.

```
var hm = require('header-metadata');
var fs = require('fs')
var sf = require('sprintf').sprintf;
var transform = require('transform');
var sm = require ('service-metadata');

var options = {
    "location": "local:///dynamicRouting_with_XSLT_For_GWS.xsl",
    "xmldom": null,
};

//  Perform the XSLT execution to obtain routing information

transform.xslt(options, function(error, routeDestination, abortinfo)
{
    if (error) {
        session.output.write("An error was returned when executing '"
+ options.location + "'");
    }
    else {
        setDynamicDestination(routeDestination);
    }
```

```
});
```

Listing 3-26 shows the remainder of the GWS. Having been passed the XML Nodelist returned by the XSLT, the setDynamicDestination function parses through the nodeList and extracts the necessary routing information. We could have used DataPower's transform.xpath() function to extract this data. With a simple use case like this, walking the DOM tree is sufficient, but for more complex uses, the transform.xpath() is a powerful tool.

Notice that we are using the service-metadata module to set the host, port, uri and the SSL Client Profile. We are not using the dp:xset-target extension element that we used in the XSLT and XQuery examples. If you remember back in Chapter 2, we discussed how the extension functions and elements could often be thought of as 'helper' functions whose purpose is to set variables within the DataPower firmware's data model. That's the case here; we are not using the extension element, but rather just setting the underlying variables. You'll see our random /circle, /star requirement is easily handled in GWS also.

Listing 3-26 Set dynamic routing and generate dynamic URI.

```
//  Set the Dynamic Routing based on XML Node returned from XSLT
Transform


function setDynamicDestination(routeDestination) {


  var host =
routeDestination.item(0).getElementsByTagName("host").item(0).textCon
tent;
```

```
  var port =
routeDestination.item(0).getElementsByTagName("port").item(0).textCon
tent;

  var sslid =
routeDestination.item(0).getElementsByTagName("sslid").item(0).textCo
ntent;


  console.debug('host is %1$s, port is %2$s, sslid is %3$s', host,
port, sslid);


//  You must set the routingUrlSslprofile before setting routingUrl
or Uri


  sm.routingUrlSslprofile = sslid;

  sm.routingUrl = "https://"+host+":"+port+randomURI();

}


//  Pseudo Random function to generate a /circle or /star URI


function randomURI(routeDestination) {

  var randomNumber = Math.floor((Math.random() * 10) + 1);

  if (randomNumber%2 == 0) {

    return "/circle";

  }

  else {

    return "/star";

  }

}
```

Once again, the execution of the GWS version of the dynamic routing process works just the same as the others. The uri contains 'js' executing the Award_Service_Using_GWS rule. The example in Figure 3-19 shows the results and hey, we got a gold star this time!

Figure 3-19 GWS dynamic routing results.

Summary

Congratulations on having performed a significant amount of the work that is required in a real world DataPower implementation! We've demonstrated the ability to request and process both XML and JSON services. You've seen how to parse documents using XPath and XQuery and how to invoke GatewayScript and XPath 2.0 processes through XSLT and vice versa. Importantly we've discussed some of the key best practices for implementing an environment neutral configuration and one that is easily transported between devices. These included the Host Alias, and the DNS Static Host. Using these will be a significant help in your configuration management efforts. We've also gone through the server and client implications of standing up an SSL/TLS service including selecting Ciphers, creating PEM and PKCS12 certificates and managing them in DataPower and your client browser.

Of course you can extend this configuration adding monitoring, logging targets and much more. But you now have the skills and some real examples to build on. So, go forth and develop!

Chapter 4 Development Tools

Messaging Patterns

Now that you have read all of the chapters on development, you realize that you may have to do some programming when configuring your services. The extent of that programming will depend on your use cases and will range from simple XML to XML transformations using XSLT to complex logic using GatewayScript. We have provided you with the basics, some advanced topics, and even some real-world examples of XSLT and GatewayScript. Even after all that, it still might seem a little intimidating. But fear not—help is on the way. As with any other programming language, a developer coding for DataPower should have a set of tools available for editing, testing, and debugging during the development process. This chapter discusses some tools available for XSLT and JavaScript development to help you along your way.

Many "old-school" developer environments consist of a basic text editor, and they might claim that's all they need. However, with today's complex programming languages, most realize the benefits of an Integrated Development Environment (IDE). An IDE can be thought of as the developer's tool box. There are many different types available for different programming languages provided by many different software vendors. Most IDEs provide a robust text editor that offers tools such as code formatting, debugging, and possibly a runtime environment. Because we are programming for the

DataPower runtime, we are interested only in XSLT and JavaScript programming and IDEs that support them. Although it is not the intent of this chapter to give you a tutorial on any one product, we will point out the key features of various IDEs that can assist you when coding for your DataPower services.

XMLSpy

If you are simply dealing with XML and XSLT, Altova XMLSpy is very popular since it is specifically designed to work with XML, XSD, and XSL documents. All of the features discussed in this section are demonstrated using the most current version of XMLSpy at the time of this writing and might not be available in all prior versions. Be sure to check the version you are using to see what features are available.

Text Editor

XMLSpy provides a rich text editor for editing your XML and XSL documents. It provides many features expected of an IDE, including auto complete, document formatting, and automatic error identification. Because this product is designed specifically to work with XML documents, it also provides a graphical hierarchical view of the document in the text editor. Each element and its children can be expanded and collapsed within the document. Figure 4-1 shows the text editor displaying an XSL document. Notice how easy it is to identify the start and end of a particular element. It is also convenient to be able to collapse a particular element when you are not working with it.

```
<?xml version="1.0" encoding="UTF-8"?>
<xsl:stylesheet version="1.0" xmlns:xsl="http://www.w3.org/1999/XSL/Transform">
    <xsl:output method="xml" version="1.0" encoding="UTF-8" indent="yes"/>
    <xsl:template match="/book">
        <xsl:variable name="author_first" select="substring-before(author, ' ')"/>
        <xsl:variable name="author_last" select="substring-after(author, ' ')"/>
        <book-request>
            <book-name>
                <xsl:value-of select="name"/>
            </book-name>
            <book-author>
                <author-first>
                    <xsl:value-of select="$author_first"/>
                </author-first>
                <author-last>
                    <xsl:value-of select="$author_last"/>
                </author-last>
            </book-author>
        </book-request>
    </xsl:template>
</xsl:stylesheet>
```

Figure 4-1 XMLSpy Text Editor.

During your development, it is likely that you will be coding some complex XPath expressions in your stylesheets. For this reason, XMLSpy comes with a convenient XPath generator tool. By simply opening the input XML document and selecting the location in the document of interest, this tool can generate the applicable XPath, where you can copy it to the clipboard and paste it into your XSLT. Figure 4-2 shows this feature where the XPath statement is generated for the <author> element, which is a child of the <book> element. This menu shown was presented when right clicking the <author> element. The generated XPath “book/author” can now be copied and pasted into the source XSLT document.

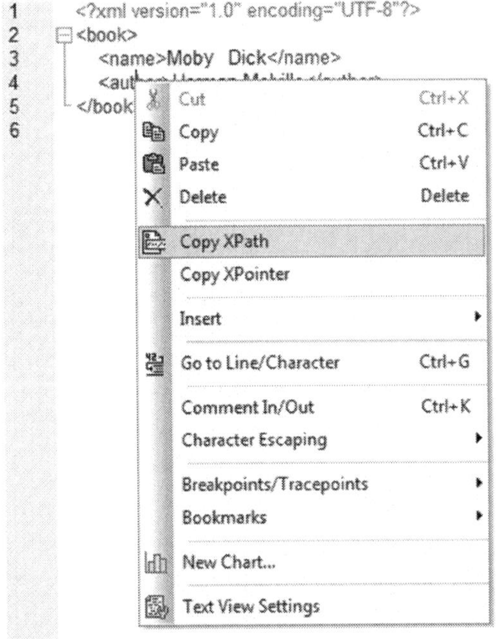

Figure 4-2 XMLSpy Generate and copy XPath.

Executing your XSLT

XMLSpy also includes a built-in XSLT runtime engine, so it is possible to test your XSLT code in this IDE. You can simply specify the input XML document and the XSL file and execute the transformation. The output of the transformation is written to a separate file and displayed. To execute your XSLT in XMLSpy, you first open the XSL file in the text editor. Then from the top menu, select XSL/XQuery→XSL Transformation. You are then asked to select the XML input file, where you can browse to the sample XML to be transformed, as shown in Figure 4-3. Keep in mind that if your XSLT utilizes DataPower custom extension functions, elements, or DataPower variables, you cannot execute this in XMLSpy. This is because the XSLT runtime in these tools does not know anything about these DataPower specific elements, functions, or variables.

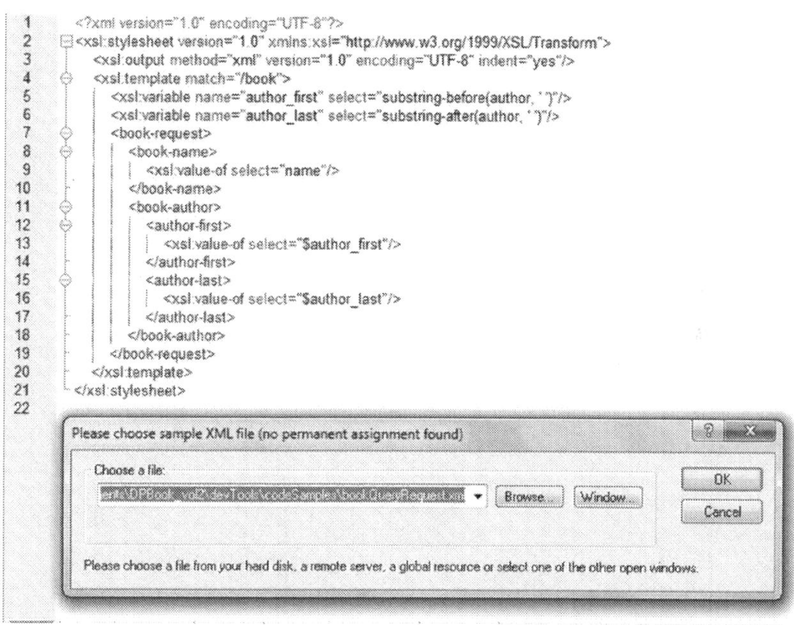
<?xml version="1.0" encoding="UTF-8"?>
<xsl:stylesheet version="1.0" xmlns:xsl="http://www.w3.org/1999/XSL/Transform">
<xsl:output method="xml" version="1.0" encoding="UTF-8" indent="yes"/>
<xsl:template match="/book">
<xsl:variable name="author_first" select="substring-before(author, ' ')"/>
<xsl:variable name="author_last" select="substring-after(author, ' ')"/>
<book-request>
<book-name>
<xsl:value-of select="name"/>
</book-name>
<book-author>
<author-first>
<xsl:value-of select="$author_first"/>
</author-first>
<author-last>
<xsl:value-of select="$author_last"/>
</author-last>
</book-author>
</book-request>
</xsl:template>
</xsl:stylesheet>
Please choose sample XML file (no permanent assignment found)
Choose a file:
Browse...
Window...
OK
Cancel
Please choose a file from your hard disk, a remote server, a global resource or select one of the other open windows.

Figure 4-3 Selecting a sample XML input file for transformation.

After selecting the input XML file, the transformation is executed, and the result file is displayed.

Of course, not all of your XSLT will be as simple as the bookRequest.xslt shown in Figure 4-1. At times you will be trying to trace through the execution path of some complex recursion or logic, trying to figure out why you are not getting the expected results. Luckily, XML Spy has a step-by-step debugging tool that can help with this troubleshooting. This feature allows for breakpoints and displaying the current context, variables, and output document as the XSL executes. To execute the stylesheet in debug mode, you select XSL/XQuery→Start Debugger/Go. You are asked again to select an input XML document. After selecting the input document, you are presented with the debugging screen where you can step through the execution line by line as shown in Figure 4-4. From this screen you can step into the execution of the XSLT where valuable information is displayed such as current context, variables, and the output document as it is being built.

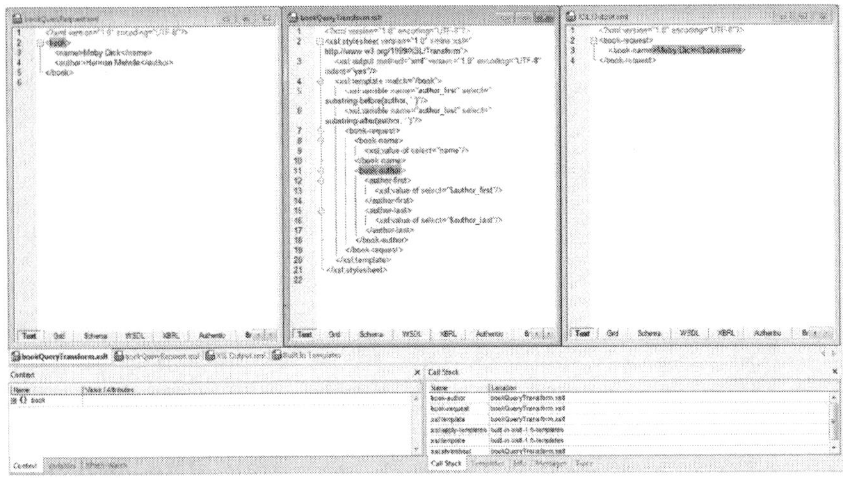

Figure 4-4 XMLSpy Debugging.

If your development for DataPower is strictly XSLT, you will find that XML Spy can be one of your biggest assets as it is built specifically for XML processing. What we have shown you here is merely scratching the surface of what this tool has to offer. As you begin using this tool, you will uncover the invaluable built-in features to make your job easier when developing your XML and XSLT.

Eclipse

If working with XML and coding XSLT was the extent of your development (remember the old days of DataPower?) then an IDE that specializes in this would suffice. Now that DataPower is "bilingual" we need tools that support both XSLT and JavaScript. I am sure you can find many IDEs that support one, or both these. Perhaps your favorite IDE does. There is one IDE that is used by many developers for almost any language in existence. That IDE is Eclipse. Eclipse is an open source project that provides all of the tools and utilities that you expect out of an IDE. There are many plugins available to help with many different tasks throughout the software development lifecycle (SDLC). You can find plugins for code assist, debugging, and even integration with your favorite source control manager. We do use source control, right? If you are feeling ambitious, you can even develop your own custom plugins. That is a topic for another book in and of itself. Many of today's licensed IDEs and development tools are actually built on Eclipse, such as WebSphere Transformation Extender (WTX) Design Studio. Because of Eclipse's versatility, extendibility, and ubiquity, we think this is a good "all around" development tool for developing for DataPower. In this section we will show you how Eclipse can be used for developing and debugging XSLT and JavaScript for DataPower. All examples in this section are using Eclipse Java EE for Web Developers, Luna Service Release 1 (4.4.1). This particular package will contain all of the plugins for XSLT and

JavaScript you should need. If not, you will see how we install some additional plugins later in this chapter.

XML and XSLT

Even with power and flexibility of GatewayScript, there is no doubting the processing power of XSLT within DataPower when processing XML documents. For these use cases you should have a full featured IDE for assisting you. Eclipse would certainly do the trick for this. Eclipse has many built-in features for programming XSLT, such as text formatting, an XSLT runtime engine, and step-by-step debugging. Keep in mind that the Eclipse runtime will only suffice when coding XSLT that does not include the use of DataPower artifacts such as extension functions and variables.

The text editor in Eclipse is where you create and edit your files. For this discussion, these will be XSLT stylesheets and XML files. This is not your typical text editor, as it has many built-in features that are available based on the extension of the file you are editing. For example, if you are editing an .xsl file, the editor knows that it is an XSLT stylesheet and enables the built-in features for editing XSLT.

When creating a new file in Eclipse, you can specify the type of file that you are creating. When you specify that the new file is an XSLT stylesheet, it will create a new XSL file with the mandatory elements and declarations as shown in Listing 4-1. You can see that a new XSL file was generated with a template for matching on the root of the document.

Listing 4-1 New XSL File Created Within Eclipse.

```
<?xml version="1.0" encoding="UTF-8"?>

<xsl:stylesheet version="1.0"
xmlns:xsl="http://www.w3.org/1999/XSL/Transform">

    <xsl:template match="/">

<!-- TODO: Auto-generated template -->

    </xsl:template>

</xsl:stylesheet>
```

After the XSL file is created, the file can be edited in the text editor pane, which is where you see the real power of this IDE. As you first start to code your XSLT, you might notice some pop-ups that display next to the cursor; these contain suggestions for completing the current line of code. For example, when you begin creating your stylesheet, you might start by creating a <xsl:template> element. As you begin to type this code, a pop-up displays with suggestions immediately after typing the '<' in the editor, as shown in Figure 4-5. Any of the elements displayed can be chosen and will be inserted automatically into your code. In this case, you can click the <xsl:template> element. Not only does this save you on some typing, but it is also handy if you don't remember the exact syntax of an element. If you find that this pop-up does not display automatically, you can press CTRL and the spacebar together to activate it.

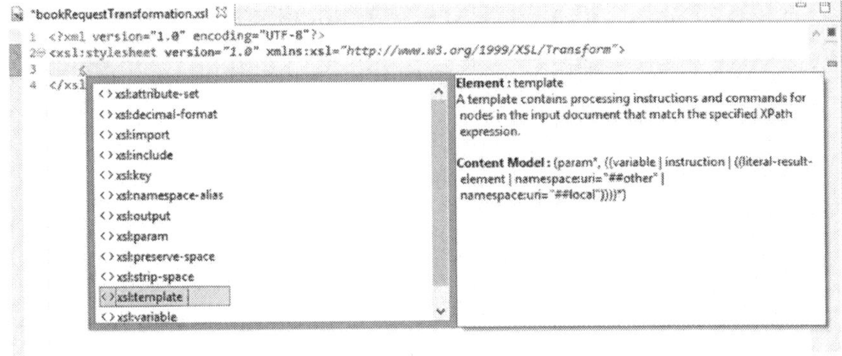

Figure 4-5 Content Assist pop-up.

In addition to the content assist capability, Eclipse also provides a way of alerting you that there is a syntax error in the code—by drawing a red squiggly line underneath the line where the error occurs. Figure 4-6 shows an example where the namespace was not added to the ending element for the template. Notice the squiggly line underneath the ending </template> tag. Hovering the cursor over this error provides more details about the error.

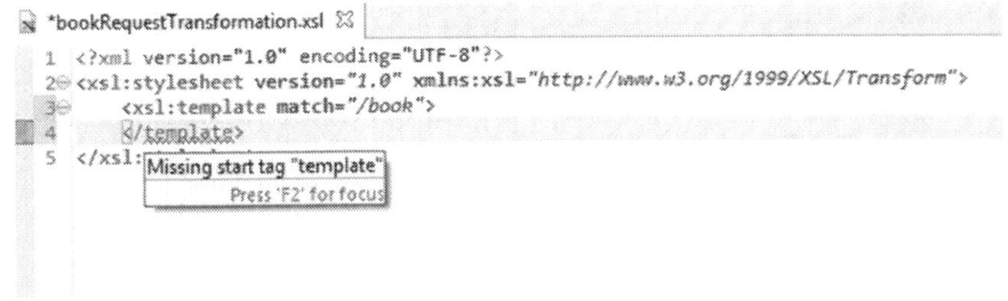

Figure 4-6 Eclipse alerting of an error.

Many developers do not take the time to write code that is properly formatted, such as indenting between elements and conditional statements. When using Eclipse, you don't have to worry about this because it provides a feature to format the code for you. You can right-click within your XSL or XML file and select Format→Document, and your document is formatted for you. Figure 4-7 shows a small piece of XSLT within the Eclipse text editor that has not been properly formatted. After using the Format option, the code is formatted so that all the nested elements are indented, as shown in Figure 4-8.

These formatting parameters are configurable, although the defaults should suffice. Notice how much easier the code is to read after it has been formatted.

bookRequestTransformation.xsl | *bookQueryTransform.xslt

```
<?xml version="1.0" encoding="UTF-8"?>
<xsl:stylesheet version="1.0" xmlns:xsl="http://www.w3.org/1999/XSL/Transform">
<xsl:output method="xml" version="1.0" encoding="UTF-8" indent="yes"/>
<xsl:template match="/book">
<xsl:variable name="author_first" select="substring-before(author, ' ')"/>
<xsl:variable name="author_last" select="substring-after(author, ' ')"/>
<book-request>
<book-name>
<xsl:value-of select="name"/>
</book-name>
<book-author>
<author-first><xsl:value-of select="$author_first"/></author-first>
<author-last><xsl:value-of select="$author_last"/></author-last></book-author></book-request>
</xsl:template>
</xsl:stylesheet>

```

Figure 4-7□XSL before auto format.

bookRequestTransformation.xsl | *bookQueryTransform.xslt

```
<?xml version="1.0" encoding="UTF-8"?>
<xsl:stylesheet version="1.0"
    xmlns:xsl="http://www.w3.org/1999/XSL/Transform">
    <xsl:output method="xml" version="1.0" encoding="UTF-8"
        indent="yes" />
    <xsl:template match="/book">
        <xsl:variable name="author_first" select="substring-before(author, ' ')" />
        <xsl:variable name="author_last" select="substring-after(author, ' ')" />
        <book-request>
            <book-name>
                <xsl:value-of select="name" />
            </book-name>
            <book-author>
                <author-first>
                    <xsl:value-of select="$author_first" />
                </author-first>
                <author-last>
                    <xsl:value-of select="$author_last" />
                </author-last>
            </book-author>
        </book-request>
    </xsl:template>
</xsl:stylesheet>
```

Figure 4-8 XSL after auto format.

When coding XSLT, it is likely that you will be writing many XPath statements to query the XML document being parsed. Many times this will be an easy task that can be accomplished by looking at the XML document itself. There are times however, that even an experienced XSLT developer can use a little help with formulating these XPath expressions for deeply nested, complex XML documents. This is where the XPath expression builder in Eclipse comes in handy.

As you are coding your XSLT, you will most likely refer back to a sample XML document representing the actual document that will be used as input for the transformation. You will refer to this document for creating XPath expressions that may be used to extract the value of an element or attribute to be used within the transformation. Using this sample document, Eclipse can help you by generating the XPath expression for you within the XPath Expression View. The XPath Expression View can be accessed from the top menu within Eclipse Window→Show View→Other→XML→XPath. The XPath View will appear as a tab under the editor. With the source XML document open in the editor, you can now click on the element that you wish to generate the XPath statement for as seen in Figure 4-9. You can also manually type in your XPath statement here to see how it evaluates against the source XML document.

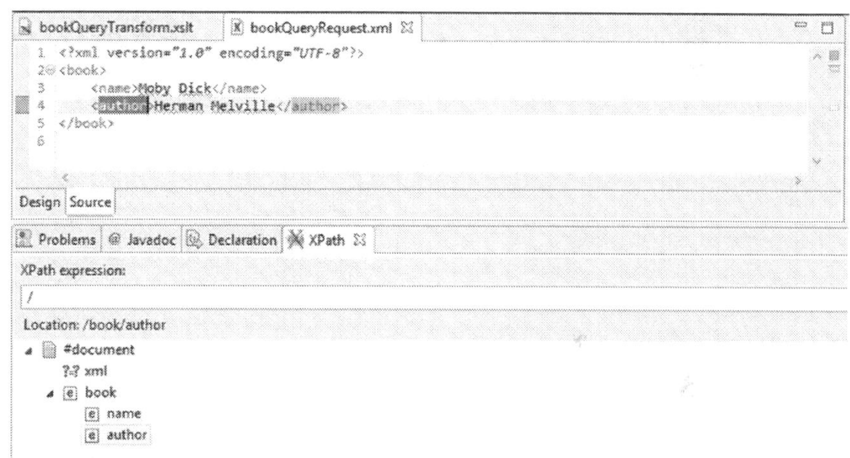

Figure 4-9 Eclipse XPath view.

After you have completed your XSLT development, you might want to test it before deploying to the DataPower runtime. Eclipse comes with an XSLT runtime for you to test your code from within the IDE itself. The easiest way to do this is to import the XML that will be used as the input to the transformation into the project. A project is simply a top-level folder containing all the files for the application being developed. When developing stylesheets for DataPower services, you might create a project for each service and store the associated files within it. This keeps your workspace more organized and makes it much easier when it is time to move the code to the DataPower device for a given service. For more information on projects and importing files, please refer to your Eclipse documentation. After importing the XML file, into the project, you can highlight the XML and XSL files in the Navigator pane of your Eclipse environment (hold down Ctrl and click each file), right-click one of them, and select Run As→XSL Transformation as shown in Figure 4-10.

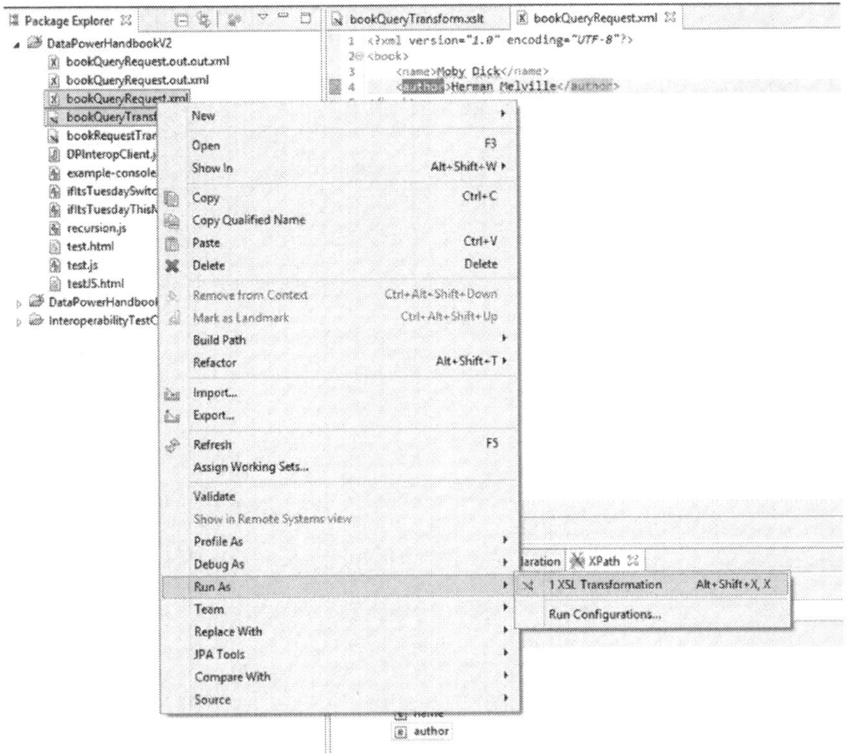

Figure 4-10 Executing XSLT within Eclipse.

After the XSL transformation is complete, the results are written to a new file and shown in the text editor pane. If any errors were encountered during the execution, they will be listed in the console that is typically located just below the text editor. Keep in mind that Eclipse does not know about any custom DataPower functions and elements that your XSLT might be utilizing during a transformation, so using these will cause the transformation to fail. After a successful execution, you might notice that the resulting XML file is written out in one single line and may be difficult to read. This is where the Format option comes in handy. As discussed earlier, to format this results document, you right-click in the document and select Format→Document. The results of an XSL transformation after formatting are shown in Figure 4-11.

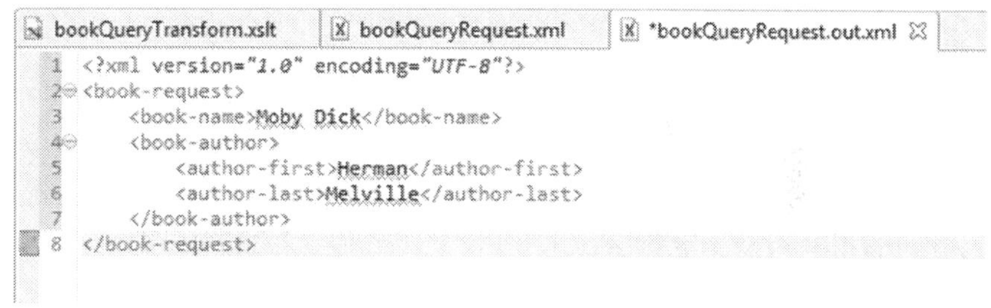
bookQueryTransform.xslt
bookQueryRequest.xml
*bookQueryRequest.out.xml
<?xml version="1.0" encoding="UTF-8"?>
<book-request>
<book-name>Moby Dick</book-name>
<book-author>
<author-first>Herman</author-first>
<author-last>Melville</author-last>
</book-author>
</book-request>

Figure 4-11□XSLT execution results.

This example produced a small, simple XML results file that is easy to read. It is likely that your results file will not always be this small. Large XML files, even when formatted, are often difficult to read. Because of this, there is a graphical viewer for your XML files in the text editor. When viewing and editing your XML files, there are two tabs at the bottom of the editor. One is labeled Source and shows you the XML in text format as shown in our examples. The second tab is labeled Design and gives you a graphical representation of the entire XML file, as shown in Figure 4-12. All nested elements can be expanded and collapsed for readability. You can see how this can make reading large XML files much easier.

Node	Content
?-? xml	version="1.0" encoding="UTF-8"
book-request	
book-name	Moby Dick
book-author	
author-first	Herman
author-last	Melville

Figure 4-12 Design view of an XML file.

Interoperability Test Service

With the introduction of firmware version 5.0.0 came an interesting new feature called the Interoperability Test Service (IOP). Once setup, this feature can be a real time saver for a developer. In this section we will show you how to set this up and some of the key features of it.

The IOP was introduced to fill the need for testing XSLT, WTX maps, FFD files, and even XPath statements without having to deploy them to a DataPower device, create a service, add the stylesheet to an action, and then submit a request to the service. This is a long way to go just to test you code and find out you have a syntax error! Once you setup and configure this new feature, this will be as simple as submitting a one line command. Let's get started here and see how to get this setup.

The IOP can be enabled and setup via the WebGUI or the CLI. If the WebGUI is your preference, you must first log into the DataPower device default domain. You can navigate to Objects→Device Management→Interoperability Test Service. Or you can simply type "Interoperability Test Service" without the quotes in the search menu and click the link.

You will be presented with the configuration page for this service as shown in Figure 4-13. Notice that is disabled by default. The first thing you must do from here is enable the service by selecting the enabled radio button next to the Administrative State field

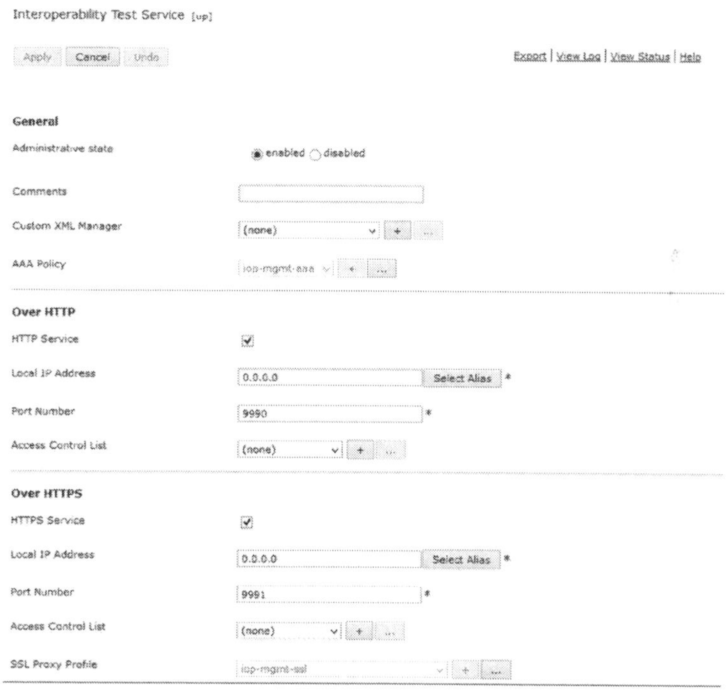

Figure 4-13□Interoperability Test Service configuration screen.

As you can see, there are many configurable parameters on this screen. You can apply a AAA policy, select a custom XML Manager, or even specify an access control list. For now, let's just get the basic configuration set so we can start using it. Selecting the HTTP and HTTPS Service options makes this accessible over HTTP and HTTPS. For each, you must assign an IP address and port that is will listen on. In addition, you must select an SSL Proxy Profile for the HTTPS configuration as shown. Much of this is provided as the default configuration, but it can be customized as you see fit.

Clicking the Apply button will enable the IOP service and it is ready to use. As always, save the domain configuration to be sure the change is persisted.

Once the IOP Service is enabled you will notice a very large warning banner at the top of the Web GUI warning you that the Interoperability Test Service is enabled and should not be enabled in a production environment or an environment that manages sensitive data. Do not take this warning lightly! Enabling this service allows all users to access it from the outside unless you configure a AAA policy for it to enforce access control. For these reasons, it is highly advisable to only enable this service for your development environments.

The next step in this process is to setup the client that will be used on the local machine that you will working from. This can be found in the resource kit that came with device or it can be downloaded from the IBM InfoCenter. The resource kit will have a file name like "ResourceKit.5000.zip". This file should be copied to your local workstation and extracted.

Within the unzipped Resource Kit directory will be a directory named “interoperability-service”. Within this directory will be a “clients” directory which will provide the executables required to access the IOP service. You will also see a “samples” directory which will contain some helpful samples to get you started.

Once the Resource Kit is copied and extracted, you are ready to start using the client to send requests to the IOP service. Let’s start taking a look at how we can use the client to access the IOP service.

Within your clients directory you will see a DPInteropClient.jar file and a DPInteropClient.sh file. Each of these files will provide the same functionality so the choice is yours whether you would like to use a shell script or Java executable. The syntax for the arguments passed will also be the same for each type. For the examples provided here, we will use the .jar file executed from a command line but the flexibility provided by both shell and Java allow for easy integration within your favorite IDE such as Eclipse.

As mentioned earlier, the IOP service provides the ability to execute a XSLT stylesheet against an input document provided. This can be incredibly useful when you are developing your stylesheets locally, which you most likely will be. Let’s take this use case as our first example here.

From a command prompt we navigate to the client directory that contains the .jar file. From here we can execute the DPInteropClient.jar file by simply entering “java –jar DPInteropClient.jar” without the quotes. Just entering this command with no arguments will give you a listing of all of the available arguments that can be passed. This will be helpful while you learn to use the IOP service. For now, we want to execute a stylesheet against an input document. For this we will need to pass some arguments to this executable. We will need to pass the XSLT file name, the input XML document, the host name or IP of the IOP service on the DataPower device, and finally the port that it is listening on. Listing 4-2 shows this command with these arguments.

Listing 4-2 Execute a stylesheet against input XML.

```
java -jar DPInteropClient.jar -x bookQueryTransform.xslt -i
bookQueryRequest.xml -h wa1vmvdp1 -p 9990
```

This command will submit a request to the IOP to transform the input doc bookQueryRequest.xml with the XSLT bookQueryTransform.xslt. As you can see the XSLT file name is preceded by a –x and the input document preceded by a –i. You will also notice the –h for host name and –p for port. Submitting this will result in the IOP client sending this request with the specified documents to the IOP service which will in turn execute the transformation and return the results. This can be seen in Figure 4-14.

```
C:\Users\Owner\Documents\DataPower\ResourceKit.5000\interoperability-service\cli
ents>java -jar DPInteropClient.jar -x bookQueryTransform.xslt -i bookQueryReques
t.xml -h walvmvdp1 -p 9990
>> Creating the xslt request...
>> Connecting to endpoint: http://walvmvdp1:9990/
>> No basic authentication is provided.
>> Receiving HTTP response: 200
<?xml version="1.0" encoding="UTF-8"?>

<book-request>
<book-name>Moby Dick</book-name>
<book-author>
<author-first>Herman</author-first>
<author-last>Melville</author-last></book-author></book-request>
C:\Users\Owner\Documents\DataPower\ResourceKit.5000\interoperability-service\cli
ents>_
```

Figure 4-14□IOP Client Request and Response.

This simple example demonstrated the usefulness and simplicity of using the IOP service to perform a transformation on an XML document using a XSLT stylesheet. Since this is actually executed on the DataPower device, it can be used when you have DataPower extension functions, elements, and variables within your stylesheets. This would not be possible in a runtime outside of DataPower such as Eclipse. It is also possible to transform multiple input documents with a single XSLT using the IOP as well if you bundle all of your input documents and stylesheets into one .zip file and specify which documents to use on the command line. There is much to discover within this tool once you start working with it.

Another handy feature of the IOP is the ability to perform schema validation against an XML document. This can also be accomplished within the IOP client by submitting the command shown in Listing 4-3. In this command the –t parameter is passed with a value of “schema” to indicate that a schema file is being passed. The –x is used to pass the actual schema, and the –i value is the XML file to validate. The IOP service will respond with a SOAP message with the content of the XML file if it passes validation.

Listing 4-3 Schema validate XML.

```
java -jar DPInteropClient.jar -t schema -x bookQuery.xsd -i
bookQueryRequest.xml -h wa1vmvdp1 -p 9990
```

As developers, you can see that this IOP service was built with remote development in mind. We have demonstrated a couple of key features of this tool but there are more. It would certainly behoove you to explore this service and all of its capabilities such as XPath evaluation, multiple input documents in a single request, and WTX map transformations which you will see in the subsequent chapter on non-XML transformations.

JavaScript/GatewayScript

We have now covered a couple of different tools for working with XML and XSLT. You have seen in the examples in this volume how JavaScript can also be a very powerful language for developing for DataPower. Since JavaScript has been around for a while and is so widely used, you will be sure to find a plethora of tools for working with it. If you are a Web developer, you probably have your own set of tools for working with JavaScript, which might even be Eclipse (or Eclipse based). If you do have your favorite JavaScript IDE, then by all means, use it. In this section we will stay with Eclipse to show how you can use one tool for all tasks and languages when developing for DataPower. You will see that there are similar features when working with any language within these tools.

Before you start coding any JavaScript with Eclipse, you should switch to the JavaScript perspective. The fact that there is a perspective in this product should give you a good idea that there are plenty of features for developing JavaScript. To open the JavaScript perspective, navigate to Window→Open Perspective→Other→JavaScript as shown in Figure 4-15.

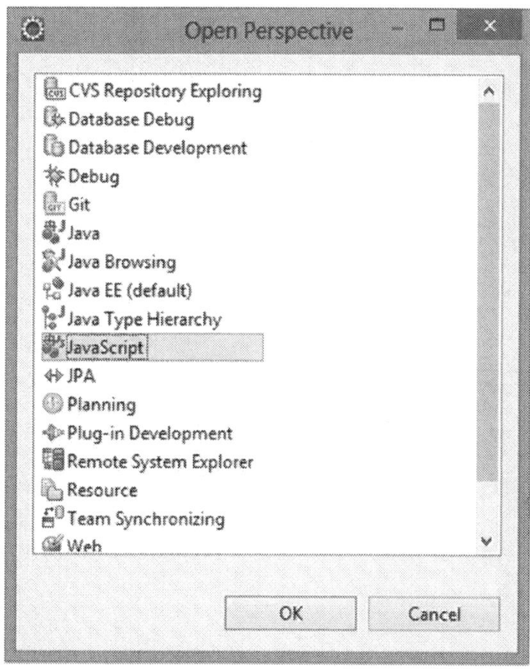

Figure 4-15 Open JavaScript perspective.

You can create a new JavaScript file in the same manner that you create a XSLT file by right clicking your project and selecting New→JavaScript Source File. This new file does not really give you much of a starting template. It only provides the new file with start and end comments. From this point you can start coding your JavaScript.

As you begin editing your JavaScript file you will again start seeing the content assist pop up when applicable as well as the syntax coloring. All of these features can be controlled by navigating to Window→Preferences→JavaScript. If you are not particular about your formatting while you code, you can always right click within the editor and select Source→Format. This will format your code automatically for you. Figure 4-16 shows the JavaScript editor with a simplified version of the "ifItsTuesdayThisMustBeBelgium" code. This code has been auto formatted so it is appropriately indented. You will also notice in the Outline pane to the right where there is a list of variables that are defined within the JavaScript file. If there were functions contained within this JavaScript, you would see them outlined here as well.

ifItsTuesdayThisMustBeBelgium.js
var date = new Date();
var dayOfWeek = date.getDay();
var TUESDAY = 4;
if (dayOfWeek == TUESDAY) {
alert("THIS must be Belgium");
} else {
alert("THIS is NOT Belgium");
}
Outline
date : Date
dayOfWeek : any
TUESDAY : Number

Figure 4-16 JavaScript editor.

Some Quality Control, Please

So you've completed your code, ran it within your DataPower service, and it does exactly what you wanted it to do. You have even formatted it properly to make it more readable, and hopefully added some descriptive comments. You're feeling pretty good about the work you've done, but is this all enough? Is your code efficient and following good JavaScript practices? Wouldn't it be nice to have a JavaScript guru review your code to ensure that it is up to par? Luckily for us, one such guru named Douglas Crockford created a nice little tool called JSLint that will analyze your code and report on any inefficiencies or potential issues it finds. For a complete explanation of the tool and all of its options, refer to the Web site http://www.jslint.com/lint.html. JSLint can be accessed and used in several different ways. The quickest way is to use the online version by simply going to www.jslint.com and copy/paste your code into the text are provided as shown in Figure 4-17. Notice all of the available options for assumptions and tolerance. Refer to the online documentation for a description of each option. For starters, it is safe to assume the defaults for each.

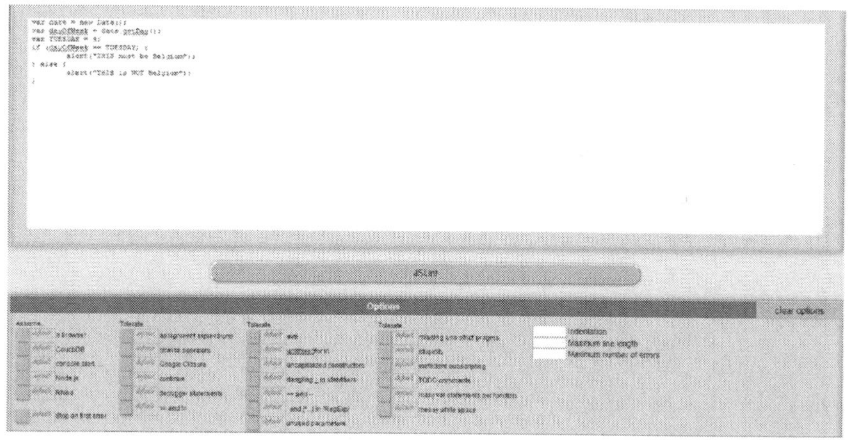

Figure 4-17 JSLint Online tool.

The second option is to download the source code from https://github.com/douglascrockford/JSLint and run this tool locally. The third option, which we will demonstrate here, is to install this within our Eclipse IDE. Again, we like to keep all of our tools in one convenient tool box!

There is no specific plugin dedicated to JSLint, however it is a subset of another plugin that we can install. Installing a plugin within Eclipse is a very simple task once you know the location URL. For this plugin, this URL is https://svn.codespot.com/a/eclipselabs.org/mobile-web-development-with-phonegap/tags/jslint4java1/download. To perform the install within your Eclipse IDE, navigate to Help→Install New Software. Next to the "Work with" text box, click the "Add" button. You are now presented with the "Add Repository" popup. Here you can enter a name within the "Name" text box to identify the repository. In the "Location" text box you will enter the URL for the download - https://svn.codespot.com/a/eclipselabs.org/mobile-web-development-with-phonegap/tags/jslint4java1/download. You can see this completed popup in Figure 4-18.

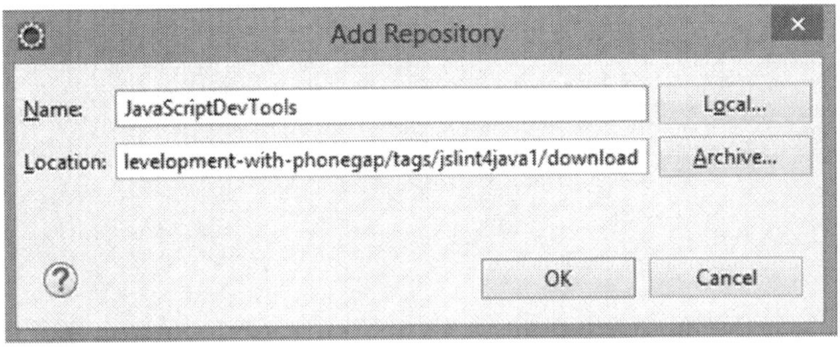

Figure 4-18 Add Repository.

Once you have filled in these two fields, click "OK". This popup will go away and you should return to the "Available

Software" screen. You may see the word "pending" while it retrieves the available downloads from the URL specified. Once this information is retrieved you will see the available plugins from this site in the large text area under the "Name" column. In this case, you should see "PhoneGap for Android with JSLint" which, when expanded, will reveal a tree structure as shown in Figure 4-19.

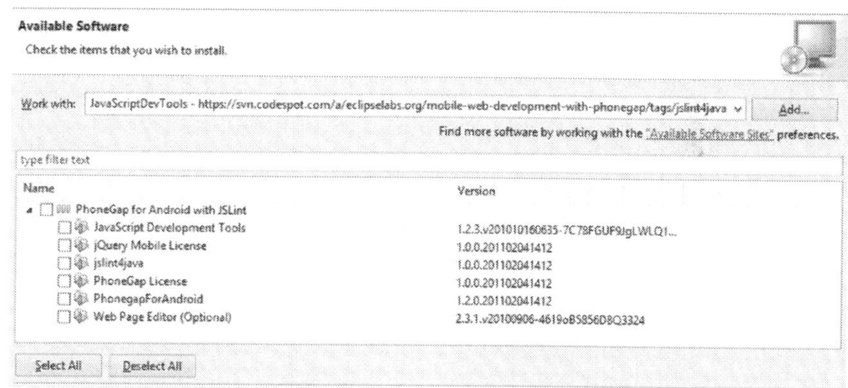

Figure 4-19 PhoneGap for Android with JSLint plugins

The plugin that we are interested in here is the jslint4Java plugin. You can go ahead and check this box and click "Next." Continue to click "Next" and then accept the license agreement and "Finish." You will receive a warning that the content is unsigned. Click ok to finish the installation. You will be prompted to restart Eclipse to finish the installation. Click "Yes" to restart.

Once the restart completes, the plugin is installed and you are ready to give it a test drive. Let's take our "ifItsTuesdayThisMustBeBelgium.js" that we have been working with and see what the quality control tool has to say about it. It's such a small, simple program, what can it have to say about it? It works right? Let's see...

To enable the JSLint plugin we simply right click on our open Project and select "Enable jslint4java". Once enabled, JSLint goes to work and analyzes all of the .js files in your project. If any potential issues are detected you will see an error or warning symbol next to the file name in the project. We open up our sample JavaScript file in our editor and reveal the issues. Figure 4-20 shows that our little JavaScript program can be better.

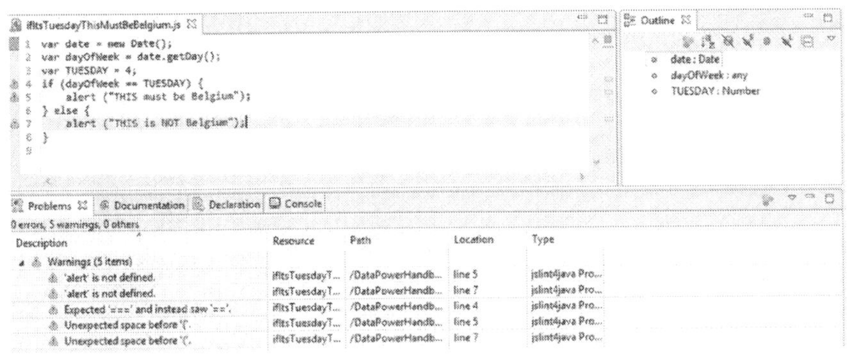

Figure 4-20 JSLint analysis.

Luckily there are no errors here but we do see some warnings. You can see the warning symbols next to each line of code where JSLint has detected that there could be an issue. In the bottom pane you can see in the "Problems" tab all of the potential issues detected. This will show all things identified in the entire project. If you do not see the "Problems" tab, navigate to Window→Show View→Other...→General→Problems.

So what are the complaints about our little JavaScript? You can hover over the warning symbol next to the line in question in the editor to reveal the issue, or you can look in the "Problems" tab. You can see in Figure 4-20 that five items in question and three general issues with them. It appears that JSLint does not like the fact that "alert" is not defined. This is reported on lines 5 and 7. We know that this does not have to be defined so we can ignore this. We also see on line 4 it does not like the fact that we used "==" instead of "===". This is one area where having this tool comes in handy. Although using "==" works in this case, it is not recommended. It is always recommended to use "===". This is because the "==" does any necessary type conversions before doing the comparison which could produce unexpected results. Using the "===" operator will not do any type conversions so if the values being compared are not of the same type, the comparison will return false.

The analysis we saw here pointed out some minor improvements that would most likely not change the outcome of our code execution. There are times, however where this could point out some potential issues that would not cause an error at runtime but produce unexpected results and cost you much time in debugging. Let's take another example where we have a switch statement within our code. As we know, in JavaScript you must have a break statement at the end of each case and before the next case statement. A very common mistake is omitting this break statement which will not cause an error but cause the execution to flow through the case statements even after one is true. This could lead to frustrating troubleshooting sessions. You can see in Figure 4-21 that our JavaScript falls victim to this very common mistake. The good news here is that JSLint picks this up right away and throws a warning. The even better news is that these warnings and errors are detected and displayed as you are typing your code! That's right, big brother is always watching!

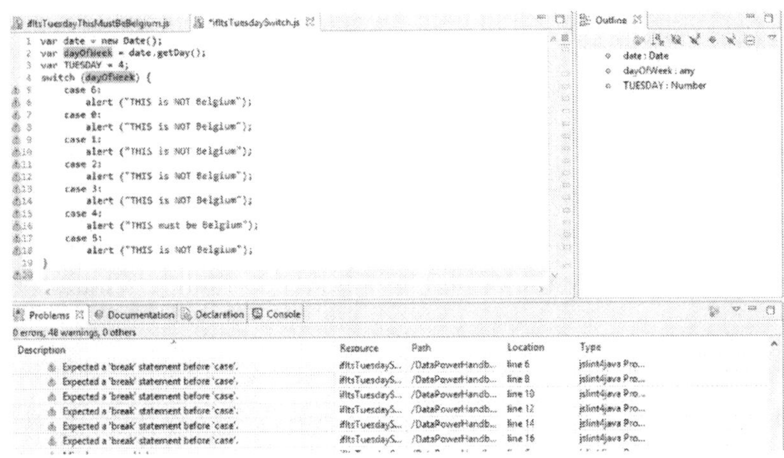

Figure 4-21 JSLint break warnings.

Now, we all know that each developer has his/her own preferences, styles, and beliefs around what is a best practice and what is a bad practice. We can take Douglas Crockford's word for it and abide by the rules and recommendations set forth in the tool, or we can change them a bit to fit our own style. Perhaps you think "==" is the right way to code this comparison and not "===" and this warning is really becoming a nuisance. If you navigate to Window → Preferences you will see jslint4Java in the list of preferences you can alter. Figure 4-22 shows this extensive list of options that you can customize. Notice that the "if === should be required" is checked. This is why we continue to see this warning. Also notice that we can eliminate the warning we saw for the "alert variable not defined" if we check the "If logging should be allowed (console, alert, etc)" box. You also have the flexibility here to specify other style preferences like number of spaces for indenting, etc. Note that after these preferences are changed, you must disable jslint4java by right clicking your project and clicking "disable jslint4java". You can then enable it in the same manner and your new preferences will take effect.

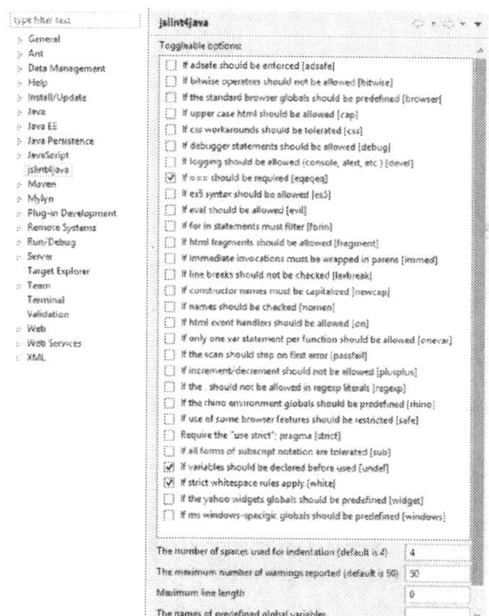

Figure 4-22 JSLint Eclipse Options.

GatewayScript Debugger

Let's face it—when developing any code, it is inevitable that there will be times where errors are thrown or the results produced are not what you expect them to be. Sometimes these will be easy to resolve by reading through the code yourself, and sometimes you just wish you could see what is going on in the code at runtime. There are several Eclipse plugins for this. Some useful plugins include ChromeDevTools, Crossfire, and others. If you are interested in these you can install them in the same way we did with jslint4java. These would all provide debugging within Eclipse, which is not where your code will ultimately run. When debugging any issue, it is important to be working within the environment where the issue will actually occur. This brings us to an exciting new feature within DataPower, introduced in firmware V7.0, the DataPower GatewayScript debugger. This new feature allows you to step through your GatewayScript as it executes within your service on DataPower.

Before jumping into debugging your GatewayScript in DataPower, there is a little bit of setup work you must do.

The first step in preparing to debug your GatewayScript is to add the "debugger;" statement at the beginning of your code. Figure 4-23 shows our "ifItsTuesdayThis MustBeBelgium.js" GatewayScript file with this debugger statement added. Notice we will be using the version of this code with the DataPower functions included since we will be running this within a DataPower service.

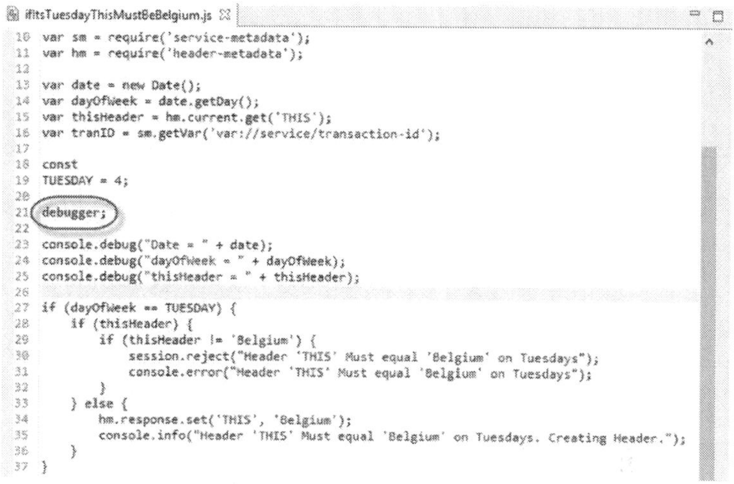

ifItsTuesdayThisMustBeBelgium.js

```
var sm = require('service-metadata');
var hm = require('header-metadata');

var date = new Date();
var dayOfWeek = date.getDay();
var thisHeader = hm.current.get('THIS');
var tranID = sm.getVar('var://service/transaction-id');

const
TUESDAY = 4;

debugger;

console.debug("Date = " + date);
console.debug("dayOfWeek = " + dayOfWeek);
console.debug("thisHeader = " + thisHeader);

if (dayOfWeek == TUESDAY) {
    if (thisHeader) {
        if (thisHeader != 'Belgium') {
            session.reject("Header 'THIS' Must equal 'Belgium' on Tuesdays");
            console.error("Header 'THIS' Must equal 'Belgium' on Tuesdays");
        }
    } else {
        hm.response.set('THIS', 'Belgium');
        console.info("Header 'THIS' Must equal 'Belgium' on Tuesdays. Creating Header.");
    }
}
```

Figure 4-23 Adding the debugger; statement.

Once you add your debugger statement in the code, you can add the code to the service in a GatewayScript action. Within the GatewayScript action configuration, you must then enable the debugger for this action by clicking the “Enable Debug” button as shown in Figure 4-24.

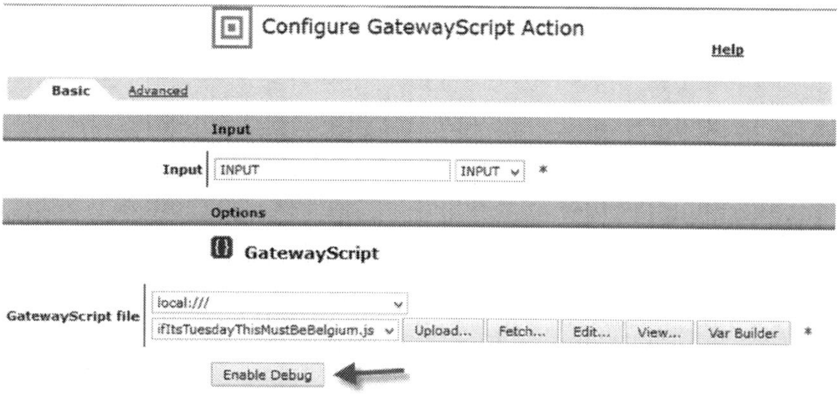

Configure GatewayScript Action
Help
Basic Advanced
Input
Input INPUT INPUT *
Options
GatewayScript
GatewayScript file local:///
ifItsTuesdayThisMustBeBelgium.js Upload... Fetch... Edit... View... Var Builder *
Enable Debug

Figure 4-24 Enable Debug.

Once the debug is enable on the GatewayScript action you will receive confirmation that it was successful and you can close the confirmation window and finish the configuration of the action. Once that is all complete and the configuration is saved, this configuration will enter debug mode when the action is invoked via a service request.

The debugger is accessed via the DataPower command line interface (CLI) so you must have access to the CLI to enter a debugging session. If you have done the initial setup on a DataPower device then you should be familiar with the DataPower CLI. If not, you can refer to your product documentation or Volume 1 of this book series *DataPower Handbook, Second Edition, Volume 1: Intro and Setup*. For now, we will provide a brief explanation of how to access the CLI.

The CLI can be accessed over Secure Shell (SSH) so you should be sure that the SSH interface is enabled on your DataPower device. You will also need an SSH client on your local workstation. There are many SSH clients that are free and easy to install. One popular client is PuTTY. Since we are developers and prefer to have all our tools in one handy place, you guessed it, there is an Eclipse plugin for that! This particular plugin is the TCF Terminal plugin. It can be downloaded from http://download.eclipse.org/tools/tcf/terminals_luna. As we have seen already, to install this within Eclipse, you can simply navigate to Help→Install New Software. Click the "Add" button, enter and name within the "Name" text box, and the download URL in the "Location" text box. Once the plugin is retrieved you can expand the TCF Terminals plugin and check the two bundles contained within. You can also check the top level plugin TCF Terminals to download all as shown in Figure2-25.

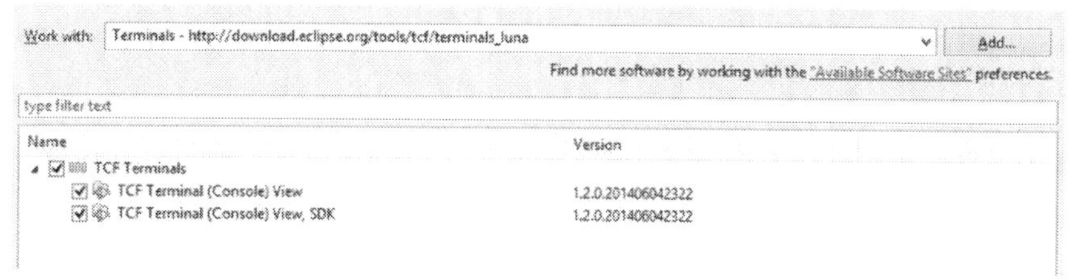

Figure 4-25 Installing the TCF Terminals Plugin.

Once the plugin has installed and Eclipse has restarted, you are ready to fire up a terminal within your IDE and connect to DataPower. To do this you can click the terminal icon in the top right of the Eclipse screen as shown in Figure 4-26, or you can use the hot keys (Ctl +Alt +T).

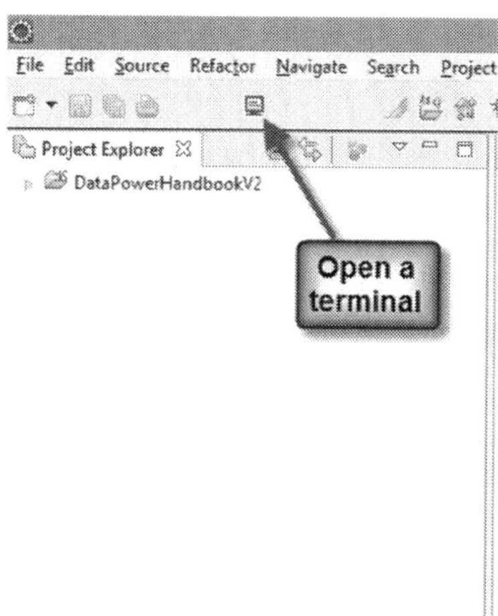

Figure 4-26 Open Terminal.

You will now be presented with a popup screen that will require some basic information about the terminal session you would like to open. First you will need to specify the type of terminal you are opening. In this case you will choose SSH. Take note of the other types of terminal sessions available as they may come in handy at a later time.

The only other two pieces of information you will need are the IP address and port that the DataPower SSH service is listening on. You can find this in the default domain under Network→Management→SSH Service. More than likely, your port will remain 22 as this is the default. Note that there is no need for user ID and/or password as you will enter them later. All other configuration parameters have been left as the default.

Once you enter this information and click “OK”, a SSH terminal session will open in a tab at the bottom of your Eclipse IDE. You will now notice that you are prompted for a login and then your password. Use your DataPower credentials to log in. If your login was successful, you should be presented with a prompt - Domain (? For all). You will enter the domain where your service that you are debugging resides.

Figure 4-27 shows an active SSH terminal session within Eclipse logged into the DataPower DPBookV2 domain.

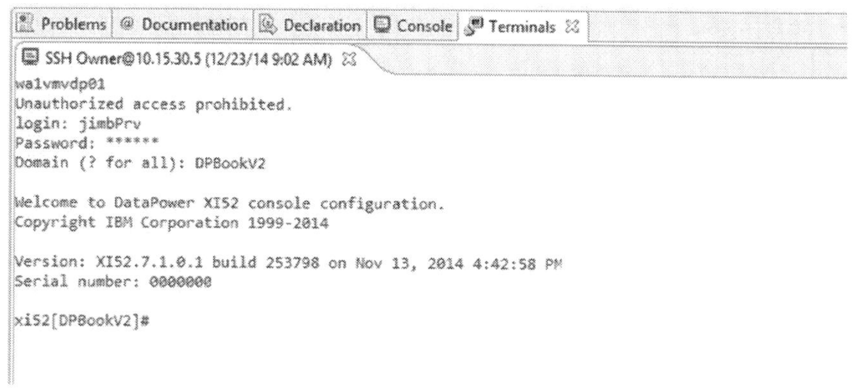

Figure 4-27 Active SSH Terminal Session.

You now have a terminal client installed in Eclipse with an open terminal session logged into DataPower in the domain you wish to debug your GatewayScript. This may seem like a long way to go for debugging but this is a one-time install and you will likely discover the power and convenience of the DataPower CLI.

For now we are interested in debugging our GatewayScript so let's get started! You can now submit a request to your service that you are debugging. Once the request hits the GatewayScript action, it will break at the debugger line in the script. At this point, you will go to your open SSH terminal session and enter into global configuration mode by typing "co" on the command line. To view all of the available sessions to debug in this domain, type "show debug-actions". Figure 4-28 shows that we have one available debug session in this domain. You can see that it is from within a service named "sampleJS" and the executing GatewayScript file is our "ifItsTuesdaySwitch.js" file.

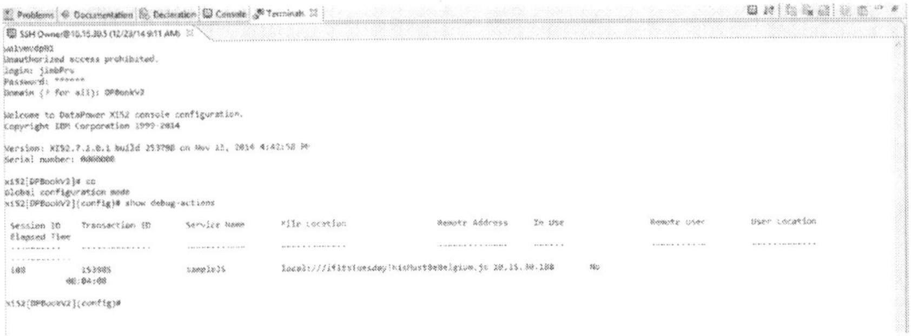

```
Problems  Documentation  Declaration  Console  Terminals
SSH Owner@10.15.30.5 (12/23/14 9:11 AM)
walyvmdp01
Unauthorized access prohibited.
login: jimbPru
Password: ******
Domain (? for all): DPBookV2

Welcome to DataPower XI52 console configuration.
Copyright IBM Corporation 1999-2014

Version: XI52.7.1.0.1 build 253798 on Nov 13, 2014 4:42:58 PM
Serial number: 0000000

xi52[DPBookV2]# co
Global configuration mode
xi52[DPBookV2](config)# show debug-actions

 Session ID   Transaction ID   Service Name   File Location                                   Remote Address   In Use   Remote User   User Location
 Elapsed Time
 ----------   --------------   ------------   -------------                                   --------------   ------   -----------   -------------
 ------------
 108          153985           sampleJS       local:///ifItsTuesdayThisMustBeBelgium.js 10.15.30.188       No
         00:04:08

xi52[DPBookV2](config)#
```

Figure 4-28 Available Debug Sessions.

This debug session is now paused at our debugger statement waiting for us to do something with it. To start working with this particular session, you will type “debug-action <session ID>” where the session ID is the Session ID shown in our CLI session. In this case, it is 108 so we will enter “debug-action 108” on the command line. Right away you will see the GatewayScript code on your screen with a “=>” at the debugger statement indicating where execution has paused as shown in Figure 4-29.

```
xi52[DPBookV2](config)# debug-action 108
  12:
  13:var date = new Date();
  14:var dayOfWeek = date.getDay();
  15:var thisHeader = hm.current.get('THIS');
  16:var tranID = sm.getVar('var://service/transaction-id');
  17:
  18:const
  19:TUESDAY = 4;
  20:
=>21:debugger;
  22:
  23:console.debug("Date = " + date);
  24:console.debug("dayOfWeek = " + dayOfWeek);
  25:console.debug("thisHeader = " + thisHeader);
  26:
  27:if (dayOfWeek == TUESDAY) {
  28:    if (thisHeader) {
  29:        if (thisHeader != 'Belgium') {
  30:            session.reject("Header 'THIS' Must equal 'Belgium' on Tuesdays");
  31:            console.error("Header 'THIS' Must equal 'Belgium' on Tuesdays");
(debug)
```

Figure 4-29 GatewayScript at initial break point.

There are many available options to choose from at this point for debugging. For this example we will demonstrate only a few. For this particular GatewayScript, we are concerned with the fact that we do not get the expected results when it is Tuesday. To best debug this, we can step through this code line by line and see where the issue could be. To do this we can enter "n" at the command line to advance to the next line. We can continue to do this until we see that we are paused at a line of interest. In this case, we can stop advancing when we get to the switch statement in our code. You can tell when the "=>" is at that line.

At this point we may want to see the values of some particular variables like "dayOfWeek" and "TUESDAY". To do this you can enter "p <variable>" where <variable> is the variable we would like to see. Figure 4-30 shows that we have paused execution at the "If" statement and printed the values of the "dayOfWeek" and "TUESDAY" variables. Well, according to my calendar, this is executing on December 23, 2014 which is indeed a Tuesday. Looking at the variables printed out, you can see that "dayOfWeek" has a value of "2" but our constant named "TUESDAY" has a value of "4". Today is Tuesday but we thought this would be equal to dayOfWeek "2". This is the reason that we are not getting our expected results. If we set the "TUESDAY" constant to "2" in our code, we should get the expected results.

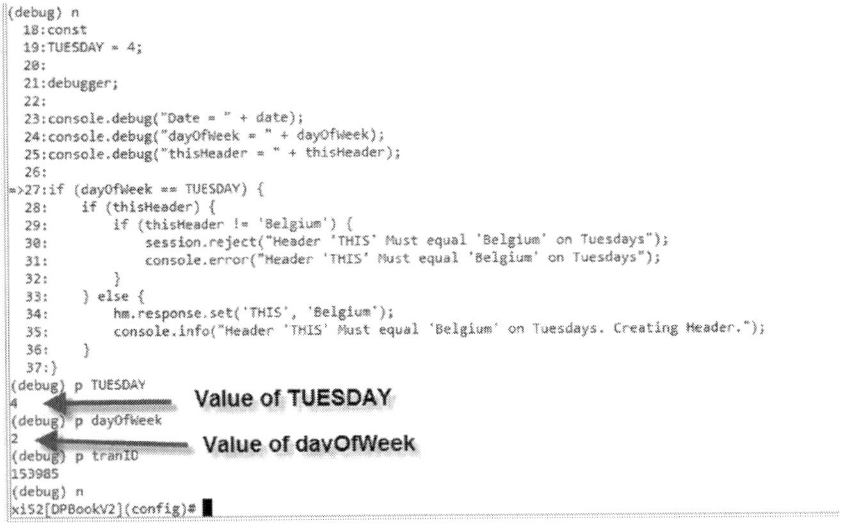

```
(debug) n
  18:const
  19:TUESDAY = 4;
  20:
  21:debugger;
  22:
  23:console.debug("Date = " + date);
  24:console.debug("dayOfWeek = " + dayOfWeek);
  25:console.debug("thisHeader = " + thisHeader);
  26:
=>27:if (dayOfWeek == TUESDAY) {
  28:    if (thisHeader) {
  29:        if (thisHeader != 'Belgium') {
  30:            session.reject("Header 'THIS' Must equal 'Belgium' on Tuesdays");
  31:            console.error("Header 'THIS' Must equal 'Belgium' on Tuesdays");
  32:        }
  33:    } else {
  34:        hm.response.set('THIS', 'Belgium');
  35:        console.info("Header 'THIS' Must equal 'Belgium' on Tuesdays. Creating Header.");
  36:    }
  37:}
(debug) p TUESDAY
4
(debug) p dayOfWeek
2
(debug) p tranID
153985
(debug) n
xi52[DPBookV2](config)#
```

Value of TUESDAY

Value of davOfWeek

Figure 4-30 Printing values of variables.

You can also see in Figure 4-30 that we are able to print out any JavaScript variables that were resolved using DataPower variables. This would not be possible if we were not executing this within a DataPower service. This example shows a basic scenario where the built-in GatewayScript debugger can be extremely useful, but I am sure you can imagine how much more useful this could be in more complex code and troubleshooting scenarios.

We have seen a simple debugging scenario here and I am sure you can start to see the benefit of this debugging tool. There are many other commands that can be used within your debugging session to help you step through and debug your code and troubleshoot your issues. A complete list of available debugger commands can be found at the IBM Infocenter - http://www-

01.ibm.com/support/knowledgecenter/SS9H2Y_7.0.0/com.ibm.dp.xg.doc/debugger_gatewayscriptdebuggercommands.html?lang=en

Using the built in GatewayScript debugger can be a tremendous help and timesaver, as you can see. Use the help command to list all of the available commands and their syntax. As useful as the debugger can be, it is important to realize that enabling a debugging session pauses the execution of all transactions executing that script which will hold all resources related to that transaction. It is critical that you are diligent in cleaning up all debug sessions by running them to completion or entering the quit command. As you can imagine, too many debug sessions running at a time could cause resource issues on the device. As with other debugging tools on DataPower, this should be limited to non-production environments only.

Testing with DataPower Functions and Elements

As you have seen in the examples throughout the development chapter, DataPower provides some extension functions and elements that you will likely find useful in your development environment. When using these in your XSLT stylesheets or even GatewayScript code, you will certainly need to test them, and testing locally as you develop is always preferable.

Until firmware version 3.8.0, testing your XSLT with DataPower elements functions was as easy as using the DataPower coproc service and Eclipse plugin provided with your device resource CD. With firmware 3.8.0 came the announcement that the coprpoc service will be deprecated along with the provided features to test your XSLT remotely via the xa.jar. Since then, there has been no official IBM provided solution to this problem. As you would expect with the IT community, present a problem or need and someone will solve it. Although it is not an official IBM solution, Hermann Stamm-Wilbrandt stepped up to this challenge and created a replacement for the deprecated tool which he calls coproc2. In addition to the original coproc service, Hermann added support for testing binary transformations, XQuery, JSONiq, and even GatewayScript!

You will find a topic on the Developerworks forum with lots of discussion, questions, answers, and the downloadable artifacts for setting up the coproc2 environment. This topic can be found at –

https://www.ibm.com/developerworks/community/forums/html/topic?id=77777777-0000-0000-0000-000014590913#f5915ec6-99ff-426d-a3d2-c71d6d96efc9&repliesPg=0

Keep in mind that you will want to read through the discussion to find the latest and greatest version of this tool. You will ultimately need to download a java file (coproc2.java) and a zip file containing an export of several DataPower services (export-coproc2all). If you want to add the support for GatewayScript, you will also need to download an additional zip file – export-coproc2gateway.zip. This file will contain another DataPower service. You should also follow the instructions in Herman's blog to install the GatewayScript functionality -

https://www.ibm.com/developerworks/community/blogs/HermannSW/entry/coproc2gatewayscript_again?lang=en

Once these files are downloaded, you will need to import the DataPower services into your DataPower device that will be used to execute your tests. You will also be required to compile the coproc2.java file on your client machine.

Once your initial setuip is complete, you can execute the coproc2 executable by passing the arguments for the location of the XSLT or GatewayScript to execute, input file to transform, and the URL of the DataPower service that will perform the execution. Keep in mind that there is a separate service for each type of processing to be performed. So the port for your DataPower URL will be different if you are executing a GatewayScript file and a XLST transformation.

There are many features available in this coproc2 service if you read through the forum and blog posts. You will even see that Hermann explains how to integrate this into Eclipse.

Although there is much power and flexibility in this solution, if compiling java code and executing via command line seems to be more that you need at this time, there is also a way to integrate Hermann's coproc2 solution into your Eclipse tooling quickly and easily. Thanks to Paul Glezen, the coproc2 solution is available via an Eclipse plugin. The installation is as easy as installing a plugin as we did with previous tools. Of course you will still be required to import the DataPower services that will do the work. A detailed explanation of the installation and execution can be found at https://github.com/pglezen/coproc2.

Summary

Development tools are created to help developers with their day-to-day activities by speeding up repeatable tasks, formatting code, pointing out potential mistakes, or debugging. Sometimes the number of tools available can be a bit overwhelming and counterproductive. We have demonstrated a small subset of tools available to you and their capabilities. Most other tools available will provide similar capabilities. The tools you choose to use may be a personal preference, company standard, or chosen for budgetary reasons.

Regardless of which tools you use, keep in mind that they are there to help you in your development efforts. If the tool becomes more cumbersome to learn or use, perhaps that is not the right tool for you. When choosing your tool set, keep in mind the entire SDLC and how you work. Think about initial development of your code, source control, unit testing, fixes and change controls, and deployment.

There are a lot of steps involved in a complete development effort and your toolset should support all of these steps by making them easier and more streamlined. The less tools you have to manage, the better off you will be so try to keep to a small set of tools that support many of these tasks. Again, they should be there to make your job less complicated, not more.

Chapter 5 Transforming Secondary Data Formats

This chapter wraps up Volume III on DataPower development. We cover the topic of processing 'secondary' data formats and show that while there are some capabilities for hand-coding in XSLT, developers generally utilize specialized tooling due to the complexity of the transforms. We cover both programmatic and non-programmatic aspects of transforming these types of data, and the use of common tools for doing so.

While DataPower is an XML and JSON-centric product, it can also apply its processing power to transforming other message types, which can be more intensive to process. By 'secondary formats', we mean anything that is not one of those two primary, first-class message-type citizens on DataPower. Some examples of secondary message formats are COBOL record layout/CICS COMMAREA, Electronic Data Interchange (EDI), comma-separated values (CSV), pure text files, and CICS Copybooks. You will often hear these data types referred to as "binary", although they are in fact often text-based and not pure binary files. In fact, DataPower has a specialized, optimized runtime engine just for processing these types of data.

In the "old" days of DataPower, you had to have a particular appliance model to do these types of transformations. In the 9004 model line, this was the XI50 or XB60. In the 9005 physical or virtual line, it was either the XI52 or XB62 (or the XG45 with the Data Integration Module). In the 9006 DataPower Gateway, the Integration Module must be purchased in order to have this capability. The DataPower models and available modules are discussed in detail in Volume 1 of this book series *IBM DataPower Handbook Volume I: DataPower Intro & Setup*.

Common Secondary Data Formats and Scenarios

Two of the tools that we discuss in this chapter use an XML schema to describe the secondary data file layout. There is currently no widely adopted standard for this (see the sidebar on DFDL), so for now, each tool uses its own proprietary schema. What they have in common is that they describe the field layouts, positioning, and other constraints and metadata such as whether each field is numeric, string, date/time, and so on.

INFO — Data Format Definition Language (DFDL)

There is an emerging Open Grid Forum standard for describing binary and textual data called Data Format Description Language (DFDL or "daffodil"). http://www.ogf.org/ogf/doku.php/standards/dfdl/dfdl. As this gains wider adoption, it will of course be considered for the feature set on IBM DataPower Gateway Appliance firmware and other IBM products.

Although sales presentations, conferences, and trade publications may lead one to believe that modern systems have fully embraced Web 2.0 and SOA, and are all XML or JSON-based, this is often not the case. Most businesses find themselves with only one foot in the door, and they have to leverage multiple data formats—perhaps a more modern Web 2.0, Java-EE or Web services front-end passing data to a legacy environment consisting of mainframes and messaging systems such as WebSphere MQ. Often, these robust backend platforms remain in place because they're reliable and work well!

Alternatively, a business may find itself in a situation where it simply doesn't have the budget or time necessary to upgrade its legacy infrastructure. To better understand, let's explore a few of those scenarios.

Legacy Backend/Pseudo Web Service Frontend

Consider a hypothetical company that has been doing business the same way for many years—it accepts and processes data from its customers (in this case, other businesses) using the EDI message format and protocol backed by mainframe platforms and messaging systems. Although the EDI message format is still viable, and many of the older protocols used for transmission have been replaced by Internet protocols, their partners have stated that they will no longer support EDI at all. The partners have moved on to more modern message formats and delivery mechanisms, such as mobile devices using JSON or SOAP-based Web services.

The first approach our company might take is to rewrite its backend applications and replace its infrastructure in order to "get with the times" and not lose the business from partners and clients. This would likely be quite an expensive and lengthy process; programmers need to be retrained, and there needs to be extensive testing and an elaborate changeover process.

A much better alternative is to use DataPower as a façade, to present a modern face to the outside world, and then accept the messages sent in by clients and transform them to the legacy formats and send over the existing protocols to the backend—which in most cases would not need to change at all!

To accomplish this, for example a WSDL file could be created to represent the agreed-upon service, port, binding, and operation details. There are many tools (for example, IBM Integration Developer and Apache Axis JAVA2WSDL) that can be used to create a WSDL from various artifacts such as JavaBeans, "plain old Java objects," and sample XML messages. This resulting WSDL can be used to create a Web Service Proxy, which we cover in our volume on DataPower services.

As part of the processing policy, a Transform Binary (xformbin) action would be used to do the data conversion (SOAP to EDI in this case). We get into the methods of creating these types of transforms and using the xformbin action later in the chapter.

And lastly, a protocol handler is configured to pass the message to the backend. Typically for Web services, this would be HTTP(s); however, in these situations it's not uncommon to see protocols such as MQ, FTP, IMS, or NFS. The capability to do this accentuates the flexibility of DataPower's protocol mediation features.

Multiple Secondary Data Formats

Some organizations, by their nature, must process several different types of information in various formats and from various sources at once. Examples are news, intelligence, and law enforcement agencies. Data can arrive via fax, email, over phone conversation transcripts, teletype terminals, or by other means, and preferably is distilled to a common format (for example, a "golden schema"), processed, and saved to a backend persistent store such as a database. One of the major use cases for the processing power of these appliances is to reduce the amount of business application code on the backend—from having to handle and transform many different formats to dealing only with this one "golden" format. As we all know, each line of application code is expensive to maintain, not to mention the huge gain in performance by doing this on a dedicated hardware platform like DataPower.

For example, a law enforcement agency typically receives daily information from weather services on impending severe weather conditions, from transportation agencies on major accidents, from environmental protection agencies on hazardous chemical spills, and from the general public on just about any "emergency," such as lost pets. The fact that these data streams may be over multiple protocols lends nicely to the use cases for the Multi-Protocol Gateway, as described in our volume on DataPower services.

Tooling for Transforming Secondary Data

There are several options for working with secondary data. These range from simple (hand-coding in XSLT) to powerful workstation development tools. In this section we familiarize you with a few of these options.

Good Old XSLT

Those familiar with Extensible Stylesheet Language (XSL) already know there are options available for processing non-XML data. XSL contains XSL Transformations (XSLT) and its sibling XSLFormatting Objects (XSL-FO) and XPath. We covered an introduction to XSLT in chapter one of this volume. XSL-FO is used to generate human-readable documents such as PDF, PostScript, Rich Text Format (RTF), and even GUI components. However, XSL-FO is not a good fit for the type of machine-to-machine translations that are the bailiwick of DataPower. XSLT is a good fit, of course, and there we also find a solution—you can declare <xsl:output method="text"> at the top of your stylesheet to indicate that the output of this transform will be text, rather than the more common XML or HTML. When using this option, a full XML result tree is formed internally, but then the string value is emitted as output. Let's review a simple example. Listing 5-1 shows an example stylesheet to operate on the XML input file shown in Listing 5-2. Note the xsl:output declaration in the stylesheet.

Listing 5-1 XSLT to Create Comma-Separated Text Output from XML Input.

```
<?xml version="1.0" encoding="UTF-8"?>

<xsl:stylesheet xmlns:xsl="http://www.w3.org/1999/XSL/Transform"
version="1.0">
```

```
   <xsl:output method="text"/>
   <xsl:template match="Customer">
      <xsl:value-of select="firstName"/>,
      <xsl:value-of select="lastName"/>,
      <xsl:value-of select="street"/>,
      <xsl:value-of select="city"/>,
      <xsl:value-of select="state"/>
   </xsl:template>
</xsl:stylesheet>
```

Listing 5-2 Sample XML Input File for XML to Text.

```
<?xml version="1.0" encoding="UTF-8" ?>
   <Customer>
      <firstName>Dean</firstName>
      <lastName>Moriarity</lastName>
      <street>42 Bleeker Street</street>
      <city>Denver</city>
      <state>CO</state>
   </Customer>
```

We configured this stylesheet on an XML Firewall service with a normal Transform action. We did not modify any values other than to change the Request Type from the default of SOAP to XML. The results are shown in Figure 5-1.

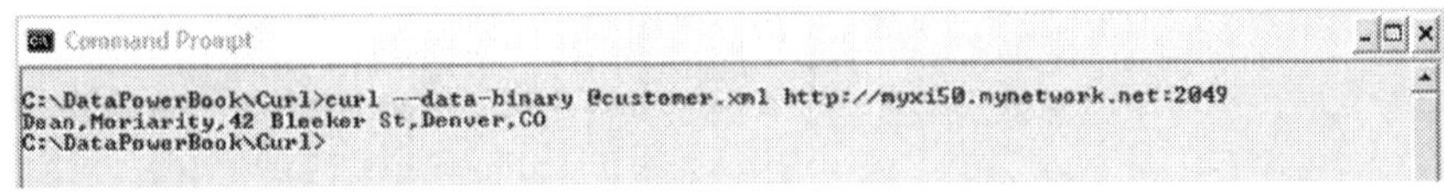

Figure 5-1 Output of XML to text example.

The first drawback of this approach is that the conversion can only be done "one way" from XML to text. The second drawback is that it would be rather tedious and cumbersome to apply this to many of the "real world" scenarios involving complex data types and large files, such as COBOL Copybooks and EDI documents. It also doesn't support other encoding types. The same approach could be used with JSON using JSONiq—handcoding this for a 'real world' use case would be non-trivial. We also have GatewayScript, which includes the readAsBinary and readAsJSON capabilities to read the input. But the only built-in mechanism within the language are to string manipulate the input and then outputting the json/binary into the output stream, which has the same limitations as our XML-to-text example.

Third-Party Development Tools for Secondary Transform Development

We have discussed how simple XML-to-text scenarios can be done with XSLT code. However, as we stated earlier, most scenarios involve large amounts of complex data. To develop these types of transformations, some type of external tooling is necessary. There are two options that are used for DataPower: Liaison Contivo Analyst and IBM WebSphere Transformation Extender (WTX).

Both products are similar in nature—they provide graphical integrated development environments (IDE) that enable various inputs and outputs to be described (such as the field delimiters and types) and to lay out the mapping from one datatype to another.

For example, one might import a XML schema definition file to the tooling to describe the input, and a COBOL Copybook definition to describe what the output should look like. From there, a graphical mapping component is used to drag and drop fields from the XML input definition to the COBOL field definition. It can really be this simple in many cases!

Another component of these tools is the testing engine. Both products are used for transformation development outside of DataPower, and contain runtime engines that can be added to an application server and other environments for this purpose. For example, the WTX runtime can be purchased as an add-on for IBM Information Bus (formerly called WebSphere Message Broker). These runtime environments are included for testing purposes with the development tools for both products that we are discussing. Both tools can test the transforms that are being developed against the local runtime as well as directly on a DataPower device. It would be most beneficial to test against the DataPower runtime to ensure that the transforms will work in the target runtime environment. For both products, there is not 100 percent compatibility between their native runtimes and the runtime implementation on DataPower.

When the testing cycle is complete, the artifacts are exported from the tooling and imported to the DataPower device as part of a Processing Policy using the Transform Binary (xformbin) action that we will discuss shortly.

Now that we've talked about what these two products have in common, let's discuss each in more detail.

Liaison Contivo Analyst

The Flat File Descriptor (FFD) is an XML schema developed by DataPower and Contivo to describe binary data files. Listing 5-3 shows a sample FFD file to describe a simple comma-separated value text file that can contain from zero to unlimited records.

Listing 5-3 Sample FFD File for Comma-Separated Values.

```
<File name="CSVFILE">
   <Group name="CSVLine" minOccurs="0"
          maxOccurs="unbounded" delim="\n">
      <Field name="id" delim=","/>
      <Field name="fname" delim=","/>
      <Field name="lname" delim=","/>
      <Field name="title" delim=","/>
      <Field name="dept" delim=","/>
      <Field name="org"/>
   </Group>
</File>
```

When you are describing data using Analyst from your workstation, the FFD files are generated for you by the tool and used in conjunction with annotated XSLT, which is also generated. The FFD files describe the data and the XSLT acts as the programmatic code to do the mapping at runtime. For testing, an XML Firewall called contivo_policy, which is included with Analyst, must be imported. This firewall is contained in the domain export contivo-analyst-policy.zip and listens on port 2321 by default. Figure 5-2 shows the Analyst configuration page for setting up DataPower as the runtime test platform.

Contivo Analyst - Options

COBOL Copybook Import
Connection Preference
Default Directories
Display
General
Interface Modeler
Map Testing
Namespace Level
Processing Instructions
Servers
Transform Settings
Tree View
XSLT Settings

Runtime
Java
XSLT
DataPower Processor
Host name or IP address http://192.168.1.35
Port Number 2321
Command File C:\Contivo\Contivo_Analyst_3_10_5_15\bin\DataPower.bat Browse
Send Message Location C:\Contivo\Contivo_Analyst_3_10_5_15\DataPower\send Browse
Response Message Location C:\Contivo\Contivo_Analyst_3_10_5_15\DataPower\response Browse

Figure 5-2 Contivo Analyst configuration for DataPower testing.

The Analyst component for describing data layouts is called the Interface Modeler. Figure 5-3 shows a COBOL Copybook description using that tool. Note the use of the OCCURS DEPENDING ON clause for repeating groups. The Layout tab is shown in this figure, but the Basic tab can be used to describe the minimum and maximum occurrences of each field individually, and the Advanced tab can be used to describe the data type of each field (integer, decimal, date/time, and so on).

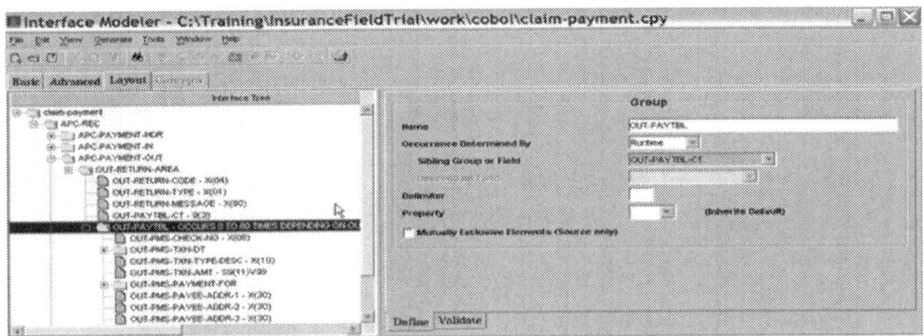

Figure 5-3 Analyst Interface Modeler describing COBOL data.

After the data types have been described, the Analyst Mapping Studio is used to define the relationships between the input and output data by dragging the fields. Figure 5-4 shows a SOAP to COBOL Copybook example using the Map tab.

When the mapping is complete, the next step is to test. Figure 5-5 shows the result of the test for the scenario we have been describing. You can see how the values have been correctly transferred from the input SOAP message to the output COBOL Copybook, indicating a successful test.

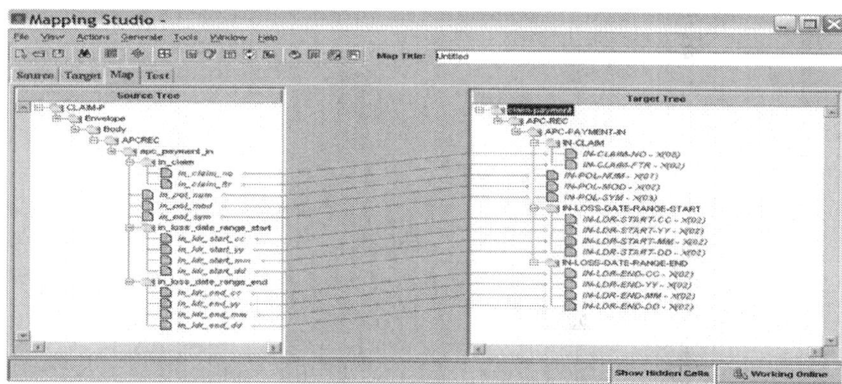

Figure 5-4 Analyst Mapping Studio drag-and-drop paradigm.

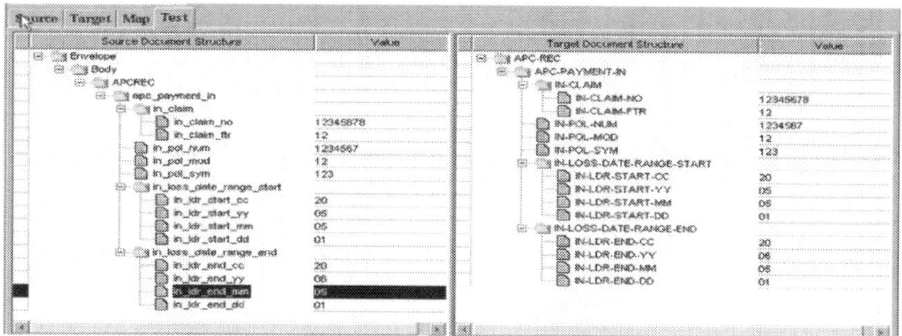

Figure 5-5 Analyst test results.

When testing is done through Analyst to the DataPower platform, a MIME package containing the FFD and XSLT files as well as the test data is sent to the contivo_policy firewall mentioned earlier. The results are processed and sent back for analysis within the Analyst development environment. There are tools for troubleshooting within Analyst, and debugging can also be done on the DataPower side, using the logs, probes, and other troubleshooting techniques described throughout this book.

WebSphere Transformation Extender Design Studio

The second product we will discuss is the IBM WebSphere Transformation Extender (WTX) Design Studio. WTX has several advantages: It runs in the open and extensible Eclipse platform, and has multiple available runtimes (making it a strategic product for shops with many different environments). WTX is actually a family of products, including runtime transformation engines for different platforms, a software development kit, an IDE called Design Studio, resource adapters for databases and other platforms, an Integration Flow Designer, and a Business-to-Business Manager. There are enterprise and industry "packs" available for things like the Health Insurance Portability and Accountability Act (HIPAA), EDI, and Financial Information Exchange (FIX).

Some of these pieces are part of the WTX runtime, which is used for much broader purposes than the "mission" of the DataPower appliances, and hence are not available for running transformations on the DataPower binary engine. For example, DataPower has its own database interface code and does not need to include the WTX runtime for that. DataPower has its own process editor—the Processing Policy. See the WTX documentation for specifics on what features are available when building transformations targeted for DataPower.

We will focus on the WTX Design Studio, which is the integrated development environment for describing data and designing maps, and the only part of the WTX suite relevant to DataPower. To be clear: If you are purchasing WTX solely to use with DataPower, you only need the Design Studio—you do not need any of the other runtime products.

The features and usage of Design Studio are similar to Contivo Analyst. Maps can be designed and debugged against the local WTX runtime engine, or they can be sent to a DataPower appliance for development testing of map execution. There are graphical tools for importing XML schema and COBOL Copybook definitions, as well as other data types.

Because many binary scenarios involve interaction with legacy back ends, a useful feature for WTX is the seamless conversion between various code pages, such as ASCII to EBCDIC, when transforming data.

An old expression states that "talk is cheap," so let's actually look at how to design binary transformations for DataPower using WTX Design Studio. Our next section does precisely that!

Creating Transformations with WebSphere TX Design Studio

Let's go back to our example scenario where a company has a backend legacy environment that processes COBOL Copybook files with employee records that are sent to them via a legacy transport or protocol. Its business partners have grown tired of the expense of supporting this platform and are insisting on a more modern infrastructure, and are threatening to discontinue doing business with the company if it does not provide an XML-based interface. This presents a big problem for the company. The expense and time involved in retraining programmers, rewriting and testing applications, and converting infrastructure are daunting. However, someone has heard about these "magical appliances" that can act as gateways and have amazing message transformation and mediation capabilities. DataPower to the rescue!

TIP — Version Coordination

Because this capability involves the use of two separate products, it's important to verify that you are using versions that are tested and integrated to work together. For example, if there is a brand new version of WTX, it may take the DataPower team until the next released version to be able to support it.

To solve this problem, we can insert an appliance (physical or virtual) between the business partner and that backend. We can then create a WSDL file to use as the basis for a partner-facing Web service and publish that interface to the business partner, who could then send SOAP messages over HTTP. (To focus on the WTX capabilities and keep to a reasonable length, we use a simple XML file and firewall for our example.) When these messages arrive at the appliance, as part of the Processing Policy, we transform them to COBOL Copybook format and transport them to the backend via any supported protocol such as MQ, TIBCO, or FTP. Of course, all other Processing Policy actions are available for things such as crypto, dynamic routing, AAA, logging, auditing, and so on.

Listing 5-4 shows the example XML input file we are using for this scenario. Of course, there is an accompanying schema that describes this document and can be used for validation purposes.

Listing 5-4 Sample XML Employees Input Data.

```
<?xml version="1.0" encoding="UTF-8"?>
```

```
<NewEmployees>
    <Employee>
        <EmployeeNumber>12345</EmployeeNumber>
        <FirstName>Joe</FirstName>
        <LastName>Smith</LastName>
        <MiddleInitial>L</MiddleInitial>
        <HireDate>20080701</HireDate>
        <StartingSalary>24000</StartingSalary>
</Employee>
    <Employee>
    <EmployeeNumber>67890</EmployeeNumber>
        <FirstName>Mary</FirstName>
        <LastName>Thomas</LastName>
        <MiddleInitial>R</MiddleInitial>
        <HireDate>20080628</HireDate>
        <StartingSalary>32500</StartingSalary>
    </Employee>
    <Employee>
        <EmployeeNumber>23897</EmployeeNumber>
        <FirstName>Laurie</FirstName>
        <LastName>Jones</LastName>
        <MiddleInitial>T</MiddleInitial>
        <HireDate>20080629</HireDate>
        <StartingSalary>22000</StartingSalary>
    </Employee>
</NewEmployees>
```

The COBOL Copybook for our output data is shown in Listing 5-5. Note that this contains a construct for repeating data—the OCCURS DEPENDING ON clause. The file should begin with a record count and then be followed by some number of employee records.

Listing 5-5 COBOL Copybook Definition for the Employee Output Data.

```
01 EMPLOYEE-RECS.
   02 EMPLOYEE-COUNT PIC 9(2) COMP.
   02 EMPLOYEE-RECORD OCCURS 0 TO 99 DEPENDING ON EMPLOYEE-COUNT.
      03 EMPLOYEENUMBER PIC 9(5).
      03 FIRSTNAME PIC A(20).
      03 MIDDLEINITIAL PIC A(1).
      03 LASTNAME PIC A(20).
      03 HIREDATE PIC 9(8).
      03 STARTSALARY PIC 9(7).
```

Now that we know what we're dealing with, the remainder of this chapter walks you through some of the major steps in creating such a solution. This being a DataPower book, our intention is not to train the reader on WTX Design Studio. The following scenario shows the major points of configuration through an intermediate example. There are many additional powerful features that can be leveraged by the combined strength of DataPower and WTX, so additional reading is recommended!

Configuring DataPower for WTX

We mentioned earlier that the Design Studio enables iterative testing and development against the DataPower runtime. After the Design Studio software is installed on your workstation, the next step is to configure the DataPower appliance. To do this, we need to enable and configure the Interoperability Test Service, as described in Chapter 4, "Development Tools." When that is done, the appliance is ready for testing WTX maps. The Interoperability Test Service also supports HTTPS for secure communications with WTX Design Studio.

Building the Scenario Transformation

At a high level, our example scenario consists of a few steps:

1. Create Type Trees to describe the input and output data format. Type Trees are hierarchical objects used by WTX for this purpose. They contain a definition for each distinct field found in the dataset and all attributes about that field, such as its type (numeric, date/time, and so on), its length, what delimiter indicates the end of the field, whether it should be padded, and so forth. Type Trees also contain group objects that can hold those fields in a defined relationship and order, such as how they might appear in an EDI file or Copybook. Type Trees can be created manually or they can be created by importing files such as XML schema definitions, Copybooks, or text/binary example files.

2. Use the Map Designer to describe how the data should be transformed from the input type tree(s) to the output type tree(s). Maps in WTX are held in a container called a Map Source. Each map has some number of input and output cards. These cards represent the datasets used for the transforms. In most cases, you will use Type Trees created earlier for these cards, although there are exceptions—for example, rather than create a Type Tree from an XSD file, you can skip that step and identify the XSD file directly on an input or output card when designing a map. When the input and output cards are defined, they can then be used to lay out the transform by dragging fields from one card to the other, or by using functions from the WTX library or creating your own.
3. Test the transformation first on the WTX runtime and then on DataPower.
4. Deploy to a DataPower domain and Processing Policy.

In our following scenario, WTX Design Studio has been installed, and the mundane steps of creating a workspace and project have been completed. We have created a project with the name XMLToCOBOL.

Creating Type Trees

To build our example scenario, first we import the file for the Copybook that was shown in Listing 5-5. Figure 5-6 shows the numerous choices for data type imports. If the data type is not a known format—for example, custom text or binary files—the type tree can be built manually by describing the field delimiters and types. Importing is much easier!

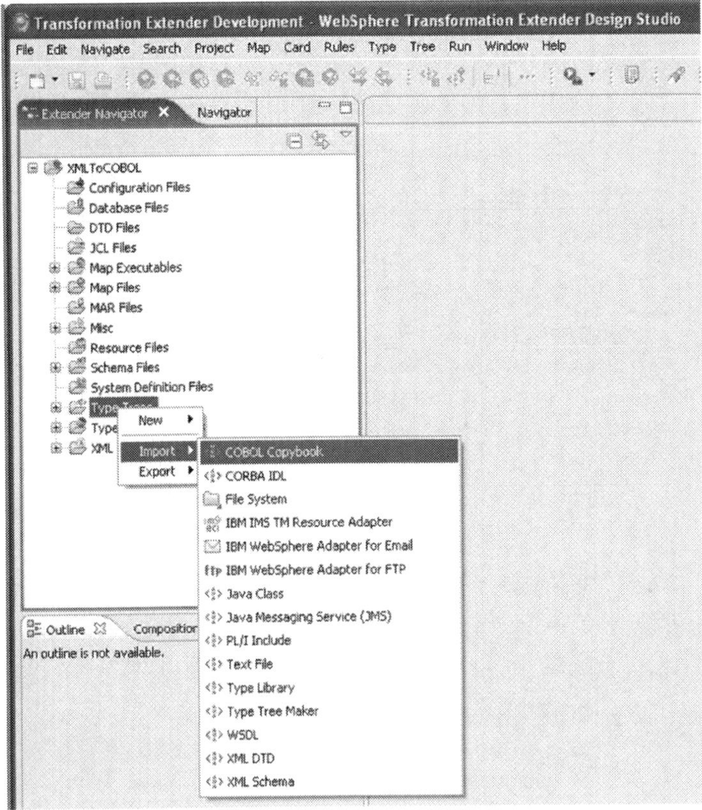

Figure 5-6 Type Tree import selections.

During the import process, we named the new type tree EmployeesCPY, which results in a generated file of the same name with an .mtt extension. The results are shown in Figure 5-7. Notice that the fields are not in the same order they are listed in the Copybook. This is because at this point they are simple, unrelated field definitions.

Clicking on each field results in a properties pane that shows the specifics, such as the field's data type and padding information. Figure 5-8 shows the properties of the STARTSALARY field. Notice that it is numeric (integer), a max length of 7, and will be padded right-justified with leading zeros. Other capabilities shown are the ability to specify the national language (Western, Italian, German, and so forth) and data language (such as Native, ASCII, EBCDIC).

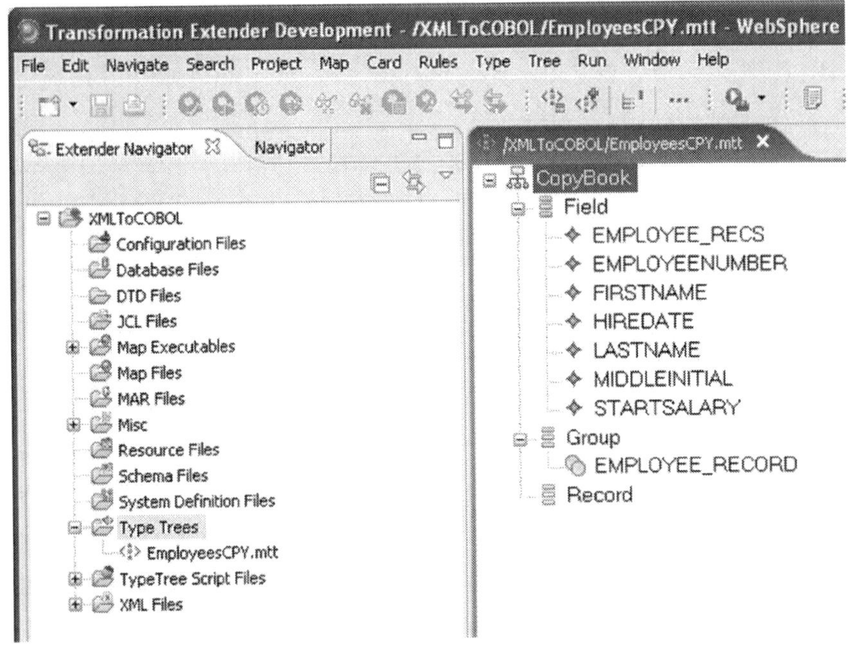

Figure 5-7 Import of COBOL Copybook to type tree.

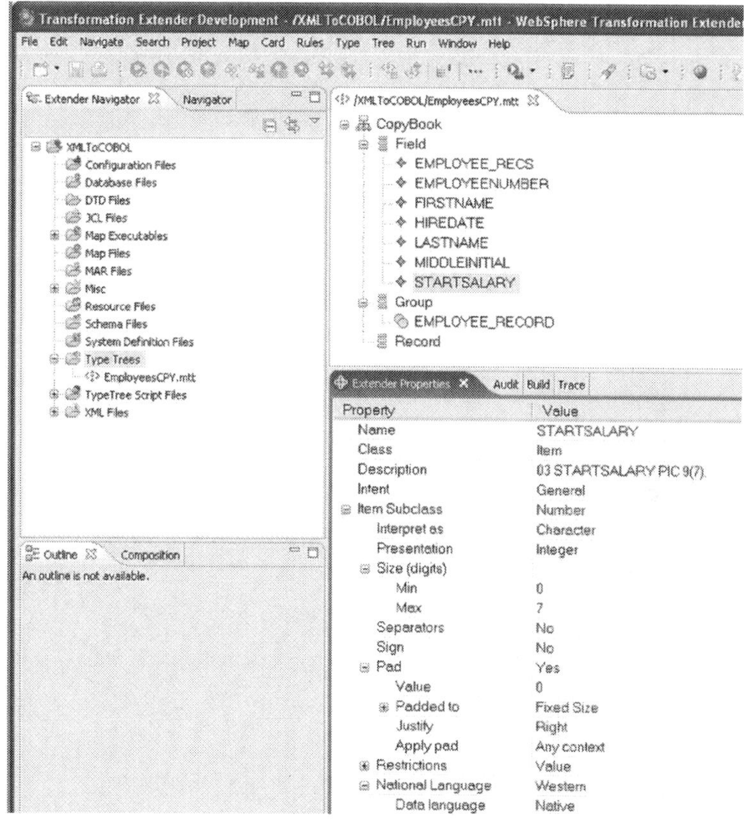

Figure 5-8 Property pane for the STARTSALARY field.

You may have noticed in Figure 5-7 that the importer created an EMPLOYEE_RECORD group object based on the record definition in the Copybook. It also generated an EMPLOYEE_RECS object that is really the entire file definition, which starts with the EMPLOYEE_COUNT record counter field and is followed by the actual records, as shown in Figure 5-9. It is also evident in this figure that the fields are now in their proper order in the record object.

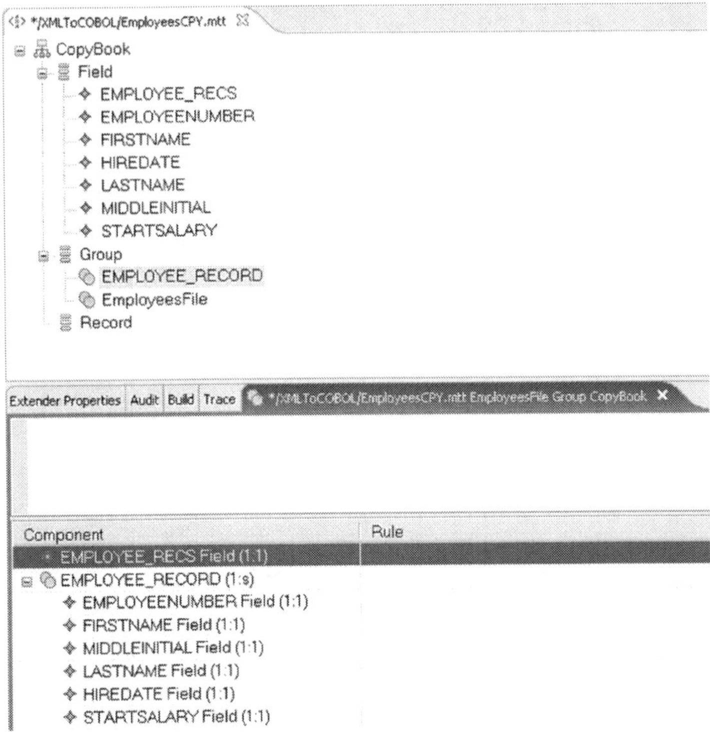

Figure 5-9 EMPLOYEE_RECS file definition object created.

At this point we have completed our definition of the type tree for the COBOL output file. The final step of this process is to analyze the logic and structure of the type tree to see if it is formatted properly. Figure 5-10 shows the menu choices used and the analysis results; in this case there are no errors or warnings.

Next we imported the XSD file to build a type tree for our XML input data. The process for this is the same one we used for importing the COBOL Copybook, only this time we chose XML Schema from the list shown in Figure 5-6. The results of the import are shown in Figure 5-11. Noticeable in Figure 5-11 are elements of the XML file, such as the prolog (where the XML version, encoding, and other attributes can be found). We have put the focus on the StartingSalary field to display its attributes, which you can see are numeric/integer per the schema definition for this field.

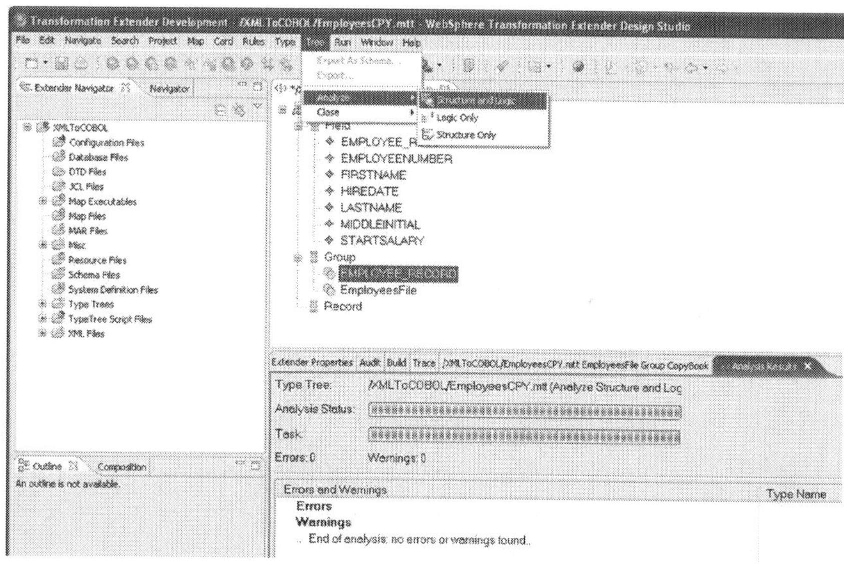

Figure 5-10 Analysis of the COBOL Type Tree with no errors.

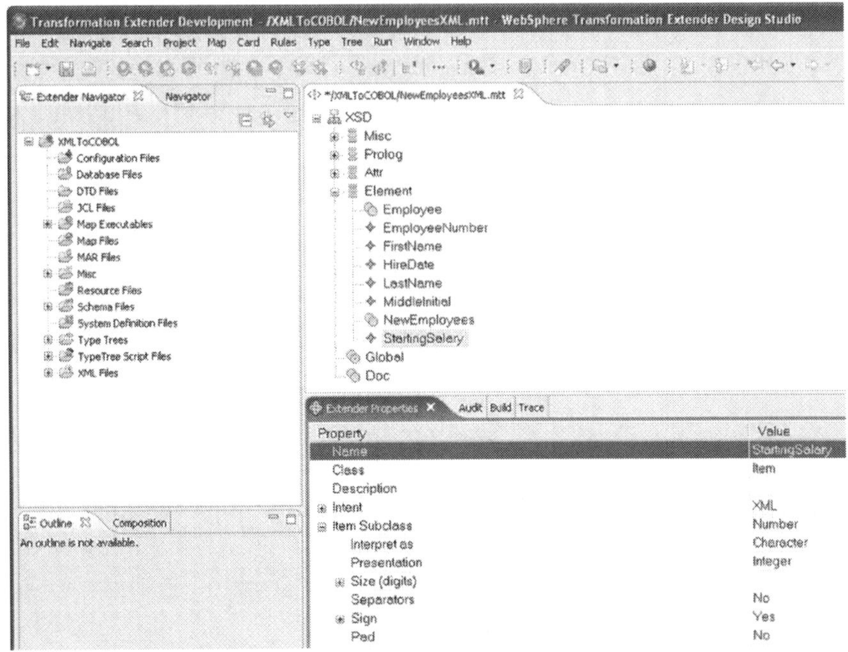

Figure 5-11 Type tree import of the XML schema definition.

Now that our input and output data have been described by the type trees we have built, we can create a map to show how we want to transform the data from XML to COBOL at runtime.

Using the Map Designer

The Map Designer is where the actual logic for the transform is described. In WTX, maps are held in containers called Map Source Files, so one of those must be created prior to any maps. Figure 5-12 shows that we have created a map source called EmployeeMaps by right-clicking on the Map Files folder in the Extender Navigator, and we subsequently created a new map under that called EmployeesXMLtoCPY in the Outline pane just below. Take note of the structure under the map file. There is a section for declaring the inputs and outputs for the map, and then an Organizer area where various logs and results can be viewed.

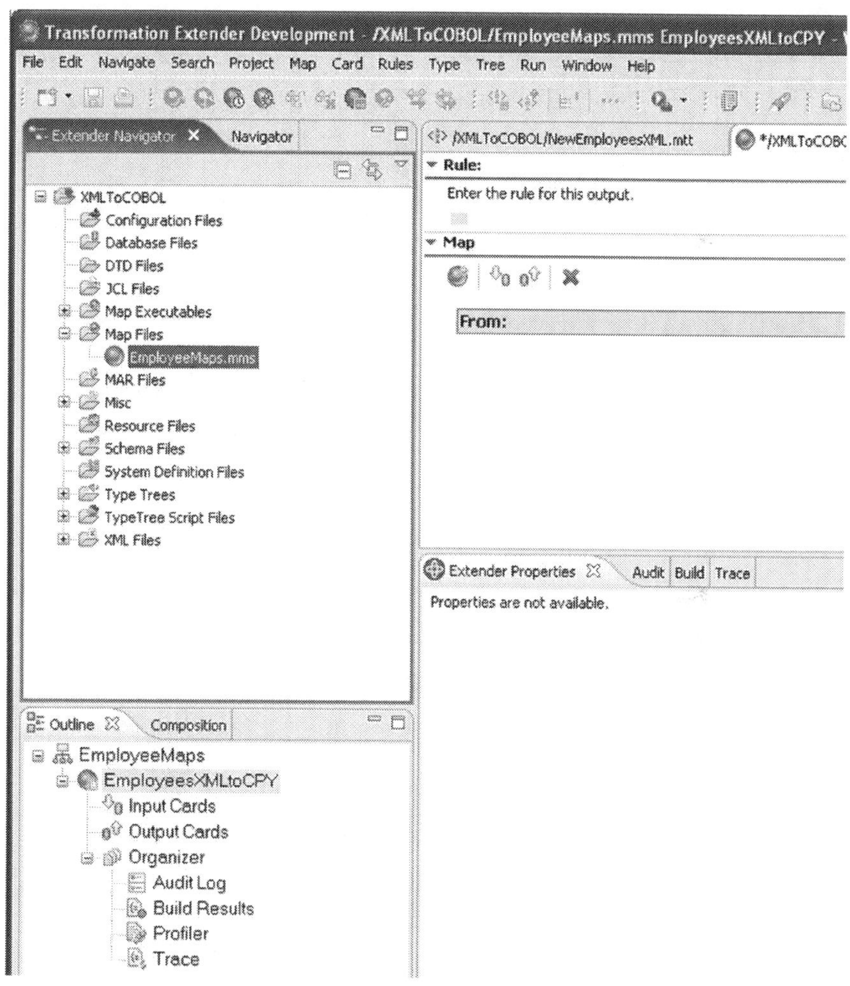

Figure 5-12 Creating a map source and map file.

TIP — Creating New Maps

After right-clicking on the Map Files folder in the Extender Navigator and selecting New to create a new map source, it may seem intuitive to right-click on the map source name and expect to create a map under that map source. However, you must do this in the Outline pane below—right-clicking on the map source there will yield the New→Map selection.

The next step is to define the input and output cards. Figure 5-13 shows the card we created by right-clicking on the Input Cards folder and selecting New. We have given this card a name of EmployeesXMLInput and selected our previously built type tree. When you have identified the type tree, you must populate the Type field to tell the map where in that type tree you want to operate. Remember that the type tree is hierarchical in nature. We have selected the Doc level element, which represents the structured data in the XML file (as can be seen in Figure 5-11). We have also selected a previously created sample input file NewEmployees.xml in the FilePath field, which will be used as input when we tell Design Studio to do a transform to test our map. The file contains the data shown in Listing 5-4.

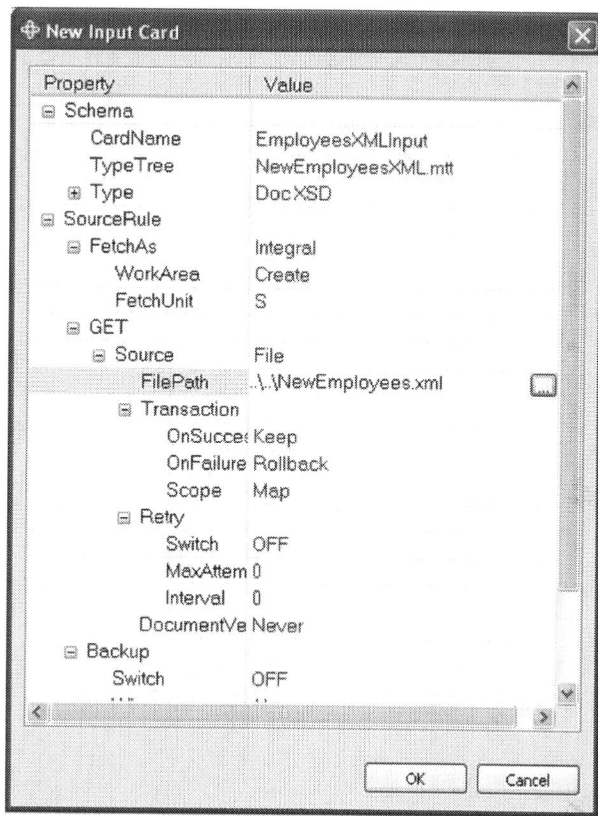

Figure 5-13 Input card for the Employee XML data.

TIP — Native Schema Support

Note that with version 8.2 and up of WTX Design Studio, the XML schema can be specified directly on the input card in the TypeTree field, rather than the .mtt file that was created by importing the schema. This enables you to avoid the step of importing the schema and creating a type tree.

Next, the output card is defined, using the same process. Figure 5-14 shows the card name, the previously created COBOL type tree, and the type and name of the output file that we would like created when we do our testing. We have chosen the file object created earlier as the type for the transform.

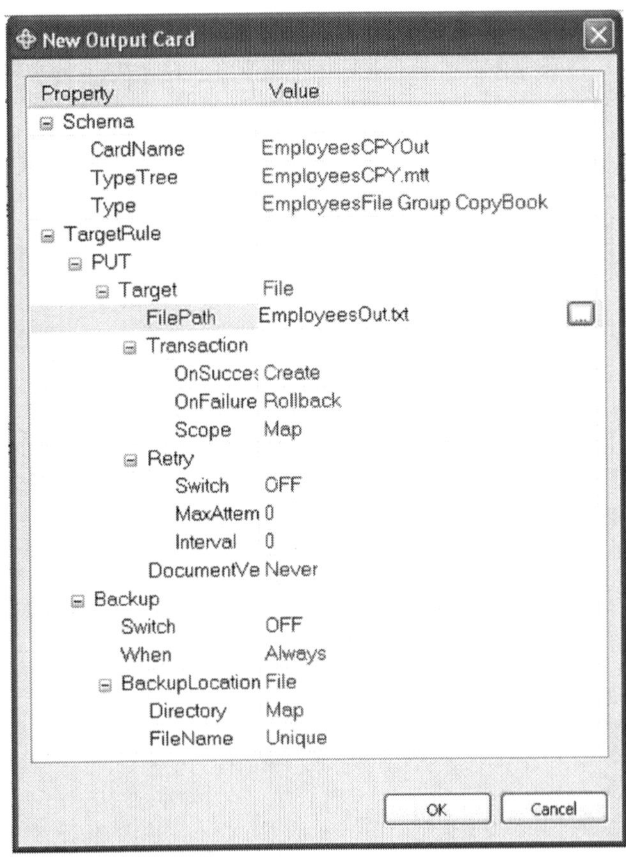

Figure 5-14 Output card defined for Employee COBOL Copybook data.

Now that the cards are defined, the actual transform logic can be described. We have double-clicked on the input and output cards and arranged them side by side to facilitate this, as shown in Figure 5-15—XML input on the left, COBOL output on the right.

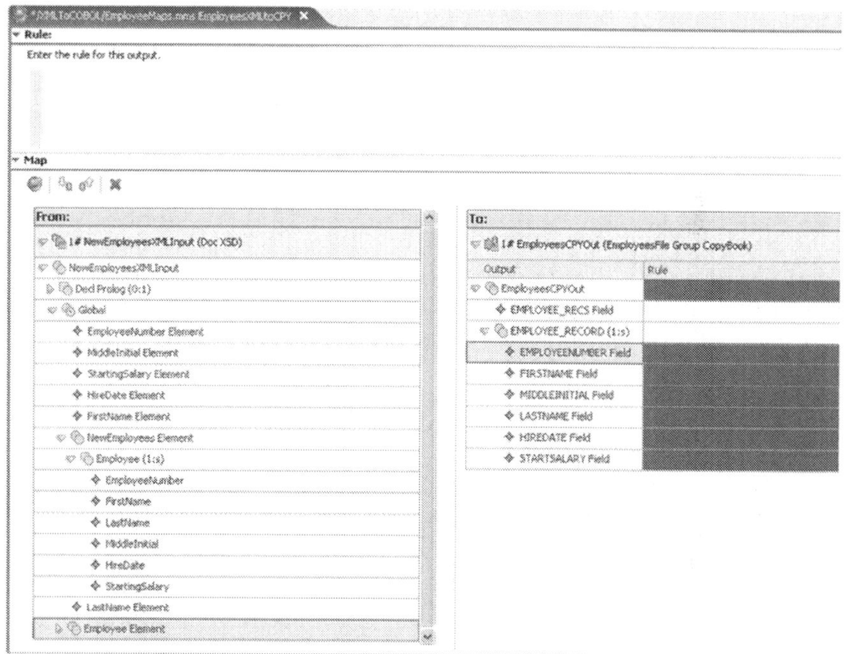

Figure 5-15 Input and output card layouts prior to designing transform logic.

This is the point at which the true power of WTX can be appreciated. What would normally be complex coding can be achieved by simply dragging and dropping. For example, we can simply drag fields such as FirstName from the input card to the corresponding output card rather than having to program those conversions.

However, this example was intentionally created to be non-trivial, containing some of the challenges you might expect in the real world. For example, it is apparent that there is no corresponding XML input field to populate the EMPLOYEE_REC record counter field in the output. This problem can be solved by using one of the WTX built-in programming functions, "COUNT." Figure 5-16 shows this function in place for that field. To create it, we placed our cursor in the Rule column next to that field in the To: card, and then typed "COUNT(" in the Rule pane above that, as seen in the figure. It takes the Employee (1:s) nodeset (which can be dragged directly up rather than typing it) from the input XML document as its input parameter, so the total count of those nodesets found in the XML will be used for the value in the output record.

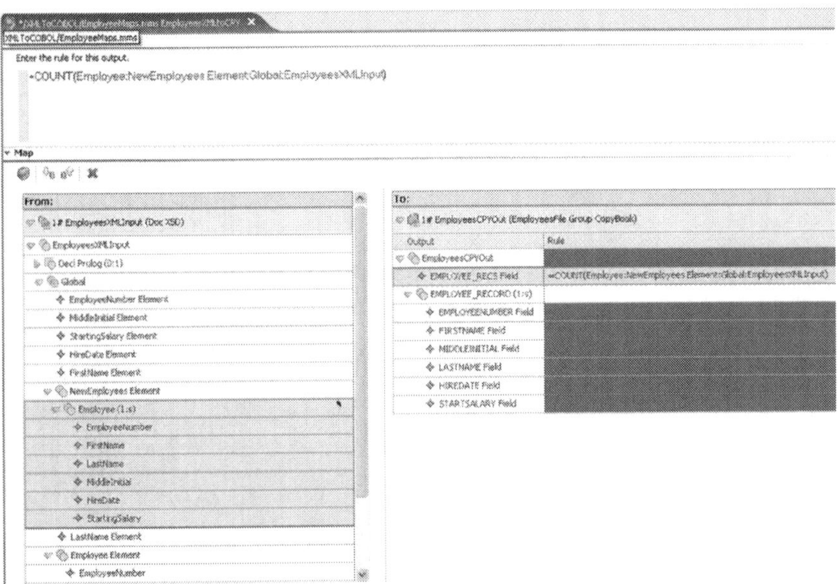

Figure 5-16 COUNT function used to generate the EMPLOYEE_RECS field.

The second challenge presented by our example scenario is that of the repeating records in the output datasets. We need some way to loop through the employee nodesets in the input document and create output COBOL records. To do this in WTX, you use something called a functional map. The standard convention is to begin any new functional map name with "F_" to indicate that this is a functional map rather than a built-in function.

Figure 5-17 shows the functional map call in place, created the same way that the COUNT function was created. However, this is just a call; the function itself has not as yet been created. This would be the next logical step.

For those with a programmatic mindset, it might seem daunting to have to create code to do this looping. You might be saying "Ah hah! Here is where we're going to be forced to write some code...." But this is not the case. By right-clicking on the call that we just created in the Rule cell of the To: card, and selecting Functional Map Wizard from the context menu, we get a dialog like the one shown in Figure 5-18; the wizard selects the proper levels of the hierarchy from both input and output cards for us. Note that this is simply a "very good guess" from the tool and should always be checked for accuracy.

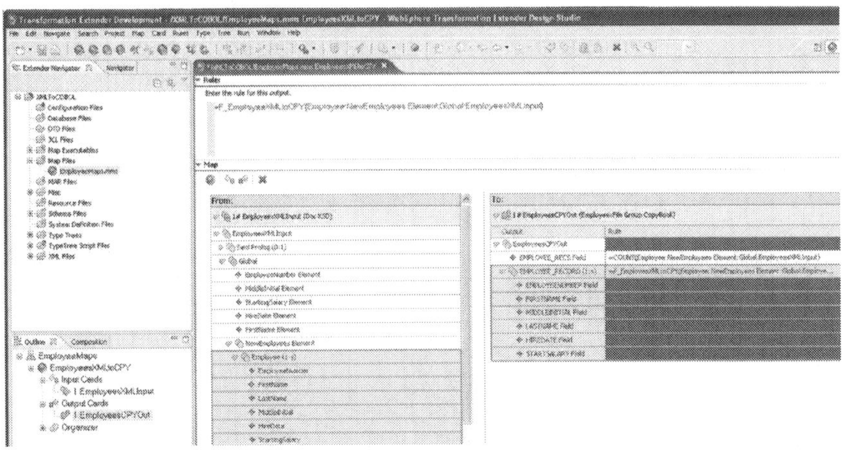

Figure 5-17 Functional Map Call for employee records.

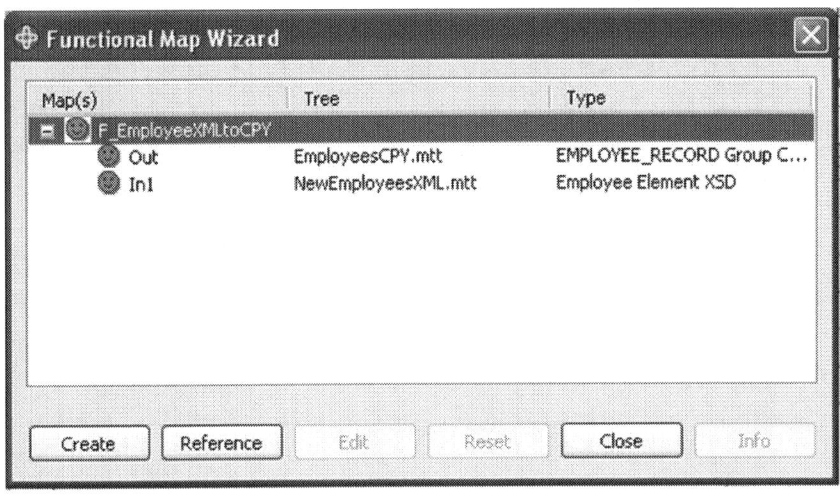

Figure 5-18 Functional Map Wizard for the employee records loop.

All we need to do at this point is click the Create button, and the functional map definition is created for us. Figure 5-19 shows the results. The functional map is shown listed under the Map Executables folder in the Extender Navigator pane, and the Outline pane now contains this new map along with the associated input and output cards, which were also generated for us. These cards are displayed in panes side by side, so that all we need to do now is drag the fields from the input card to the output card to finish defining the transform logic. This has already been done in the figure.

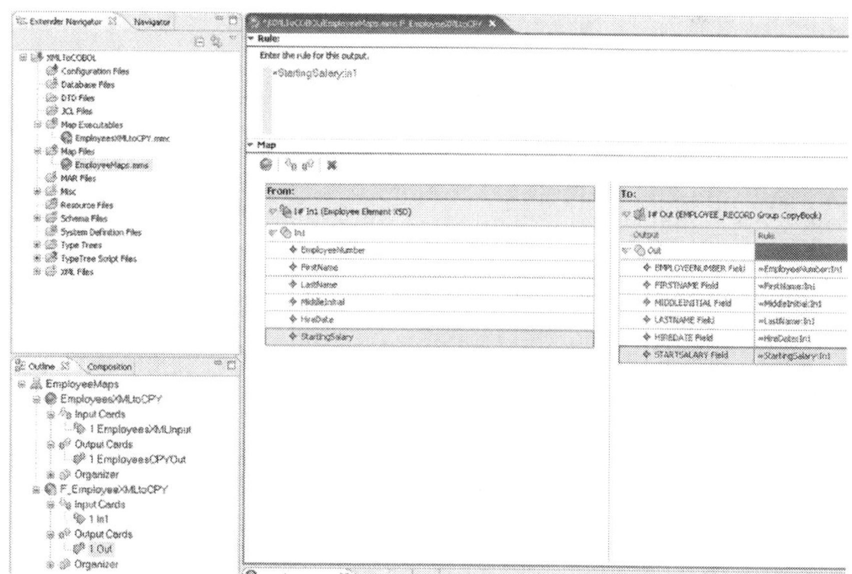

Figure 5-19 Functional map with transform design complete.

Our map is complete at this point, so now on to testing! In Figure 5-19, you might have noticed that the icon next to our map is the purple ball, which represents WTX. This means that WTX is the current runtime designated for this map. We can build the map (in essence, this is a compile step) by right-clicking on the map name in the Outline pane and choosing Build. If there are no errors, the build dialog will flash momentarily and then disappear. We can then run the map by again going to the context menu and choosing Run.

The result at this point is an error that says “One or more inputs was invalid.” Something is wrong. What a great time to investigate some of the troubleshooting tools! By right-clicking on the map name in the Outline pane and choosing Map Settings, you can access the map trace settings. Figure 5-20 shows how we have enabled the trace with all settings On.

After the map is rebuilt and rerun, the tools under the Organizer folder can be leveraged. Double-clicking on the Trace folder will load the trace into a new pane for inspection, as shown in Figure 5-21.

Reading this, it becomes evident that the runtime is trying to read the schema file, which has not been imported into the project. When we built the type tree based on this schema earlier, it did not get imported automatically as a result.

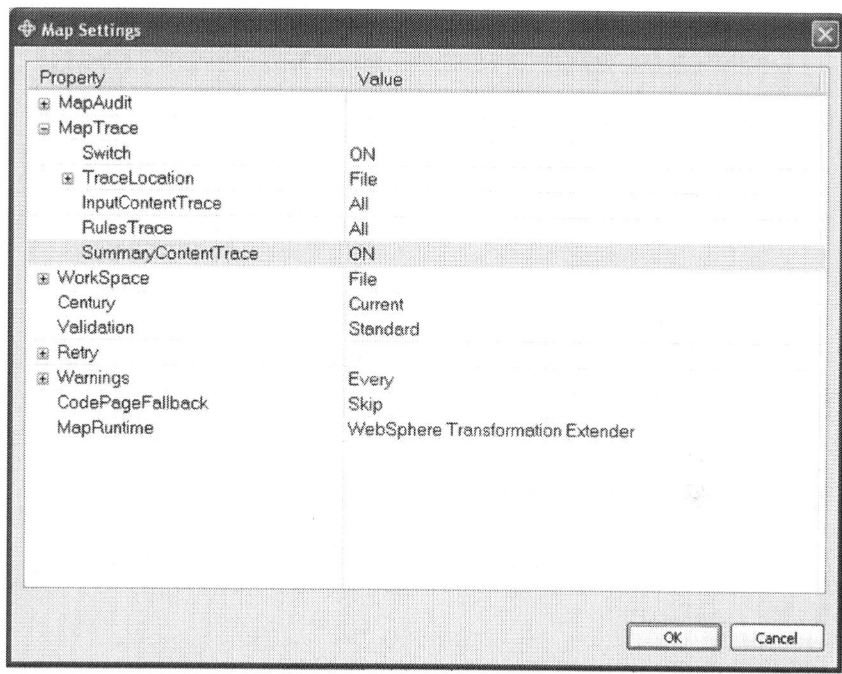

Figure 5-20 Map trace set on for our employee Map transformation.

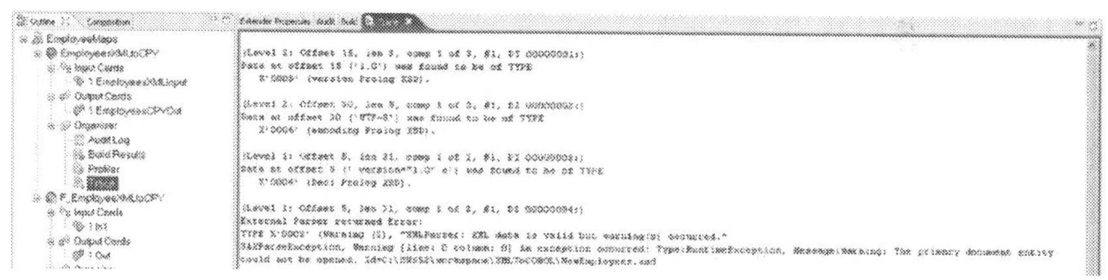

Figure 5-21 Trace output for debugging WTX transform problems.

If we go to the Extender Navigator and right-click on the Schema Files directory, import the schema, and then build and run the map once more, we get a much better result, as seen in Figure 5-22.

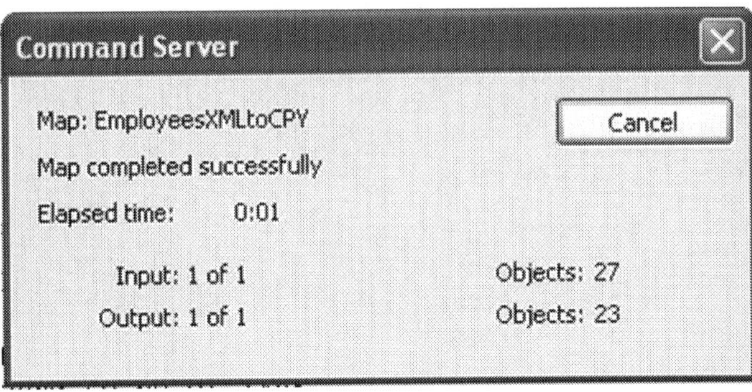

Figure 5-22 A successful map execution for the employee transformation.

Seeing is believing, as they say. To look at the actual results of this run, right-click the map name again and choose Run Results. Figure 5-23 shows the desired results: the binary two-byte field for our record counter followed by several employee records. The output COBOL data matches what our XML input data had.

Figure 5-23 Run results for the employee XML to COBOL transformation.

Keep in mind what we said earlier that not all WTX runtime functions are supported on DataPower. So testing against WTX as a first step is fine, particularly since you can take advantage of the debugging and profiling tools in that mode. But keep in mind that the maps may work there, but not against DataPower. For this reason, you may want to specify DataPower as the runtime engine as a default and leave it that way.

To change the runtime for a map, you must right-click the map and go to the map settings, as shown in Figure 5-24.

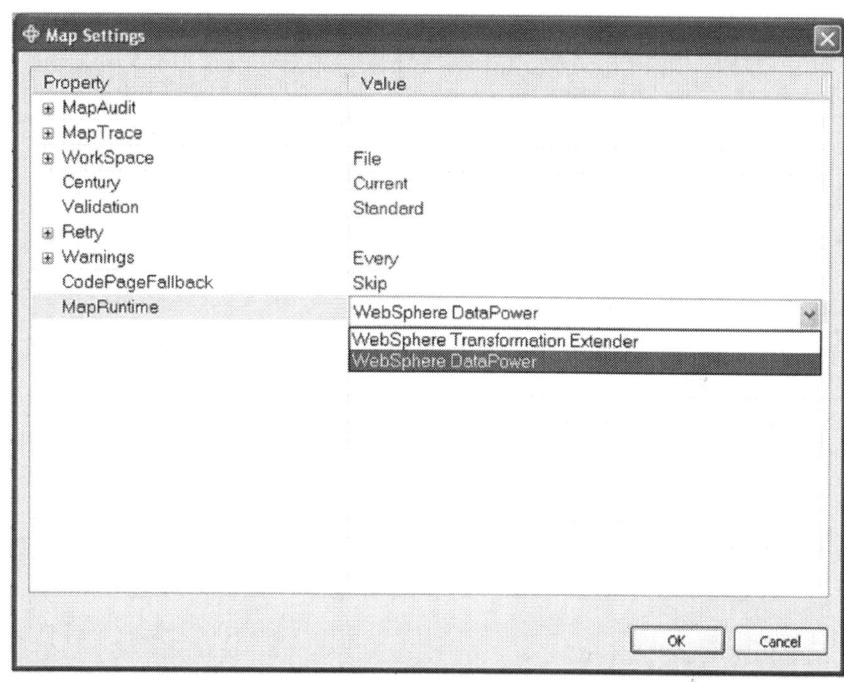

Figure 5-24 Changing the map runtime from WTX to DataPower.

After making this change, you will notice that the icon next to the map has changed from the WTX purple ball to the DataPower logo. This indicates that when the map is run, it will execute against the DataPower runtime. Obviously, we must tell the Design Studio where our device is located. This can be accomplished by going to the Window→Preferences menu and navigating to the DataPower settings, as shown in Figure 5-25.

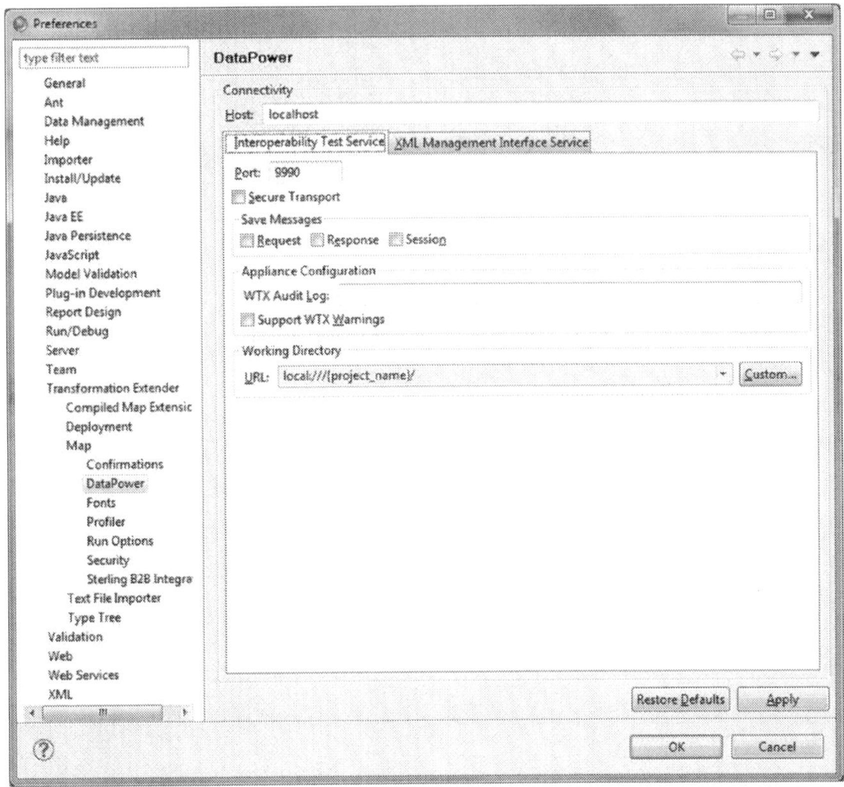

Figure 5-25 Configuring WTX Design Studio for DataPower runtime.

Rebuilding and running the map now results in a successful run. There is indication on the results dialog that the test was run against the appliance, as shown by the IP address and port in Figure 5-26. The results can be inspected again and are the same. The DataPower logs can also be viewed for additional confirmation or debugging.

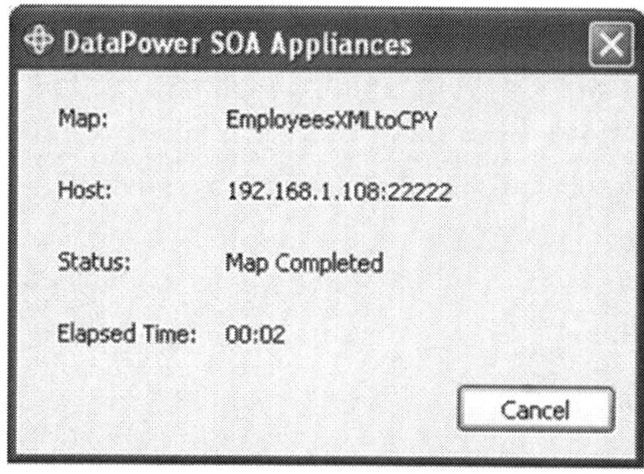

Figure 5-26 Successful map execution on DataPower.

Deploying to DataPower

As we've seen, changing, testing, and debugging to fine-tune the maps can be done very easily in an iterative fashion, with very little effort by the developer. But at some point, the developer will be satisfied with the changes and will want to move the transform to a real DataPower service running in some domain.

The first step is to locate the generated .dpa file in the Design Studio workspace directory for your project, and upload it to the DataPower appliance.

This file can then be used to create a Binary Transform action in a request or response rule in a Processing Policy. Figure 5-27 shows how this is accomplished. First a Transform action is dragged onto the rule and configured. The "Transform binary" option is chosen, which you may notice changes the action title and icon from Transform to Transform Binary. Next, the DPA file that was just uploaded must be specified in the WTX Map file field. There is no need to specify the MTS files anywhere—they are contained in the DPA file.

After placing this transform into a service, testing can be done using any of the normal means. Figure 5-28 shows the results when we test the policy using curl.

Configure Transform binary Action

Help

Basic Advanced

Input

Input (auto) (auto) *

Options

Transform binary

Use Document Processing Instructions
- Transform binary
- Transform with a processing control file, if specified
- Transform with embedded processing instructions, if available
- Transform with XSLT style sheet

Transform File local:/// (none) Upload... Fetch... Edit... View... Var Builder

WTX Map file local:/// EmployeesXMLtoCPY.dpa Upload... Fetch... Edit... View... Var Builder

WTX Map Mode DPA

WTX Audit Log

URL Rewrite Policy (none) + ...

Asynchronous on off

Output

Output (auto) (auto)

Delete Done Cancel

Figure 5-27 Configuring a Transform Binary action in the Processing Policy.

Figure 5-28 Run results for sample binary transforming firewall.

Advanced WTX Transform Features

There are often complex requirements for binary transformations, like any other business scenario. Let's explore some of the more advanced techniques in this area.

Multiple Input and Output Cards

The scenario we showed you was simple: one input and one output dataset. In the real world, one scenario might be to have multiple input or output datasets. As you know by now, the advanced features for any DataPower object can be found in the WebGUI only by accessing it through the Navigation menu. Figure 5-29 shows our example Transform Binary action (accessed from Objects→XML Processing→Processing

Action), and it is obvious how much more there is in the way of configuration than what we saw earlier when opening this through the policy editor. Locate Named Inputs and Outputs dropdown shown in this screen shot has the choices default, dynamic, and explicit.

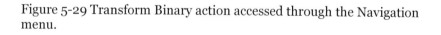

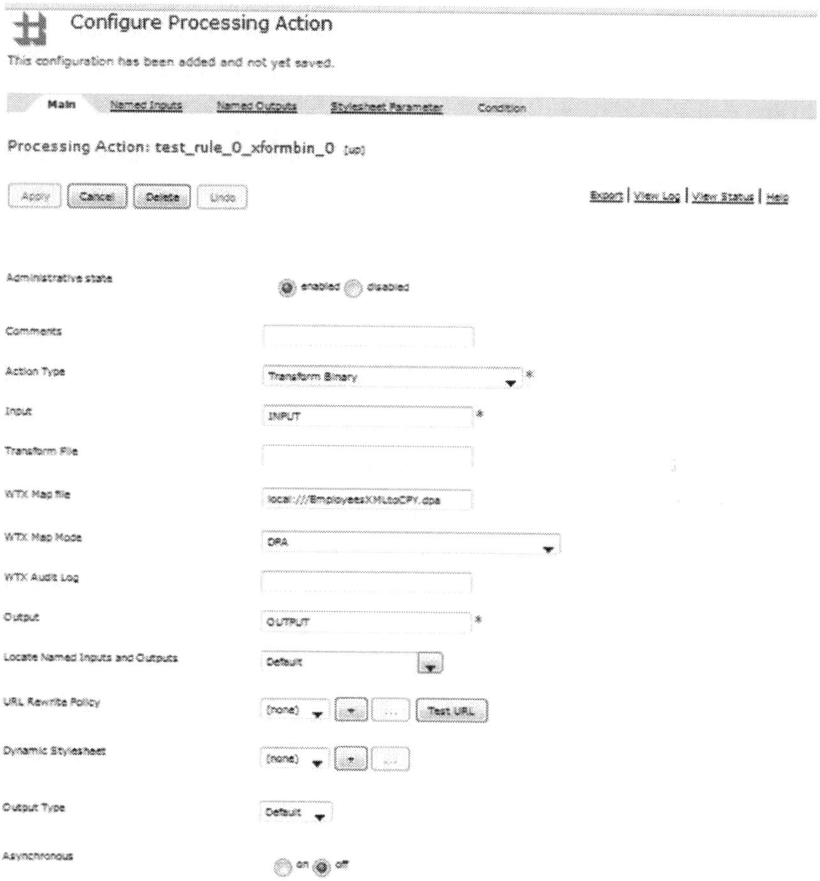

Figure 5-29 Transform Binary action accessed through the Navigation menu.

The default choice enables one input and one output context, as used in our example scenario. The explicit choice requires you to name the inputs and outputs directly. This can be done by using the Named Inputs and Named Outputs tabs shown in the figure.

As an example, if you had a transform that requires input from an EDI file and an MQ message, your configuration might appear as shown in Figure 5-30. This would require you to have cards named EDIFileCard and MQMessageCard in the map you built in WTX, and to have contexts named EDIFileContext and MQMessageContext with the appropriate data available to the action and visible at runtime when the policy executes. Multiple outputs would be configured similarly.

To use the dynamic option, you must at runtime populate one or more DataPower variables in the form var://local/named-input/map-input-name, where map-input-name corresponds to a named card in the WTX map (such as the EDIFileCard we used in the last explicit example). You can have one or more of these variables. The value of this variable should be the name of the context that will hold the data at runtime (for example, EDIFileContext as shown previously). There is a corresponding named-output variable for the outputs. This dynamic content could come from message attachments, external sources, content enrichment techniques such as data fetched with the dp:url-open() extension function, using the Fetch action, or any number of ways, making this quite powerful.

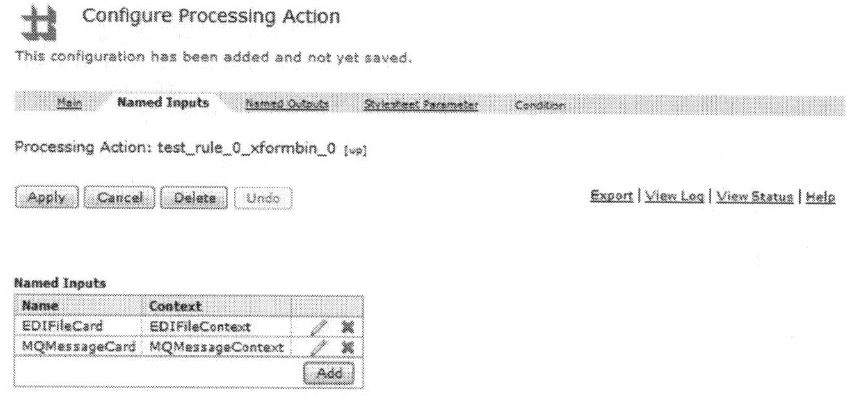

Figure 5-30 Multiple named inputs for a Transform Binary action.

Precompiling Maps for DataPower

WTX Design Studio comes with a number of useful tools, one of which is a command-shell utility for precompiling maps. This has a parameter to compile maps for DataPower, which might be useful in batch deployment scenarios. The result of this is the same DataPower Compiled Maps (dpa) that are generated when you choose the Build command from the Design Studio context menu for the map. An example is shown in Figure 5-31.

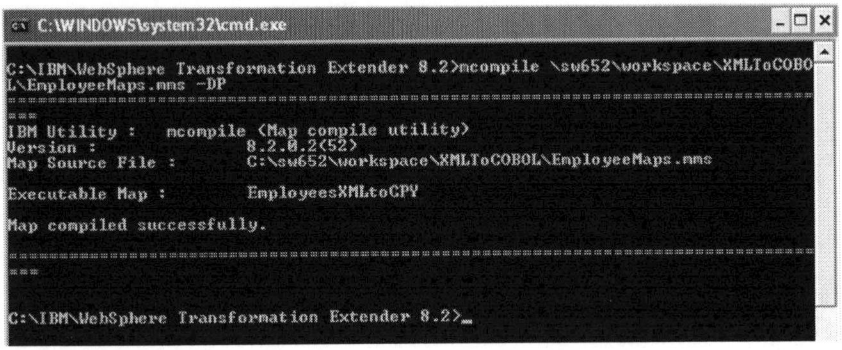

```
C:\WINDOWS\system32\cmd.exe

C:\IBM\WebSphere Transformation Extender 8.2>mcompile \sw652\workspace\XMLToCOBO
L\EmployeeMaps.mms -DP
================================================================================
===
IBM Utility :   mcompile (Map compile utility)
Version :              8.2.0.2(52)
Map Source File :      C:\sw652\workspace\XMLToCOBOL\EmployeeMaps.mms

Executable Map :       EmployeesXMLtoCPY

Map compiled successfully.

================================================================================
===

C:\IBM\WebSphere Transformation Extender 8.2>_
```

Figure 5-31 Batch compilation of DataPower maps with mcompile.

Detecting File Formats

In some situations, the message content may need to be analyzed dynamically at runtime to determine whether it is XML, JSON or a secondary format, or perhaps if it is a secondary format, to look for certain values inside the file to determine which transform should be used.

One way to determine whether the file is XML is to set up a Transform Binary action to look for the XML declaration within an incoming message, and then use a callable rule to fire the appropriate processing rule for XML or secondary data.

Another approach would be to use the match action using xpath="/" would be the easiest way to check if it is XML. The dp:parse() extension function could also be used to detect this, but it is not recommended since it adds extra cycles by trying to parse the data explicitly, and will result in errors being thrown.

Run Maps

WTX has a RUN function that allows you to execute another compiled map from a component or map rule. You can use RUN to dynamically name source or destination files, or both, or to dynamically pass data to a map. You can also use the RUN function to split the output data into separate files based on some value in the input. There are certain situations where we may need to look at a snippet of data to determine the nature of transformation. In those cases, usage of RUN will simplify the map design. RUN maps should be uploaded to the appliance for parent maps to invoke.

PARSE Function

In version 8.4.1 (available on DataPower firmware 7.2 and above), WTX introduced the PARSE function. The idea of PARSE is to provide the same functionality as an input card, but as a function. This allows users to parse a section of data at any point in the mapping process instead of making the decision up-front. The documentation for this new feature is at http://www-01.ibm.com/support/knowledgecenter/SSVSD8_8.4.1/com.ibm.websphere.dtx.funcexp.doc/references/r_funcs_express_PARSE.htm?lang=en.

Audits

A map audit log is created when a map is executed. The log information is based on a particular map and provides information about map execution, map settings, card settings, and specific data objects. Map audit logs are in XML format and the contents can be mapped in such a way as to provide performance statistics and information about the content of your data. Audit allows generating reports for a map transformation. Please refer to the WTX InfoCenter for more details for Audit information.

WTX Packs

IBM WebSphere Transformation Extender Industry Pack solutions can provide out-of-the-box capabilities to integrate a range of industry-standard data formats with an enterprise infrastructure. Industry packs help developers accelerate the delivery of transformation solutions by providing predefined type tree templates and conversion maps and, in many cases, offering validation maps and tools to help reduce risk in projects that require conformity to mandatory and advisory guidelines. DataPower supports a number of WTX packs including HL7, X12, EDIFACT and FIX

INFO — Using WTX for Primary Data Formats

WTX does support the primary data formats used on DataPower (XML and JSON), so you may have been thinking 'Why not just use this nice graphical tool for all of my transforms involving XML and JSON?' This is quite possible; however there would be certain tradeoffs such as performance and the inability to use DataPower's internal threat-checking and schema engine. For these reasons, we recommend using the native facilities (XSLT, XPath, XQuery and JSONiq) for transforms that do not involve secondary data formats.

Summary

This chapter has taken you deep into the world of secondary data type transformations on DataPower. We have discussed some of the tools and techniques that are involved. When the transforms are built, they can be used with any service, commonly the Multi-Protocol Gateway due to its many supported protocols, and the Web Service Proxy as in some of the scenarios we've discussed.

This is a topic that can be quite complex, and perhaps even merit a book of its own. There is an additional DataPower sample under the install directory for Design Studio that has a scenario for converting a comma-separated text contact information file to mailing labels. Another invaluable source of information on this topic is the excellent technical blog by Hermann Stamm-Wilbrandt, which was mentioned earlier in this volume. Hermann commonly covers the complex topics involved in transforming and transmitting secondary formats and non-standard protocols. He also has a webcast on this topic at http://www-01.ibm.com/support/docview.wss?uid=swg27022977.

As we see further adoption of DFDL, these capabilities will surely change over time, as they are added into WTX and perhaps even adoption of DFDL as a first-class part of the DataPower runtime. Time will tell.

Many shops have data specialists that focus on the taxonomy of the data structures used by their applications. This is further evidence that working with DataPower often requires cooperation among the many factions that comprise an enterprise IT shop!

Appendix A: Resources

To download code listings shown in this book, please go to http://wildlakepress.com/books/15-information-technology/18-datapower-handbook-resources

Development Resources

XQuery 1.0 and XPath 2.0 Data Model (XDM):

http://www.w3.org/TR/XPath-datamodel/

JSON: http://www.jsoniq.org/

JSONiq draft specification 0.4.42:

http://www.jsoniq.org/docs/JSONiqExtensionToXQuery/pdf/Language_Specification-0.4.42-JSONiq-en-US.pdf

World Wide Web Consortium: http://www.w3.org

CommonJS 1.0:

http://wiki.commonjs.org/wiki/Modules/1.0

JSONx specification:

https://tools.ietf.org/html/draft-rsalz-jsonx-00

Hermann Stamm-Wilbrandt's Blog:

https://www.ibm.com/developerworks/community/blogs/HermannSW/?lang=en

DataPower Resources

IBM DataPower Handbooks:

Volume I: DataPower Intro & Setup:

http://amzn.to/1IjrEBb

Volume II: DataPower Networking:

http://amzn.to/1Ijrzh3

Volume IV: DataPower B2B and File Transfer:

http://amzn.to/1Ijrzh3

IBM DataPower Knowledge Center:

http://www-01.ibm.com/support/knowledgecenter/SS9H2Y/welcome

IBM DataPower Information Center:

http://www.ibm.com/software/integration/datapower/library/documentation

IBM DataPower Internet/WWW Main Product Page:

http://www.ibm.com/datapower

DataPower GitHub:

https://github.com/ibm-datapower

Twitter:

https://twitter.com/IBMGateways

YouTube:

https://www.youtube.com/channel/UCV2_-gdea5LM58S-E3WCqew

LinkedIn:

https://www.linkedin.com/groups?home=&gid=4820454

developerWorks Discussion Forum:

https://www.ibm.com/developerworks/community/forums/html/forum?id=11111111-0000-0000-0000-000000001198

Weekly DataPower Webcast:

https://www14.software.ibm.com/webapp/iwm/web/signup.do?source=swg-wdwfw

SlideShare:

http://www.slideshare.net/ibmdatapower/

How-to find appropriate DataPower product information:

http://www-01.ibm.com/support/docview.wss?uid=swg21377654

DataPower Product Support Website:

Contains firmware, documentation, support procedure, technotes and other helpful material:

http://www.ibm.com/software/integration/datapower/support/

Redbooks:

http://www.redbooks.ibm.com/cgi-bin/searchsite.cgi?query=datapower

Software Services for WebSphere:

Top-notch DataPower consulting from IBM WebSphere.

http://www.ibm.com/developerworks/websphere/services/findbykeyword.html?q1=DataPower

Hermann Stamm-Wilbrandt's Blog:

Hermann is one of the brightest minds in DataPower-land, and his blog on development topics is incredibly valuable, featuring tips and techniques that can't be found elsewhere.

https://www.ibm.com/developerworks/community/blogs/HermannSW/?lang=en

WebSphere Global Community DataPower Group:

http://www.webspehereusergroup.org/datapower

IBM WebSphere DataPower Support:

http://www.ibm.com/software/integration/datapower/support/

Support Flashes RSS Feed:

http://www-947.ibm.com/systems/support/myfeed/xmlfeeder.wss?feeder.requid=feeder.create_public_feed&feeder.feedtype=RSS&feeder.maxfeed=25&OC=SS9H2Y&feeder.subdefkey=swgws&feeder.channel.title=WebSphere%20DataPower%20SOA%20Appliances&feeder.channel.descr=The%20latest%20updates%20about%20WebSphere%20DataPower%20SOA%20Appliances

IBM DataPower Support Technotes:

http://www.ibm.com/search/csass/search?q=&sn=spe&lang=en&filter=collection:stgsysx,dblue,ic,pubs,devrel1&prod=U692969C82819Q63

IBM Education Assistant DataPower Modules:

http://www-01.ibm.com/support/knowledgecenter/websphere_iea/com.ibm.iea.wdatapower/plugin_coverpage.dita

WAMC Technote:

http://www-01.ibm.com/support/docview.wss?uid=swg24032265

DataPower Feature Grid:

We consider the Feature Grid to be an invaluable resource, and we are excited to provide it to you. It yields the answers to the most commonly asked questions about DataPower ("Is feature/protocol/spec X supported on my Y appliance?") We had initially included the entire table here, spread across several pages. However, due to its density, it was hard to read, and it was literally changing under us as product management made changes for the impending announcements.

We debated and felt that the best thing we could do for our readers would be to provide a URL hyperlink, so that the most up to date information (and not stale or incorrect information!) is available to you. There are detriments to this approach, such as the dreaded 'busted URL', but in this day and age it's likely that you are reading this on a device with an Internet connection, or have one within reach, and as well we have the capability to update this book as soon as we find that something is amiss. You can find the features grid at:

http://www.slideshare.net/ibmdatapower/ibm-data-power-gateways-features-comparison

Acknowledgements

The Author Team:

We thank the IBM management team for allowing us to access the resources necessary to write the book.

The author team would like to thank the following people for technical contributions, clarifications, and suggestions for this book: Jaime Ryan (first edition co-author), Sunil K Dandamudi, Arif Siddiqui, Bhargav Perepa, Chris Cross, Shiu-Fun Poon, Russell Butek, Trey Williamson, Colt Gustafson, David Maze, David Shute, Eugene Kuznetsov, Gari Singh, Greg Truty, Henry Chung, Joel Smith, John de Frietas, John Graham, Ken Hygh, Keys Botzum, Rich Groot, Marcel Kinard, Steve Hanson, Naipaul Ojar, Jon Harry, and Paul Glezen.

John Rasmussen:

I was lucky enough to have joined DataPower during its initial startup phase, and to have worked with some truly talented and inspirational people through its acquisition by IBM. The list is too long, but I'd like to thank Eugene Kuznetsov for making this all possible and for providing me with the opportunity to participate, Rich Salz for his generosity of time and knowledge and the many contributions he made to DataPower, Brian Del Vecchio for making building the WebGUI fun. And the many individuals who I came to respect and to rely on in tough times including; Jan-Christian Nelson, Gari Singh, David Maze, John Shriver, Tony Ffrench, James Ricotta, Shiu-Fun Poon and many others within and beyond the DataPower and IBM families. To my fellow authors, with a special word of appreciation to Bill Hines, as there is no doubt that without Bill's tremendous effort and continuous dedication these books would not have happened.

Bill Hines:

Special thanks for Sunil K Dandamudi for all of his help with the WTX chapter. I'd like to thank Keys Botzum and Kyle Brown for being role models for work ethic and integrity, and mentoring me throughout my IBM career. I'd like to thank my immediate and extended family for being supportive and understanding during the tough times. Last, I'd like to thank my author team for sticking with this project during the many months, nights, and weekends of heated debates and stress. You were all picked for a reason, and I think the fact that you have all put up with me, and we have been through what we have and emerged still good friends with tremendous respect for each other, attests to those decisions being good ones. I'm extremely proud of the job you've done.

Jim Brennan:

I would like to thank all of my co-authors for including me in the writing of this book and for making it the best that it could be. I would especially like to thank Bill Hines for getting the band back together to get the latest information out there in this, and future volumes. I would like to thank my family and friends for being understanding and supportive when the stress seemed to be getting the best of me.

Ozair Sheik:

I would like to thank my co-authors for giving me the opportunity to contribute to this book. A special thanks to Bill Hines whose hard work and leadership made this book a reality. I have been fortunate to work with a talented group of people during my career. Special thanks to my managers who recognized my contributions and provided me with opportunities to grow. I would also like to thank my IBM colleagues, Arif Siddiqui, Robert Conti, Ken Hygh, Tony Ffrench, Shiu-Fun Poon, Rachel Reinitz, Salman Moghul and Fred Tucci. I would like to thank my family and friends for supporting me in reaching my career goals.

About the Authors

John Rasmussen

John is a Senior Engineer within the IBM DataPower organization. John has been with IBM and DataPower since 2001 and has worked as a product development engineer (where he created and developed the original WebGUI Drag and Drop Policy Editor) and as a product specialist assisting many clients in the implementation of DataPower devices. John has an extensive career in software development, including work with McCormack & Dodge/D&B Software, Fidelity Investments and as an independent consultant. John has a degree from the University of Massachusetts at Amherst, and lives in Gloucester, Massachusetts.

Bill Hines

Bill is an IBM Executive I/T Specialist. His current role is as North America Cloud Integration and SaaS Technical Leader, working out of Lake Hopatcong, NJ. He has many years of IBM WebSphere solution design and implementation experience in both customer engagements and developing and delivering internal training within IBM. He is the lead author of the acclaimed IBM Press book IBM WebSphere DataPower SOA Appliance Handbook (first and second editions) and co-author of IBM WebSphere: Deployment and Advanced Configuration, as well as many articles published in WebSphere Technical Journal and developerWorks.

Jim Brennan

Jim is a partner and president of an independent consulting firm, McIndi Solutions. McIndi Solutions is an IBM business partner based out of Hackettstown, NJ specializing in DataPower administration and configuration. Jim has assisted in developing and delivering internal DataPower education material to IBM consultants and engineers. Jim has also been an application developer working with several different programming languages and platforms ranging from COBOL to Java. Jim has been a JEE developer for several years specializing in JEE development for WebSphere Application Server. He also has several years of experience with WebSphere Application Server installation, configuration, troubleshooting, and administration. Jim has more than ten years of I/T experience with a certificate from the Chubb Institute of Technology and also attended Felician College in Lodi, NJ.

Ozair Sheikh

Ozair is a Senior Product Line Manager for IBM DataPower Gateways and certified IBM IT Specialist. He is an experienced SOA/ESB/Mobile IT professional with over 10 years in managing, consulting, instructing and developing enterprise solutions using WebSphere technologies. He is avid speaker at several worldwide conferences; topics ranging from Mobile security, API Management and architecting mission-critical ESB systems.

In his current role, Ozair helps drive new innovative solutions for the DataPower gateway platform that reflect customer requirements and market trends. Ozair holds a bachelor of Mathematics with specialization in Computer Science from the University of Waterloo. In his spare time, he is an avid hockey and basketball fan, and enjoys writing mobile apps to solve his everyday problems.

Afterword

Afterword by Eugene Kuznetsov

"The proper planning of any job is the first requirement. With limited knowledge of a trade, the job of planning is doubly hard, but there are certain steps that any person can take towards proper planning if he only will."

—Robert Oakes Jordan, Masonry

I founded a company called DataPower® in the spring of 1999 to build products based on several distinct ideas. The first idea involved applying reconfigurable computing and dynamic code generation to the problem of integrating disparate applications. The second idea centered on the concept of data-oriented programming (DOP) as the means to achieve direct and robust data interchange. The third idea involved delivering middleware as a network function, enabled by the DOP technology and inspired by the successful models of ubiquitous connectivity. The product's journey since has been remarkable, and this great book is another milestone for the entire team behind DataPower. Before more discussion of the book itself, a few words on these three ideas.

Rapidly adapting to change is key for everything and everyone in today's world, and IBM appliances are no exception. Whether it's a policy, a transformation map, a schema, or a security rule, DataPower will try to put it into effect with as little delay and interruption as possible. Popular methods for maintaining this kind of flexibility come with a large performance penalty. However, by dynamically generating code and reconfiguring hardware based on the current message flow, it became possible to achieve both flexibility and near-optimal performance. At any given point, the device operates as a custom engine for a particular task, but when the task changes, it can rapidly become a different custom engine underneath the covers.

This dynamic adaptability is especially useful when combined with DOP. Stated briefly, DOP emphasizes formally documenting data formats and using them directly, instead of encapsulation or abstraction, to integrate or secure different modules or systems. Today, XML is probably one of the most successful and readily recognized examples of DOP, but the principles are more universal than any particular technology. Another example of DOP is the way DataPower XI52 processes binary data, by using high-level format descriptors instead of adaptors.

These, in turn, enable the creation of network hardware (also known as appliance) products that operate on whole application messages (rather than network packets) to integrate, secure, or control applications. Greater simplicity, performance, security, and cost-effectiveness were envisioned—and are now proven—with the appliance approach. Beyond the appliance design discipline, the success of IP & Ethernet networking in achieving universal connectivity has much to teach about the best way to achieve radically simplified and near-universal application integration.

Reading this book will enable you to benefit from the previous three ideas in their concrete form: the award-winning

IBM products they became. From basic setup to the most powerful advanced features, it covers DataPower appliances in a readable tone with a solid balance of theory and examples. For example, Chapter 6 does a great job in explaining the big-picture view of device operation, and Chapter 22 gives a detailed how-to on extending its capabilities. With some of the most experienced hands-on DataPower practitioners among its authors, it provides the kind of real-world advice that is essential to learning any craft.

When learning IBM DataPower, there is one thing that may be more helpful and rewarding than remembering every particular detail, and that is developing an internal "mental model" of how the devices are meant to operate and fit into the environment. Especially when troubleshooting or learning new features, this "mental model" can make device behavior intuitive. Reading the following pages with an eye toward not just the details but also this mental model will speed both productivity and enjoyment.

In conclusion, I would like to use this occasion to thank the entire team, past and present, who made and continues to make DataPower possible. Their work and the passion of DataPower users is an inspiring example of how great people and a powerful idea can change the world for the better.

—Eugene Kuznetsov, Cambridge, MA Founder of DataPower Technology, Inc. served as President, Chairman, and CTO at various points in the company's history, and then served as director of Product Management and Marketing, SOA Appliances at IBM Corporation.

DataPower's first office is on the right. Photo courtesy of Merryman Design.

Afterword by Jerry Cuomo

It all started when I was asked to co-host an IBM Academy Conference on “Accelerators and Off-Loading” in 2004. I was feeling a little out of my element, so I decided to take some of the focus off me and put it on others. I had been reading about some of the new XML-centered hardware devices and was intrigued. I have always been interested in system performance. With XML dominating our emerging workloads (e.g., Service Oriented Architecture), the impact of XML performance on system performance was becoming increasingly important. Hence, I thought it would be a good idea to invite a handful of these XML vendors to our conference.

At the conference, the DataPower presentation was quite different from the others. It wasn’t about ASICs or transistors; it was about improving time to value and total cost of operation. The DataPower presentation focused on topics that were also near and dear to me, such as systems integration, configuration over programming, and the merits of built-for-purpose systems. In essence, Eugene Kuznetsov, the DataPower founder and presenter, was talking about the value of appliances. While very intriguing, I couldn't help but feel curious about whether the claims were accurate. So, after the conference I invited Eugene to come to our lab in Research Triangle Park in North Carolina to run some tests.

I have to admit now that in the back of my mind, I operated on the principle of "keeping your friends close and your enemies closer." Behind my intrigue was a feeling of wanting to understand their capabilities so that we could outperform vendors with WebSphere® Application Server. The tests went well; however, the DataPower team was somewhat reluctant to dwell on the raw XML performance capabilities of their appliance. Feeling a little suspicious, I had my team run some raw performance experiments. The results were off the charts. Why wasn't the DataPower team flaunting this capability? This is when I had my "ah-ha" moment. While performance measured in transactions per second is important and part of the value equation, the overall performance metrics found while assessing time to value and overall cost of operation and ownership are the most critical performance metrics to a business. This is where the DataPower appliances outperform. I read a paper, written by Jim Barton, CTO and co-founder of Tivo, called "Tivo-lution." The paper was inspiring as it confirmed the motivations and aspirations that I've had ever since I led IBM's acquisition of DataPower in 2005. In the paper, Barton describes the challenges of making complex systems usable and how "purpose-built" computer systems are one answer to the challenge:

"One of the greatest challenges of designing a computer system is in making sure the system itself is 'invisible' to the user. The system should simply be a conduit to the desired result. There are many examples of such purpose-built systems, ranging from modern automobiles to mobile phones."

The concept of purpose-built systems is deeply engrained in our DNA at IBM. The name of our company implies this concept: International Business Machines.

IBM has a long history of building purposed machines, such as the 1933 Type 285, an electric bookkeeping and accounting machine. I can imagine this machine being delivered to an accountant, plugging it in, immediately followed by number crunching. The accountant didn't have to worry about hard drive capacity, operating system levels, compatibility between middleware vendors, or application functionality. It just did the job. I can also imagine it followed the 80/20 rule. It probably didn't do 100% of what all accountants needed. But it probably did 80% of what all accountants needed very well. Users just dealt with the remaining 20%, or learned to live without it.

"Business Machines, Again" is my inspiration. Our customers respond positively to the re-emergence of this approach to engineering products. It's all about time-to-value and total cost of operation and ownership. Appliances such as our WebSphere DataPower are leading the way in delivering on these attributes.

At the extreme, purpose-built systems, such as a Tivo DVR and an XI52, are built from the ground up for their purposes. While they might use off-the-shelf parts, such as an embedded Linux® OS, it is important that all parts are "right sized" for the job. Right-sizing source code in a hardware appliance is more like firmware (with strong affinity to the underlying hardware) than it is software. As such, the Tivo-lution paper describes the need to own every line of source code to ensure the highest level of integration and quality:

"...by having control of each and every line of source code...

Tivo would have full control of product quality and development schedules. When the big bug hunt occurred, as it always does, we needed the ability to follow every lead, understand every path, and track every problem down to its source."

The Tivo team even modified the GNU C++ compiler to eliminate the use of exceptions (which generate a lot of code that is seldom used) in favor of rigid checking of return code usage in the firmware. DataPower similarly contains a custom XML compiler that generates standard executable code for its general-purpose CPUs, as well as custom code for the (XG4) XML coprocessor card.

A physical appliance has the unparalleled benefit of being hardened for security. Jim talks about this in his Tivo paper:

"Security must be fundamental to the design...We wanted to make it as difficult as possible, within the economics of the DVR platform, to corrupt the security of any particular DVR."

The DataPower team has taught me the meaning of “tamper-proof” appliances, or more precisely “tamper-evident.” Like the 1982 Tylenol scare, we can’t stop you from opening the box, but we can protect you, if someone does open it. In fact, the physical security characteristics of DataPower make it one of the only technologies some of our most stringent customers will put on their network Demilitarized Zone (DMZ). If a DataPower box is compromised and opened, it basically stops working. An encrypted flash drive makes any configuration data, including security keys, difficult to exploit. “DP is like the roach motel; private keys go in, but never come out” is the way we sometimes describe the tamper-proof qualities of DataPower.

But the truth is, DataPower is not a DVR. DataPower is a middleware appliance. Middleware is a tricky thing to make an appliance out of. Middleware is enabling technology and by its nature is not specific to any application or vendor. The Tivo appliance is a specific application (TV and guide) that makes it somewhat easier to constrain:

“Remember, it’s television. Everybody knows how television works.”

“Television never stops, even when you turn off the TV set. Televisions never crash.”

Hence, the challenge (and the art) in building a middleware appliance involves providing the right amount of constraint, without rendering the appliance useless. For example, DataPower does not run Java™ code (which is the primary means of customizing much of the WebSphere portfolio); instead, it uses XML as the primary mode of behavior customization. So, at some level, DP is not programmed, but instead it is configured. Now, for those who have used XML (and its cousin XSLT), you know that it's more than configuration; however, it is a constraint over Java programming, which has unbounded levels of customizability. The combined team of IBM and DataPower have been bridging this gap (of special to general purpose) effectively. We have recently added features to DP to allow it to seamlessly connect to IBM mainframe software (IMS™ and DB2®) as well as capabilities to manage a collection of appliances as if they were one.

IBM has a healthy general-purpose software business. Our WebSphere, Java-based middleware is the poster child for general-purpose middleware (write once, run almost everywhere). However, there is a place for business machines that are purposed built and focus on providing the 80 part of the 80/20 rule. We are heading down this path in a Big Blue way.

This book represents an important milestone in the adoption of DataPower into the IBM family. The authors of this book represent some of IBM's most skilled practitioners of Service Oriented Architecture (SOA). This team is a customer facing team and has a great deal of experience in helping our customers quickly realize value from our products. They have also been among the most passionate within IBM of adopting the appliance approach to rapidly illustrating the value of SOA to our customers. The authors have unparalleled experience in using DataPower to solve some of our customers' most stringent systems integration problems. This book captures their experiences and best practices and is a valuable tool for deriving the most out of your WebSphere DataPower appliance.

—Jerry Cuomo, IBM Fellow, WebSphere CTO

Afterword by Kyle Brown

I can still remember the day in late 2005 when Jerry Cuomo first called me into his office to tell me about an acquisition (then pending) of a small Massachusetts company that manufactured hardware devices.

"Wait a minute. Hardware??!?"

That's the first incredulous thought that went through my mind. Jerry was the CTO of the WebSphere brand in IBM, which had become the industry-leading brand of middleware based on Java. Why were we looking at a company that made hardware? Echoing the immortal words of Dr. "Bones" McCoy from the classic Star Trek series, I then thought,

"I'm a software engineer, not a hardware engineer, dang it!"

But as I sat in his office, Jerry wove me a story (as he had for our executives) that soon had me convinced that this acquisition did, in fact, make sense for WebSphere as a brand and for IBM as a whole. Jerry had the vision of a whole new way of looking at SOA middleware—a vision that encompassed efficient, special-purpose appliances that could be used to build many of the parts of an SOA. Key to this vision was the acquisition of DataPower, which gave us not only a wealth of smart people with deep experience in Networking, XML, and

SOA, but an entry into this field with the DataPower family of appliances—notably the Integration appliance.

Since that day, I've never regretted our decision to branch out the WebSphere brand well beyond its Java roots. The market response to the introduction of the DataPower appliances to the brand has been nothing short of phenomenal. Far from distracting us, the ability to provide our customers with an easy-to-use, easy-to-install, and remarkably efficient hardware-based option for their ESB and security needs has turned out to be an asset that created synergy with our other product lines and made the brand stronger as a whole. It's been an incredible journey, and as we begin to bring out new appliances in the DataPower line, we're only now beginning to see the fundamental shift in thinking that appliance-based approaches can give us.

On this journey, I've been accompanied by a fantastic group of people—some who came to us through the DataPower acquisition and some who were already part of the WebSphere family—who have helped our customers make use of these new technologies. Bill, John, and the rest of the author team are the true experts in this technology, and their expertise and experience show in this book.

This book provides a wealth of practical information for people who are either novices with the DataPower appliances, or who want to learn how to get the most from their appliances. It provides comprehensive coverage of all the topics that are necessary to master the DataPower appliance, from basic networking and security concepts, through advanced configuration of the Appliance's features. It provides copious, detailed examples of how the features of the appliances work, and provides debugging help and tips for helping you determine how to make those examples (and your own projects) work. But what's most helpful about this book is the way in which the team has given you not just an explanation of how you would use each feature, but also why the features are built the way they are. Understanding the thinking behind the approaches taken is an enormous help in fully mastering these appliances. The team provides that, and provides you with a wealth of hints, tips, and time-saving advice not just for using and configuring devices, but also for how to structure your work with the devices.

This book is something the DataPower community has needed for a long time, and I'm glad that the authors have now provided it to the community. So sit back, crack open the book, open up the admin console (unless you have yet to take the appliance out of the box—the book will help you there, too!) and begin. Your work with the appliances is about to get a whole lot easier, more comprehensible, and enjoyable as well.

—Kyle Brown, Distinguished Engineer, IBM Software Services and Support

Made in the USA
San Bernardino, CA
23 January 2016